Praise for *The Dog Who Healed a Family*

"These touching and engaging vignettes will make animal lovers out of us all."

—*Publishers Weekly*

"Great gifts for animal lovers, or anyone who wants to be reminded what a poignant, funny and enriching gift that animals are to the human spirit."

—*Tulsa World*

Praise for *The Dog with the Old Soul*

"Brimming with tears, laughter and love, *The Dog with the Old Soul* reminds us of the life-altering connection that animals can make in our lives."

—*Talkin' Pets*

"The friendly, first-person presentations reflect wise, warm and compelling storytelling that captures both the combustible and complex feel of the human-animal bond."

—**Seattle Kennel Club**

The
Little Book
— OF —
Puppy Love

True Animal Stories
to Warm the Soul

Jo Coudert and
Jennifer Basye Sander

PREVIOUSLY PUBLISHED AS *THE DOG WHO HEALED A FAMILY*
AND *THE DOG WITH THE OLD SOUL*

HANOVER
SQUARE
PRESS

ISBN-13: 978-1-335-21600-7

The Little Book of Puppy Love: True Animal Stories to Warm the Soul

The following stories were first published in Reader's Digest: "Goose Steps"; "The Pig Who Loved People"; "The Good Shepherd"; "I Love You, Pat Myers"; "Sister Smog and the Windshield Viper"; "An Experiment in Love" and "Frankie Buck."

The following stories were first published in Woman's Day: "The Dog Who Healed a Family"; "Woman (and Dog) to the Rescue"; "Connie and the Dog"; "How Do You Spank a Duck?"; "Where's Bubba?"; "Saving Trouper" and "A Swan Called Porcelain."

"Sweet Elizabeth" was first published in McCall's.

"The Puppy Express" was first published in Family Circle.

HANOVER
SQUARE
PRESS™

This publication contains opinions and ideas of the author. It is intended for informational and educational purposes only. The reader should seek the services of a competent professional for expert assistance or professional advice. Reference to any organization, publication or website does not constitute or imply an endorsement by the author or the publisher. The author and the publisher specifically disclaim any and all liability arising directly or indirectly from the use or application of any information contained in this publication.

This edition published by arrangement with Harlequin Books S.A.

Library of Congress Cataloging-in-Publication Data has been applied for.

Hanover Square Press
22 Adelaide St. West, 40th Floor
Toronto, Ontario M5H 4E3, Canada
HanoverSqPress.com
BookClubbish.com

Printed in U.S.A.

CONTENTS

The Dog Who Healed a Family

The Dog with the Old Soul

The Dog
Who Healed
a Family

Preface

All the stories in this book are about animals, and all are true. What the stories have in common is the love and caring that can exist between animals and people. Nancy Topp struggled for weeks to get a seventeen-year-old dog home across fifteen hundred miles. Gene Fleming fashioned shoes for a goose born without feet and supported the goose in a harness until he learned to walk. Months after their javelina disappeared, Patsy and Buddy Thorne were still roaming ranch lands in Texas, Bubba's favorite chocolate in their pockets, searching for their wild pig.

The Thornes recently sent a clipping from their local newspaper describing how a group of men out hunting with bows and arrows came upon a javelina. The animal stood still, gazing at the men, while they shot at it three times. When all three arrows failed to strike home, one of the men ventured close enough to pet the animal and found it was tame and welcomed the attention.

What is amazing about the report is not that the animal was Bubba—it was not—but that the hunters shot three times at a creature that was not big enough or wild enough to be a threat to them and that did not provide sport by running. And because the meat of a javelina is too strong-tasting to be palatable, they were not interested in it for food.

The hunters shot at the javelina because it was there, which is the same reason a neighbor who lives downriver from me catches all the trout within hours of the time the state fish and wildlife service stocks the stream. An amiable man who loves his grandchildren, the neighbor has built the children a tree platform where they can sit silently and shoot at the deer who come to the river to drink at twilight. He also sets muskrat traps in the river and runs over woodchucks and possums on the road.

The family doesn't eat the deer; the frozen body of a doe has been lying all winter in the field in back of my woods. Nor does anyone eat the trout the man catches; he tosses them into a little pond on his property where they stay until they become too numerous and die from lack of oxygen. When I once asked this ordinary, pleasant fellow why he'd gone out of his way to run over a raccoon crossing the road, he looked at me in surprise. "It's an animal!" he said as though that quite explained it.

To many people it is sufficient explanation. After all, did not Jehovah tell Noah and his sons that all the beasts of the earth and fish of the sea were delivered into the hands of man? Surely this is a license to destroy them even if we have no better reason at the time than the fact that they exist and we wish to.

Or is it? Belatedly we are beginning to realize that the duality of people and animals, us and them, is false, just as we have discovered that there is no split between us and the world. The world is us and we are the world. We cannot simply exploit and destroy, either the world or the animals in it, if we are not at the same time to do ourselves irreparable harm.

Consider what a Native American, Chief Seattle, said in 1854: "What is man without the beasts? If all the beasts were gone, man would die from a great loneliness of spirit. For whatever happens to the beasts, soon happens to man. All things are connected. This we know: The Earth does not belong to man; man belongs to the Earth. This we know: All things are connected like the blood which unites one family. All things are connected. Whatever befalls the Earth befalls the sons of the Earth. Man did not weave the web of life. He is merely a strand in it. Whatever he does to the web, he does to himself."

The world belongs to the animals just as much as to us. Let us be unselfish enough to share it with them openly and generously. Which is to say, when you come upon a lost dog or an orphaned fawn or a goose born without feet, give it nothing to fear from you, grant it safety, offer to help if you can, be kind. In return, as the stories here show, you will sometimes find a welcome companionship, and surprisingly often love.

Jo Coudert
Califon, New Jersey

The Puppy Express

Curled nose to tail, the little dog was drowsing in Nancy Topp's lap as the truck rolled along the interstate. Suddenly Nancy felt her stiffen into alertness. "What's the matter, old girl?" Nancy asked. At seventeen, Snoopy had a bit of a heart condition and some kidney problems, and the family was concerned about her.

Struggling to her feet, the dog stared straight ahead. She was a small dog, with a dachshund body but a beagle head, and she almost seemed to be pointing. Nancy followed the dog's intent gaze, and then she saw it, too. A wisp of smoke was curling out of a crack in the dashboard. "Joe!" she shouted at her husband at the wheel. "Joe, the engine's on fire!"

Within seconds the cab of the ancient truck was seething with smoke. Nancy and Joe and their two children—Jodi, twelve, and Matthew, fifteen—leaped to the shoulder of the road and ran. When they were well clear, they turned and waited for the explosion that would blow everything they owned sky-high. Instead, the engine coughed its way into silence, gave a last convulsive shudder and died.

Joe was the first to speak. "Snoopy," he said to the little brown and white dog, "you may not hear or see so good, but there's nothing wrong with your nose."

"Now if you could just tell us how we're going to get home," Matthew joked. Except it wasn't much of a joke. Here they were, fifteen hundred miles from home, stranded on a highway in Wyoming, with the truck clearly beyond even Joe's gift for repairs. The little dog, peering with cataract-dimmed eyes around the circle of faces, seemed to reflect their anxiety.

The Topps were on the road because five months earlier a nephew had told Joe there was work to be had in the Napa Valley and Joe and Nancy decided to take a gamble on moving out there. Breaking up their home in Fort Wayne, Indiana, they packed up the kids and Snoopy and set out for California. But once there, the warehousing job Joe hoped for did not materialize, Nancy and the kids were sharply homesick and their funds melted away. Now it was January and, the gamble lost, they were on their way back home to Fort Wayne.

The truck had gotten them as far as Rock Springs, Wyoming, but now there was nothing to do but sell it to a junk dealer for $25 and hitch a ride to the bus station. Two pieces of bad news greeted them there. Four tickets to Fort Wayne came to more money than they had, much more, and dogs were not allowed on the bus.

"But we've got to take Snoopy with us," Nancy pleaded with the ticket seller, tears welling in her eyes. It had been a disastrous day, but this was the worst news of all.

Joe drew her away from the window. It was no use getting upset about Snoopy, he told her, until they figured out how to get themselves on the bus. With no choice but to ask for help, they called Travelers Aid, and with kind efficiency the local representative arranged for a motel room for them for the night. There, with their boxes and bags piled in a corner, they put in a call to relatives back home, who promised to get together money for the fare and wire it the next day.

"But what about Snoopy?" Matthew said as soon as his father hung up the phone.

"We can't go without Snoopy," Jodi stated flatly.

Joe picked up the little dog. "Snoopy," he said, tugging her floppy ears in the way she liked, "I think you're going to have to hitchhike."

"Don't tease, Joe," Nancy said curtly.

"I'm not teasing, honey," he assured her, and tucked Snoopy into the crook of his arm. "I'm going to try to find an eastbound truck to take the old girl back for us."

At the local truck stop, Joe sat Snoopy on a stool beside him while he fell into conversation with drivers who stopped to pet her. "Gee, I'd like to help you out," one after another said. "She's awful cute and I wouldn't mind the company, but I'm not going through Fort Wayne this trip." The only driver who might have taken her picked Snoopy up and looked at her closely. "Naw," the man growled, "with an old dog like her, there'd be too many pit stops. I got to make time." Still hopeful, Joe tacked up a sign asking for a ride for Snoopy and giving the motel's phone number.

"Somebody'll call before bus time tomorrow," he predicted to the kids when he and Snoopy got back to the motel.

"But suppose nobody does?" Jodi said.

"Sweetie, we've got to be on that bus. The Travelers Aid can only pay for us to stay here one night."

The next day Joe went off to collect the wired funds while Nancy and the kids sorted through their possessions, trying to decide what could be crammed into the six pieces of luggage they were allowed on the bus and what had to be left behind. Ordinarily Snoopy would have napped while they worked, but now her eyes followed every move Nancy and the children made. If one of them paused to think, even for a minute, Snoopy nosed at the idle hand, asking to be touched, to be held.

"She knows," Jodi said, cradling her. "She knows something awful is going to happen."

The Travelers Aid representative arrived to take the belongings they could not pack, for donation to the local thrift shop. A nice man, he was caught between being sympathetic and being practical when he looked at Snoopy. "Seventeen is really old for a dog," he said gently. "Maybe you just have to figure she's had a long life and a good one." When nobody spoke, he took a deep breath. "If you want, you can leave her with me and I'll have her put to sleep after you've gone."

The children looked at Nancy but said nothing; they understood there wasn't any choice, and they didn't want to make it harder on their mother by protesting. Nancy bowed her head. She thought of all the walks, all the romps, all the picnics, all the times she'd gone in to kiss the children goodnight and Snoopy had lifted her head to be kissed, too.

"Thank you," she told the man. "It's kind of you to offer. But no. No," she repeated firmly. "Snoopy's part of the family, and families don't give up on each other." She reached for the telephone book, looked up kennels in the yellow pages and began dialing. Scrupulously she started each call with the explanation that the family was down on their luck. "But," she begged, "if you'll just keep our little dog until we can find a way to get her to Fort Wayne, I give you my word we'll pay. Please trust me. Please."

A veterinarian with boarding facilities agreed finally to

take her, and the Travelers Aid representative drove them to her office. Nancy was the last to say goodbye. She knelt to take Snoopy's frosted muzzle in her hands. "You know we'd never leave you if we could help it," she whispered, "so don't give up. Don't you dare give up. We'll get you back somehow, I promise."

Once back in Fort Wayne, the Topps found a mobile home to rent, one of Joe's brothers gave them his old car, sisters-in-law provided pots and pans and bed linens, the children returned to their old schools and Nancy and Joe found jobs. Bit by bit the family got itself together. But the circle had a painful gap in it. Snoopy was missing. Every day Nancy telephoned a different moving company, a different trucking company, begging for a ride for Snoopy. Every day Jodi and Matthew came through the door asking if she'd had any luck and she had to say no.

By March they'd been back in Fort Wayne six weeks and Nancy was in despair. She dreaded hearing from Wyoming that Snoopy had died out there, never knowing how hard they'd tried to get her back. One day a friend suggested she call the Humane Society. "What good would that do?" Nancy said. "Aren't they only concerned about abandoned animals?" But she had tried everything else, so she telephoned Rod Hale, the director of the Fort Wayne Department of Animal Control, and told him the story.

"I don't know what I can do to help," Rod Hale said when she finished. "But I'll tell you this. I'm sure going to try." A week later, he had exhausted the obvious approaches. Snoopy was too frail to be shipped in the unheated baggage compartment of a plane. A professional animal transporting company wanted $655 to bring her east. Shipping companies refused to be responsible for her. Rod hung up from his latest call and shook his head. "I wish the old-time Pony Express was still in existence," he remarked to his assistant, Skip Cochrane. "They'd have passed the dog along from one driver to another and delivered her back home."

"It'd have been a Puppy Express," Skip joked.

Rod thought for a minute. "By golly, that may be the answer." He got out a map and a list of animal shelters in Wyoming, Nebraska, Iowa, Illinois and Indiana, and picked up the phone. Could he enlist enough volunteers to put together a Puppy Express to transport Snoopy by stages across five states? Would people believe it mattered enough for a seventeen-year-old dog to be reunited with her family that they'd drive a hundred or so miles west to pick her up and another hundred or so miles east to deliver her to the next driver?

In a week he had his answer, and on Sunday, March 11, he called the Topps. "How are you?" he asked Nancy.

"I'd feel a lot better if you had some news for me."

"Then you can begin feeling better right now," Rod told her jubilantly. "The Puppy Express starts tomorrow. Snoopy's coming home!"

Monday morning, in Rock Springs, Dr. Pam McLaughlin checked Snoopy worriedly. The dog had been sneezing the day before. "Look here, old girl," the vet lectured as she took her temperature, "you've kept your courage up until now. This is no time to get sick just when a lot of people are about to go to a lot of trouble to get you back to your family."

Jim Storey, the animal control officer in Rock Springs, had volunteered to be Snoopy's first driver. When he pulled up outside the clinic, Dr. McLaughlin bundled Snoopy in a sweater and carried her to the car. "She's got a cold, Jim," the vet said, "so keep her warm. Medicine and instructions and the special food for her kidney condition are in the shopping bag."

"She's got a long way to go," Jim said. "Is she going to make it?"

"I wish I could be sure of it," the doctor admitted. She put the little dog on the seat beside Jim and held out her hand. Snoopy placed her paw in it. "You're welcome, old girl," the vet said, squeezing it. "It's been a pleasure taking care of you. The best of luck. Get home safely."

Jim and Snoopy drove 108 miles to Rawlings, Wyoming. There they rendezvoused with Cathy English, who had come 118 miles from Casper to meet them. Cathy laughed when she saw Snoopy. "What a funny-looking, serious little creature you are to be traveling in such style," she teased. "Imagine, private chauffeurs across five states." But that evening, when she phoned Rod Hale to report that Snoopy had arrived safely in Casper, she called her "a dear old girl" and admitted that "If she were mine, I'd go to a lot of trouble to get her back, too."

Snoopy went to bed at Cathy's house—a nondescript little brown and white animal very long in the tooth—and woke the next morning a celebrity. Word of the seventeen-year-old dog with a bad cold who was being shuttled across mid-America to rejoin her family had gotten to the news media. After breakfast, dazed by the camera and lights but, as always, polite, Snoopy sat on a desk at the Casper Humane Society and obligingly cocked her head to show off the new leash that was a gift from Cathy. And that night, in Fort Wayne, the Topps were caught between laughter and tears as they saw their old girl peer out at them from the television set.

With the interview behind her, Snoopy set out for North Platte, 350 miles away, in the company of Myrtie Bain, a Humane Society official in Casper who had volunteered for the longest single hop on Snoopy's journey. The two of them stopped overnight in Alliance, and Snoopy, taking a stroll before turning in, got a thorn in her paw. Having come to rely on the kindness of strangers, she held quite still while Myrtie removed it, and then continued to limp until Myrtie accused her of doing it just to get sympathy. Her sneezes, however, were genuine, and Myrtie put her to bed early, covering her with towels to keep off drafts.

In North Platte at noon the next day, more reporters and cameramen awaited them, but as soon as she'd been interviewed, Snoopy was back on the road for a 138-mile trip to Grand Island. Twice more that day she was passed along, arriving in Lincoln, Nebraska, after dark and so tired that she curled up in the first doggie bed she spotted despite the growls of its rightful owner.

In the morning her sneezing was worse and she refused to drink any water. Word of this was sent along with her, and as soon as she arrived in Omaha on the next leg, she was checked over by the Humane Society vet, who found her fever had dropped but she was dehydrated. A messenger was dispatched to the nearest store for Gatorade, to the fascination of reporters, who from then on headlined her as "Snoopy, the Gatorade Dog."

With a gift of a new wicker sleeping basket and a note in the log being kept of her journey—"Happy to be part of the chain reuniting Snoopy with her family"—Nebraska passed the little dog on to Iowa. After a change of car and driver in Des Moines, Snoopy sped on and by nightfall was in Cedar Rapids. Pat Hubbard, in whose home she spent the night, was sufficiently concerned about her to set an alarm and get up three times in the night to force-feed her Gatorade. Snoopy seemed stronger in the morning, and the Puppy Express rolled on.

As happens to travelers, Snoopy's outfit grew baggy and wrinkled, her sweater stretching so much that she tripped on it with almost every step. This did not go unnoticed, and by the time she reached Davenport, she was sporting a new sweater, as well as a collection of toys, food and water dishes and her own traveling bag to carry them in. The log, in addition to noting when she had been fed and walked, began to fill with comments in the margin: "Fantastic little dog!" "What a luv!" "Insists on sitting in the front seat, preferably in a lap." "Likes the radio on." "Hate to give her up! Great companion!"

At nightfall of her fifth and last full day on the road, Snoopy was in Chicago, her next-to-last stop. Whether it was that she was getting close to home or just because her cold had run its course, she was clearly feeling better. Indeed, the vet who examined her told the reporters, "For an old lady who's been traveling all week and has come more than thirteen hundred miles, she's in grand shape. She's going to make it home tomorrow just fine." The Topps, watching the nightly update of Snoopy's journey on the Fort Wayne TV stations, broke into cheers.

The next day was Saturday, March 17. In honor of St. Patrick's Day, the little dog sported a new green coat with a green derby pinned to the collar. The Chicago press did one last interview with her, and then Snoopy had nothing to do but nap until Skip Cochrane arrived from Fort Wayne to drive her the 160 miles home.

Hours before Snoopy and Skip were expected in Fort Wayne, the Topps were waiting excitedly at the Humane Society. Jodi and Matthew worked on a room-sized banner that read "Welcome Home, Snoopy! From Rock Springs, Wyoming, to Fort Wayne, Indiana, via the Puppy Express," with her route outlined across the bottom and their signatures in the corner. Reporters from the Fort Wayne TV stations and newspapers, on hand to report the happy ending to Snoopy's story, interviewed the Topps and the shelter's staff, in particular Rod Hale, whose idea the Puppy Express had been. One interviewer asked him why the volunteers had done it. Why had thirteen staff members of ten Humane Societies and animal shelters gone to so much trouble for one little dog?

Rod told him what one volunteer had said to him on the phone. "It would have been so easy to tell Nancy Topp that nothing could be done. Instead, you gave all of us a chance to make a loving, caring gesture. Thank you for that."

Somewhere amid the fuss and confusion, Rod found time to draw Nancy aside and give her word that Snoopy would be arriving home with her boarding bill marked "Paid." An anonymous friend of the Humane Society in Casper had taken care of it.

"I thought I was through with crying," Nancy said as the warm tears bathed her eyes. "Maybe it was worth our little dog and us going through all this just so we'd find out how kind people can be."

The CB radio crackled and Skip Cochrane's voice filled the crowded room. "Coming in! The Puppy Express is coming in!"

Nancy and Joe and the children rushed out in the subfreezing air, the reporters on their heels. Around the corner came the pickup truck, lights flashing, siren sounding. "Snoopy's here!" shouted the children. "Snoopy's home!"

And there the little dog was, sitting up on the front seat in her St. Patrick's Day outfit, peering nearsightedly out of the window at all the commotion. After two months of separation from her family, after a week on the road, after traveling across five states for fifteen hundred miles in the company of strangers, Snoopy had reached the end of her odyssey.

Nancy got to the truck first. In the instant before she snatched the door open, Snoopy recognized her. Barking wildly, she scrambled into Nancy's arms. Then Joe was there, and the children. Laughing, crying, they hugged Snoopy and each other. The family that didn't give up on even its smallest member was back together again.

★ ★ ★ ★ ★

Sweet Elizabeth

J ane Bartlett first saw the white rabbit in a pet shop window at Easter time. The other rabbits were jostling for places at a bowl of chow, but this one was sitting up on her haunches, gazing solemnly back at the faces pressed against the glass staring at her. One ear stood up stiff and straight, as a proper rabbit's ear should, but the other flopped forward over one eye, making her look as raffish as a little old lady who has taken a drop too much and knocked her hat askew.

An executive of the company in which Jane was a trainee came by, stopped to say hello and chuckled at the sight of the rabbit. Mr. Corwin was a friendly, fatherly man, and as they stood there smiling at the funny-looking creature, Jane found herself telling him stories about Dumb Bunny, the white rabbit she'd had as a small child who drank coffee from her father's breakfast cup and once leaped after a crumb in the toaster, singeing his whiskers into tight little black corkscrews. Some of the homesickness Jane was feeling at being new in New York City must have been in her voice, for on Easter morning her doorbell rang and a deliveryman handed her a box.

She set it on the floor while she read the card, and Robert, her tomcat, always curious about packages, strolled over to sniff it. Suddenly he crouched, tail twitching, ready to spring. Jane cautiously raised the lid of the box and up popped the rabbit with the tipsy ear. The cat hissed fiercely. Peering near-sightedly at him, the rabbit shook her head, giving herself a resounding thwack in the nose with her floppy ear, hopped out of the box and made straight for the cat. He retreated. She pressed pleasantly forward. He turned and fled. She pursued. He jumped up on a table. She looked dazedly around, baffled by the disappearance of her newfound friend.

Jane picked her up to console her, and the rabbit began nuzzling her arm affectionately. "Don't try to butter me up," Jane told her sternly. "A city apartment is no place for a rab-bit. You're going straight back to the pet shop tomorrow." The rabbit was a tiny creature, her bones fragile under her skin, her fur as white as a snowfield and soft as eiderdown. Gently Jane tugged the floppy ear upright, then let it slip like velvet through her fingers. How endearing the white rabbit was. Could she possibly... Jane shifted her arm and discov-ered a hole as big as a half-dollar chewed in the sleeve of her sweater. "That does it," Jane said, hastily putting the rabbit down. "You've spoiled your chances." With a mournful shake of her head, the rabbit hopped off in search of the cat.

Jane had a careful speech planned when she arrived at her office the next morning, but the kind executive looked so pleased with himself that the words went out of her head. "What have you named her?" he asked, beaming. She said the first thing that came to mind: "Elizabeth."

"Sweet Elizabeth," he said. "Wonderful!"

Sweet Elizabeth, indeed. Jane was tempted to tell him that Sweet Elizabeth had dined on her best sweater and spent the night in the bathroom, where she had pulled the towels off the racks and unraveled the toilet paper to make a nest for herself. Instead, she began to describe the rabbit's crush on Robert the cat, and soon half the office had gathered around, listening and laughing. It was the first time anyone had paid the least bit of attention to her, and Jane began to wonder whether she wasn't being too hasty about getting rid of Elizabeth. She did go to the pet shop on her lunch hour, however, just to sound them out. Their no-return policy was firm. The best they would do was sell Jane a wooden cage painted to look like a country cottage to keep the rabbit in.

"Don't get the wrong idea," she told Elizabeth that evening as she settled her into it. "It's just temporary until I find a home for you."

In the night it wasn't the sound of the rabbit butting off the roof of the cottage that awakened Jane. She slept through that. It was the crash of the ficus tree going over when Sweet Elizabeth, having nibbled away the tasty lower leaves, went after the higher ones. The next day Jane bought a latch for the cottage. That night Elizabeth worked it loose and ate the begonias on the windowsill. The following day Jane bought a lock. That night Elizabeth gnawed a new front door in her cottage.

It was not hunger or boredom that fueled Elizabeth's determination to get loose; it was her passion for Robert. The minute Jane let her out, she hopped to him and flung herself down between his paws. He, of course, boxed her soundly for her impertinence, but her adoration wore him down, and one day he pretended to be asleep when she lay down near enough to touch him with one tiny white paw. Soon, as though absentmindedly, he was including her in his wash-ups, with particular attention paid to the floppy ear where it had dusted along the floor.

All of this made marvelous stories for Jane to tell in the office, and she discovered it wasn't so hard to make friends after all. She even began to gain something of a reputation for wit when she described how Robert, finding that Elizabeth did not understand games involving catnip mice, invented a new one for the two of them.

Since Elizabeth followed him about as tenaciously as a pesky kid sister, he could easily lure her out onto Jane's tiny terrace. Then he dashed back inside and hid behind a wastebasket. Slowly Elizabeth would hop to the doorway and peer cautiously about. Not seeing the cat anywhere, she'd jump down the single step, whereupon Robert would pounce, rolling them both over and over across the living room rug until Elizabeth kicked free with her strong hind legs. Punch-drunk from the tumbling about, she'd stagger to her feet, shake herself so that her tipsy ear whirled about her head, then scramble off and happily follow the cat outside again.

This game was not all that Elizabeth learned from Robert. He taught her something far more important, at least from Jane's point of view. Out on the terrace were flower boxes that were much more to Robert's liking than his indoor litter box. Time after time, while Robert scratched in the dirt, Elizabeth watched, her head cocked, her ear swinging gently. She was not a swift thinker, but one day light dawned. Robert stepped out of the flower box and she climbed in, which is how Elizabeth, with a little help from her friend, came to be housebroken.

With that problematic matter taken care of and all the plants eaten to nubbins anyway, Jane gave up trying to confine Elizabeth to her cottage and let her stay free. She met

Jane at the door in the evening, just as Robert did, and sat up to have her head patted. She learned her name; she learned what "no" meant if said loudly and accompanied by a finger shaken under her nose; she learned what time meals were served and that food arrived at the apartment in paper bags. When Jane came home with groceries and set a bag even momentarily on the floor, Elizabeth's strong teeth quickly ripped a hole in it. That is, unless she smelled carrots, in which case she tugged the bag onto its side and scrambled into it. If Jane got to the carrots before Elizabeth did and put them away on the bottom shelf of the refrigerator, the rabbit bided her time until Jane opened the door again, then she stood up on her hind legs and yanked the carrots back out. It got so that Jane never dared slam the refrigerator door without first making sure Elizabeth's head was not inside it.

But then dinner would be over, the food put away, and Jane settled down to read in her easy chair. First Robert would come, big and purring and kneading with his paws to make a satisfactory spot for himself in her lap. Then Elizabeth would amble over, sit up on her haunches, her little paws folded primly on her chest, and study the situation to decide where there was room for her. With a flying leap, she'd land on top of Robert, throw herself over and push with her hind legs until she'd managed to wedge herself in between the cat and Jane. Soon the twitching of her nose would slow, then cease, and she would be asleep.

At such times, it was easy for Jane to let her hand stray over the soft fur, to call her Sweet Elizabeth, to forgive her all her many transgressions—the sock chewed into fragments, the gnawed handle on a pocketbook, the magazine torn into scraps. But one day Elizabeth went too far; she chewed the heels off Jane's best pair of shoes. Jane decided she had to go.

And she had a prospective family to adopt her: a young couple with three small children. She invited the parents, along with two other couples, to dinner.

All that rolling around on the rug with Robert had turned the white rabbit rather gray, and, wanting Elizabeth to look her most beguiling, Jane decided to give her a bath. She filled a dishpan with warm water and plopped Elizabeth into it. The rabbit sprang out. Jane hustled her back in and this time got a firm grip on her ears. Elizabeth kicked and Jane let go. On the third try, Jane got her thoroughly soaped on the back but Elizabeth's powerful hind legs would not let her near her stomach. Persuading herself that no one would look at the rabbit's underside, Jane rinsed her off as best she could and tried to dry her with a towel. Wet, the rabbit's silky fur matted into intricate knots. Jane brushed; Elizabeth licked. Jane combed; Elizabeth licked. Hours later, Elizabeth's fur was still sticking out in every direction and it was obvious that a soggy mass on her stomach was never going to dry. Afraid Elizabeth would get pneumonia, Jane decided to cut out the worst of the knots. With manicure scissors, she began carefully to snip. To her horror, a hole suddenly appeared. Elizabeth's skin was as thin as tissue paper and the scissors had cut right through it. Jane rushed to get Mercurochrome and dab it on the spot. In the rabbit's wet fur, the Mercurochrome spread like ink on blotting paper. Now Jane had a damp rabbit with a dirty-gray stomach dyed red.

The sight of her sitting up at the door to greet each new arrival sent Jane's guests into gales of laughter, which Elizabeth seemed to enjoy. She hopped busily about to have her ears scratched. Jane was keeping a wary eye on her, of course, and saw the moment Elizabeth spotted the stuffed celery on the hors d'oeuvres tray. But Jane wasn't quite quick enough.

Elizabeth leaped and landed in the middle of the tray. Even that simply occasioned more laughter, and there were cries of protest when Jane banished Elizabeth to her cottage.

After dinner, Jane yielded and released her. Quite as though Elizabeth had used the time in her cottage to think up what she might do to entertain the party, she hopped into the exact center of the living room floor and gazed seriously around the circle of faces. When silence had fallen and she had everyone's full attention, she leaped straight into the air, whirled like a dervish and crash-landed in a sprawl of legs and flying ears. The applause was prolonged. Peeping shyly from behind her ear, Elizabeth accepted it, looking quite pleased with herself.

The children's father adored her, and when in the course of the evening he saw that Elizabeth went to the terrace door and scratched to be let out, he couldn't wait to take her home. "She's housebroken," he reminded his wife, who was hesitating, "and the kids'll love her." Elizabeth, returning, climbed into his lap, and it was settled: Elizabeth was to go to her new family. Until the end of the evening. "What have you spilled on yourself?" the man's wife asked. The edge of his suit jacket, from lapel to bottom button, was white. Elizabeth had nibbled it down to the backing.

"You rat," Jane scolded her when the guests had gone. "I found a good home for you, and you blew it." Elizabeth shook her head remorsefully, beating herself with her floppy ear, and wandered away. After Jane had cleaned up the kitchen and was ready for bed, she went looking for Elizabeth to put her in her cottage. She hunted high, low and in between. Where was she? Beginning to be frantic, she went through the apartment a second time. She even looked over the terrace railing, wondering for one wild moment if Elizabeth had been so contrite she'd thrown herself off. Only because there was nowhere else to search did Jane open the refrigerator door. There Elizabeth was, on the bottom shelf, having a late-night snack of carrot sticks and parsley.

For quite a while after that, nothing untoward happened, and Elizabeth, Robert and Jane settled into a peaceful and loving coexistence. When Jane watched Elizabeth sunbathing on the terrace beside Robert or sitting on her haunches to wash her face with her dainty paws or jumping into her lap to be petted, she found herself wondering how she could have imagined giving Elizabeth up. Until the day she did a thorough housecleaning and moved the couch. The rug had been grazed down to the backing.

"She's eating me out of house and home. Literally," Jane wailed to a college friend over lunch. "I'm going to have to turn her in to the ASPCA."

"Don't do that. I'll take her," Jane's friend replied, surprising her because Jane knew she did not approve of pets in the house. "She can live in our garage. Evan's ten now. It'll be good for him to have the responsibility of caring for an animal."

Jane's bluff had been called. Could she really envision life without Sweet Elizabeth? She was silent. Her friend said, "Come on. We'll go get her right now."

Elizabeth met them at the door, sitting up as usual to have her ears scratched. "Oh, she's cute," said the friend, but so perfunctorily that Jane knew she had missed the point of Elizabeth. "Never mind," Jane whispered into Elizabeth's soft fur, "it'll be all right. She'll come to love you, just as I did, and you'll be happy in the country." Elizabeth shook her head slowly. Was there reproach in her eyes? Jane gave one last kiss to that foolish ear.

Robert was restless that evening, going often out on the terrace. "Oh, Robbie," Jane told him, "I'm so sorry. She was your friend, too, and I didn't think of that." As Jane hugged him, the old emptiness returned, the emptiness of the time before Sweet Elizabeth when Jane used to imagine that everyone else's phone was ringing, that everyone else had friends to be with and places to go. A little white rabbit who gave Jane the courage to reach out had made a surprising difference in her life.

It was weeks before she slammed the refrigerator door without a second thought, stopped expecting an innocent white face to come peeking around the terrace door, gave up listening for the thump of those heavy back feet. For a long time she didn't trust herself even to inquire about Elizabeth. Then one day she was driving to Boston and, on impulse, decided to stop off in Connecticut to see her. No one was home, but the garage door was open. It was some time before Jane's eyes got accustomed to the dark and she could distinguish the white blur that was Elizabeth. The little rabbit was huddled in a corner of her cottage, shaking with cold. The straw on the floor was soaking wet. The draft from the open door was bitter. Her food and water bowls were empty. Jane spoke her name and Elizabeth crept into her arms. Wrapping her in a sweater, Jane canceled her trip to Boston and headed back home.

She called her college friend the next day and told her she'd missed Elizabeth so much that she'd kidnapped her. That was all right, her friend said; what with the basketball season and all, her son hadn't had much time for the rabbit. That left Jane with just one other phone call to make—the one canceling the order for a new rug. Then she settled back to watch Elizabeth and Robert rolling across the floor together.

★ ★ ★ ★ ★

Frankie Buck

On a narrow road twisting along beside a mountain stream lay a deer, struck and killed by a car.

A motorist happening along the infrequently traveled road swerved to avoid the deer's body. As the driver swung out, he noticed a slight movement and stopped. There, huddled beside the dead doe, was a fawn, a baby who must have been born as its mother died, for the umbilical cord was still attached. "I don't suppose you have a chance," the motorist told the tiny creature as he tied off the cord, "but at least I can take you where it's warm."

The nearest place was the power plant of a state geriatric institution on a wooded mountaintop overlooking the town of Glen Gardner, New Jersey. Maintenance men there quickly gathered rags to make a bed for the fawn behind the boiler. When the fawn tried to suck the fingers reaching out to pet it, the men realized it was hungry and took a rubber glove, pricked pinholes in one finger, diluted some of the evaporated milk they used for their coffee and offered it to the fawn, who drank eagerly.

The talk soon turned to what to name the deer. Jean Gares, a small, spare man who was the electrician at the institution, had a suggestion. "If it's a female, we can call her Jane Doe," he proposed. "If it's a male, Frank Buck." The others laughed and agreed.

With the maintenance men taking turns feeding it around the clock, the little deer's wobbly legs—and its curiosity—soon grew strong enough to bring it out from behind the boiler. The men on their coffee breaks petted and played with the creature, and as soon as they were certain that Frank Buck was the name that fit, they shortened it to Frankie and taught him to answer to it. The only one who didn't call him Frankie, oddly enough, was Jean Gares. He, his voice rough with affection, addressed him as "you little dumb donkey," as in "Come on and eat this oatmeal, you little dumb donkey. I cooked it specially for you."

When Jean came to work at six each morning, always in his right-hand pocket was a special treat, an apple or a carrot, even sometimes a bit of chocolate, which Frankie quickly learned to nuzzle for. On nice days the two of them stepped outside, and Jean rested his hand on Frankie's head and stroked his fur as they enjoyed the morning air together.

At the far end of the field in front of the power plant, deer often came out of the woods to graze in the meadow. When Frankie caught their scent, his head came up and his nose twitched. "We'd better tie him up or we're going to lose him," one of the men commented. Jean shook his head. "He'll know when it's time to go," he said. "And when it is time, that's the right thing for him to do."

The first morning Frankie ventured away from the power plant, it wasn't to join the deer in the meadow but to follow Jean. The two-story white stucco buildings at Glen Gardner were originally built at the turn of the century as a tuberculosis sanitarium and are scattered at various levels about the mountaintop. Cement walks and flights of steps connect them, and Jean was crossing on his rounds from one building to another one morning when he heard the tapping of small hooves behind him. "Go on home, you dumb donkey," he told Frankie sternly. "You'll fall and hurt yourself." But Frankie quickly got the hang of the steps, and from then on the slight, white-haired man in a plaid flannel shirt followed by a delicate golden fawn was a familiar early morning sight.

One day, one of the residents, noticing Frankie waiting by the door of a building for Jean to reappear, opened the door and invited him in. Glen Gardner houses vulnerable old people who have been in state mental hospitals and need special care. When Frankie was discovered inside, the staff rushed to banish him. But then they saw how eagerly one resident after another reached out to touch him.

"They were contact-hungry," says staff member Ruby Durant. "We were supplying marvelous care, but people need to touch and be touched as well." When the deer came by, heads lifted, smiles spread and old people who seldom spoke asked the deer's name. "The whole wing lit up," remembers Ruby. "When we saw that and realized how gentle Frankie was, we welcomed him."

His coming each day was something for the residents to look forward to. When they heard the quick *tap-tap* of Frankie's hooves in the corridor, they reached for the crust, the bit of lettuce or the piece of apple they had saved from their own meals to give him. "He bowed to you when you gave him something," says one of the residents. "That would be," she qualifies solemnly, "if he was in the mood." She goes on to describe how she offered Frankie a banana one day, and after she had peeled it for him, "I expected him to swallow the whole thing, but he started at the top and took little nibbles of it to the bottom, just like you or me."

As accustomed as the staff became to Frankie's presence, nevertheless, when a nurse ran for the elevator one day and found it already occupied by Frankie and a bent, very old lady whom she knew to have a severe heart condition, she was startled. "Pauline," she said nervously, "aren't you afraid Frankie will be frightened and jump around when the elevator moves?"

"He wants to go to the first floor," Pauline said firmly.

"How do you know?"

"I know. Push the button."

The nurse pushed the button. The elevator started down. Frankie turned and faced front. When the doors opened, he strolled out.

"See?" said Pauline triumphantly.

Discovering a line of employees in front of the bursar's window one day, Frankie companionably joined the people waiting to be paid. When his turn at the window came, the clerk peered out at him. "Well, Frankie," she said, "I wouldn't mind giving you a paycheck. You're our best social worker. But who's going to take you to the bank to cash it?"

Frankie had the run of Glen Gardner until late fall, when superintendent Irene Salayi noticed that antlers were sprouting on his head. Fearful he might accidentally injure a resident, she decreed banishment. Frankie continued to frequent the grounds, but as the months passed he began exploring farther afield. An evening came when he did not return to the power plant. He was a year old and on his own.

Every morning, though, he was on hand to greet Jean and explore his pocket for the treat he knew would be there. In the afternoon he would reappear, and residents would join him on the broad front lawn and pet him while he munched a hard roll or an apple. A longtime resident named George, a solitary man with a speech defect who didn't seem to care whether people understood what he said or not, taught Frankie to respond to his voice, and the two of them often went for walks together.

When Frankie was two years old—a sleek creature with six-point antlers and a shiny coat shading from tawny to deepest mahogany—there was an April snowstorm. About ten inches covered the ground when Jean Gares came to work on the Friday before Easter, but that didn't seem enough to account for the fact that for the first time Frankie wasn't waiting for him. Jean sought out George after he'd made his rounds and George led the way to a pair of Norway spruces where Frankie usually sheltered when the weather was bad. But Frankie wasn't there or in any other of his usual haunts, nor did he answer to George's whistle. Jean worried desperately about Frankie during the hunting season, as did everyone at Glen Gardner, but the hunting season was long over. What could have happened to him?

Jean tried to persuade himself that the deep snow had kept Frankie away, but he didn't sleep well that night, and by Saturday afternoon he decided to go back to Glen Gardner and search for him. He got George, and the two of them set out through the woods. It was late in the day before they found the deer. Frankie was lying on a patch of ground where a steam pipe running underneath had thawed the snow. His right front leg was shattered. Jagged splinters of bone jutted through the skin. Dried blood was black around the wound. Jean dropped to his knees beside him. "Oh, you dumb donkey," he whispered, "what happened? Were dogs chasing you?

Did you step in a woodchuck hole?" Frankie's eyes were dim with pain, but he knew Jean's voice and tried to lick his hand.

Word that Frankie was hurt flicked like lightning through the center, and residents and staff waited anxiously while Jean made call after call in search of a veterinarian who would come to the mountain on a holiday weekend. Finally one agreed to come, but not until the next day, and by then Frankie was gone from the thawed spot. George tracked him through the snow, and when the vet arrived, he guided Jean and the grumbling young man to a thicket in the woods.

For the vet it was enough just to glimpse Frankie's splintered leg. He reached in his bag for a hypodermic needle to put the deer out of his misery. "No," said Jean, catching his arm. "No. We've got to try to save him."

"There's no way to set a break like that without an operation," the vet said, "and this is a big animal, a wild animal. I don't have the facilities for something like this."

He knew of only one place that might. Exacting a promise from the vet to wait, Jean rushed to the main building to telephone. Soon he was back with an improvised sled; the Round Valley Veterinary Hospital fifteen miles away had agreed at least to examine Frankie if the deer was brought there. Cradling Frankie's head in his lap, Jean spoke to him quietly until the tranquilizing injection the vet gave him took hold. When the deer drifted into unconsciousness, the three men lifted him onto the sled, hauled him out of the woods and loaded him into Jean's pickup truck.

X-rays at the hospital showed a break so severe that a stainless-steel plate would be needed to repair it. "You'll have to stand by while I operate," Dr. Gregory Zolton told Jean. "I'll need help to move him." Jean's stomach did a flip-flop, but he swallowed hard and nodded.

Jean forgot his fear that he might faint as he watched Dr. Zolton work through the three hours of the operation. "It was beautiful," he remembers, his sweetly lined face lighting up. "So skillful the way he cleaned away the pieces of bone and ripped flesh and skin, then opened Frankie's shoulder and took bone from there to make a bridge between the broken ends and screwed the steel plate in place. I couldn't believe the care he took, but he said a leg that wasn't strong enough to run and jump on wasn't any use to a deer."

After stitching up the incision, Dr. Zolton had orders for Jean. "I want you to stay with him until he's completely out of the anesthetic to make sure he doesn't hurt himself. Also, you've got to give him an antibiotic injection twice a day for the next seven days. I'll show you how."

There was an unused stable on the Glen Gardner grounds. Jean took Frankie there and settled him in a stall, and all night long Jean sat in the straw beside him. "Oh, you dumb donkey," he murmured whenever Frankie stirred, "you got yourself in such a lot of trouble, but it's going to be all right. Lie still. Lie still." And he stroked Frankie's head and held him in his arms when Frankie tried to struggle to his feet. With the soothing, known voice in his ear, Frankie each time fell back asleep, until finally, as the sun was coming up, he came fully awake. Jean gave him water and a little food, and only when he was sure Frankie was not frightened did he take his own stiff bones home to bed.

When word came that Frankie had survived the operation, a meeting of the residents' council at Glen Gardner was called. Ordinarily it met to consider recommendations and complaints it wished to make to the staff, but on this day Mary, who was its elected president, had something different on her mind. "You know as well as I do that there's no operation without a big bill. Now, Frankie's our deer, right?" The residents all nodded. "So it stands to reason we've got to pay his bill, right?" The nods came more slowly.

"How are we going to do that?" Kenneth, who had been a businessman, asked.

After considerable discussion, it was decided to hold a sale of cookies that they would bake in the residents' kitchen. Also, they would take up a collection, with people contributing what they could from their meager earnings in the sheltered workshop or the small general store the patients ran on the premises. "But first, before we do any of that," a resident named Marguerite said firmly, "we have to send Frankie a get-well basket."

The residents' council worked the rest of the day finding a basket, decorating it and making a card. The next day a sack of apples was purchased at the general store and each apple was polished until it shone. Mary, Marguerite and George were deputized to deliver the basket. Putting it in a plastic garbage bag so the apples wouldn't roll down the hill if they slipped in the snow, the three of them set out. They arrived without mishap and quietly let themselves into the stable. Frankie was sleeping in the straw, but he roused when they knelt beside him. Mary read him the card, Marguerite gave him an apple to eat, George settled the basket where he could see it but not nibble it and the three of them returned to the main building to report that Frankie was doing fine and was well pleased with his present.

By the seventh day after the operation, Jean called Dr. Zolton to say it was impossible to catch Frankie and hold him still for the antibiotic injections. Dr. Zolton chuckled. "If he's that lively," he told Jean, "he doesn't need antibiotics." But he warned it was imperative that Frankie be kept inside for eight weeks, for if he ran on the leg before it knit, it would shatter again.

Concerned about what to feed him for that length of time, Jean watched from the windows of his own house in the woods and on the grounds of Glen Gardner to see what the deer were eating. As soon as the deer moved away from a spot, Jean rushed to the place and gathered the clover, alfalfa, honeysuckle vines, young apple leaves—whatever it was the deer had been feeding on. Often George helped him, and each day they filled a twenty-five-pound sack. Frankie polished off whatever they brought, plus whatever residents coming to visit him at the stable had scavenged from their own meals in the way of rolls, carrots, potatoes and fruit.

"We'd go to see him, and oh, he wanted to get out so bad," remembers Marguerite, a roly-poly woman with white hair springing out in an aura around her head. "Always he'd be standing with his nose pressed against a crack in the door. He smelled spring coming, and he just pulled in that fresh air like it was something wonderful to drink."

When the collection, mostly in pennies and nickels, had grown to $135, the council instructed Jean to call Dr. Zolton and ask for his bill so they could determine if they had enough money to pay it. The day the bill arrived, Mary called a council meeting. The others were silent, eyes upon her, as she opened it. Her glance went immediately to the total at the bottom of the page. Her face fell. "Oh, dear," she murmured bleakly, "we owe three hundred and ninety-two dollars." Not until she shifted her bifocals did she see the handwritten notation: "Paid in Full—Gregory Zolton, DVM."

When the eight weeks of Frankie's confinement were up, Mary, Marguerite, George, Jean and Dr. Zolton gathered by the stable door. It was mid-June, and the grass was knee-deep in the meadow. Jean opened the barn door. Frankie had his nose against the crack as usual. He peered out from the interior darkness. "Come on, Frankie," Jean said softly. "You can go now." But Frankie was so used to someone slipping in and quickly closing the door that he didn't move. "It's all right," Jean urged quietly. "You're free." Frankie took a tentative step and looked at Jean. Jean stroked his head. "Go on, Frankie," he said, and gave him a little push.

Suddenly Frankie understood. He exploded into a run, flying over the field as fleetly as a greyhound, his hooves barely touching the ground.

"Slow down, slow down," muttered Dr. Zolton worriedly.

"He's so glad to be out," Mary said wistfully. "I don't think we'll ever see him again."

At the edge of the woods, Frankie swerved. He was coming back! Still as swift as a bird, he flew toward them. Near the stable he wheeled again. Six times he crossed the meadow. Then, flanks heaving, tongue lolling, he pulled up beside them. Frankie had tested his leg to its limits. It was perfect. "Good!" said George distinctly. Everyone cheered.

Soon Frankie was back in his accustomed routine of waiting for Jean by the power plant at six in the morning and searching his pockets for a treat, then accompanying him on at least part of his rounds. At noontime he canvassed the terraces when the weather was fine, for the staff often lunched outdoors. A nurse one day, leaning forward to make an impassioned point, turned back to her salad, only to see the last of it, liberally laced with Italian dressing, vanishing into Frankie's mouth. Whenever a picnic was planned, provision had to be made for Frankie, for he was sure to turn up, and strollers in the woods were likely to hear a light, quick step behind them and find themselves joined for the rest of their walk by a companionable deer. One visitor whom nobody thought to warn became hysterical at what she took to be molestation by a large antlered creature until someone turned her pockets out and gave Frankie the after-dinner mints he had smelled there and of which he was particularly fond.

In the fall, Jean, anticipating the hunting season, put a red braided collar around Frankie's neck. Within a day or two it was gone, scraped off against a tree in the woods. Jean put another on, and it, too, disappeared. "He doesn't like red," Pauline said. "He likes yellow."

"How do you know?"

"I know."

Jean tried yellow. Frankie kept the collar on. Jean was glad of this when Frankie stopped showing up in the mornings. He knew that it was rutting season and it was natural for Frankie to be off in the woods staking out his territory. The mountain was a nature preserve and no hunting was allowed, but still he worried about Frankie because poachers frequently sneaked into the woods; Frankie might wander off the mountain following a doe he fancied.

One day a staff member on her way to work spotted a group of hunters at the base of the mountain. Strolling down the road toward them was Frankie. She got out of her car, turned Frankie around so that he was headed up the mountain, then drove along behind him at five miles an hour. Frankie kept turning to look at her reproachfully, but she herded him with her car until she got him back to safety. On another memorable day, a pickup truck filled with hunters drove up to the power plant. When the tailgate was lowered, Frankie jumped from their midst. The hunters had read about Frankie in the local paper, and when they spotted a tame deer wearing a yellow collar, they figured it must be Frankie and brought him home.

After the rutting season, Frankie reappeared, but this time when he came out of the woods, three does were with him. And that has been true in the years since. The does wait for him at the edge of the lawn, and when he has visited with Jean and made his tour of the terraces and paused awhile under the crab apple tree waiting for George to shake down some fruit for him, Frankie rejoins the does and the little group goes back into the woods.

Because the hunting season is a time of anxiety for the whole of Glen Gardner until they know Frankie has made it through safely, George and the other people at Glen Gardner debate each fall whether to lock Frankie in the stable for his own safety. The vote always goes against it. The feeling is that Frankie symbolizes the philosophy of Glen Gardner, which is to provide care but not to undermine independence. "A deer and a person, they each have their dignity," Jean says. "It's okay to help them when they need help, but you mustn't take their choices away from them."

So, Frankie Buck, the wonderful deer of Glen Gardner, remains free. He runs risks, of course, but life itself is risky, and if Frankie should happen to get into trouble, he knows where there are friends he can count on.

★ ★ ★ ★ ★

I Love You, Pat Myers

Pat Myers was returning home after four days in the hospital for tests. "Hi, Casey. I'm back," she called as she unlocked the door of her apartment. Casey, her African gray parrot, sprang to the side of his cage, chattering with excitement. "Hey, you're really glad to see me, aren't you?" Pat teased as Casey bounced along his perch. "Tell me about it."

The parrot drew himself up like a small boy bursting to speak but at a loss for words. He jigged. He pranced. He peered at Pat with one sharp eye, then the other. Finally he hit upon a phrase that pleased him. "Shall we do the dishes?" he exploded happily.

"What a greeting." Pat laughed, opening the cage so Casey could hop onto her hand and be carried to the living room. As she settled in an easy chair, Casey sidled up her arm; Pat crooked her elbow and the bird settled down with his head nestled on her shoulder. Affectionately Pat dusted the tips of her fingers over his velvety gray feathers and scarlet tail. "I love you," she said. "Can you say 'I love you, Pat Myers'?"

Casey cocked an eye at her. "I live on Mallard View."

"I know where you live, funny bird. Tell me you love me."

"Funny bird."

A widow with two married children, Pat had lived alone for some years and devoted her energy to running a chain of dress shops. It was a happy and successful life. Then one evening she was watching television when, without warning, her eyes went out of focus. Innumerable tests later, a diagnosis of arteritis was established. Treatment of the inflammation of an artery in her temple lasted for more than a year and led to an awkward weight gain, swollen legs and such difficulty in breathing that Pat had to give up her business and for months was scarcely able to leave her apartment, which more and more grew to feel oppressively silent and empty. Always an outgoing, gregarious woman, Pat was reluctant to admit, even to her daughter, just how lonely she was, but finally she broke down and confessed, "Annie, I'm going nuts here by myself. What do you think—should I advertise for someone to live with me?"

"That's such a lottery," her daughter said. "How about a pet?"

"I've thought of that, but I haven't the strength to walk a dog, I'm allergic to cats and fish don't have a whole lot to say."

"Birds do," said her daughter. "Why not a parrot?"

That struck Pat as possibly a good idea, and she telephoned an ornithologist to ask his advice. After ruling out a macaw as being too big and a cockatoo or cockatiel as possibly triggering Pat's allergies, he recommended an African gray, which he described as the most accomplished talker among parrots. Pat and Annie visited a breeder and were shown two little featherless creatures huddled together for warmth. The breeder explained that the eggs were hatched in an incubator and the babies kept separate from their parents so that they would become imprinted on humans and make excellent pets. "After your bird's been with you for a while," the breeder assured Pat, "he'll think you're his mother."

"I'm not sure I want to be the mother of something that looks like a plucked chicken," Pat said doubtfully. But Annie persuaded her to put a deposit down on the bird with the brightest eyes, and when he was three months old, feathered out and able to eat solid food, she went with Pat to fetch Casey home.

It was only a matter of days before Pat was saying to Annie, "I didn't realize I talked so much. Casey's picking up all kinds of words."

"I could have told you," her daughter said with a smile. "Just be sure you watch your language."

"Who, me? I'm a perfect lady."

The sentence Casey learned first was "Where's my glasses?" and coming fast on its heels was "Where's my purse?" Every time Pat began circling the apartment, scanning tabletops, opening drawers and feeling behind pillows, Casey set up a litany: "Where's my glasses? Where's my glasses?"

"You probably know where they are, smarty-pants."

"Where's my purse?"

"I'm looking for my glasses."

"Smarty-pants."

When Pat found her glasses and her purse and went to get her coat out of the closet, Casey switched to "So long. See you later." And when she came home again, after going to the supermarket in the Minnesota weather, she called out, "Hi, Casey!" and Casey greeted her from the den with "Holy smokes, it's cold out there!" She joked, "You took the words right out of my mouth."

"What fun it is to have him," Pat told Annie. "It makes the whole place feel better."

"You know what?" Annie said. "You're beginning to feel better, too."

"So I am. They say laughter's good for you, and Casey gives me four or five great laughs a day."

Like the day a plumber came to repair a leak under the kitchen sink. In his cage in the den, Casey cracked seeds and occasionally eyed the plumber through the open door. Suddenly the parrot broke the silence by reciting, "One potato, two potato, three potato, four…"

"What?" demanded the plumber from under the sink.

Casey mimicked Pat's inflections perfectly. "Don't poo on the rug," he ordered.

The plumber pushed himself out from under the sink and marched into the living room. "If you're going to play games, lady, you can just get yourself another plumber." Pat looked at him blankly. The plumber hesitated. "That was you saying those things, wasn't it?"

Pat began to smile. "What things?"

"'One potato, two potato…'"

"Ah, well, that's not too bad."

"And 'Don't poo on the rug.'"

"Oh, dear, that's bad." Pat got up. "Let me introduce you to Casey."

Casey saw them coming. "Did you do that?" he said in Pat's voice. "What's going on around here?"

The plumber looked from the bird to Pat and back again. "You sure you're not a ventriloquist, ma'am? I thought parrots just squawked and said 'Polly wants a cracker.'"

"Not this parrot."

At that moment Pat sneezed. Casey immediately duplicated

the sneeze, added a couple of coughs in imitation of Pat at her allergic worst, finished up with "Wow!" as she often did, then threw in a favorite new phrase he'd picked up when the leak started: "What a mess!" The plumber shook his head slowly, speechlessly, and retired back under the sink.

Casey was so good at imitating Pat that when she telephoned her daughter's house and got one of her grandchildren on the phone, Casey would say, sounding just like her, "Hi. What's going on over there?" It got so that Annie, if she happened to answer the phone, would say, "Hello, Casey. Put Mom on," even when it was Pat herself speaking.

The three grandchildren doted on Casey. Because it amused them vastly, they had learned to belch at will and taught Casey to imitate the sound. The bird would belch loudly and follow it up immediately with "That's gross" in tones of utter disgust. Either that or he'd demand in Pat's voice, "Did you do that?"

When a bout of pneumonia put Pat back in the hospital and Casey stayed at Annie's house, he came home yelling, "Joey, are you up yet? Joey!" Pat remarked to her youngest grandson with some amusement, "Well, I guess I know what goes on at your house in the morning."

In her own house, when Pat woke up in the mornings, she'd hear Casey chittering to himself in his cage in the den. She'd tiptoe to the bathroom, but Casey had acute hearing, and no matter how soundless she'd been, the chittering would stop, there'd be a silence while he listened and then he would call out, "Is the paper here yet?"

Pat usually took the paper and her coffee back to bed. One morning the phone rang. She picked up the extension by her bed and got a dial tone. The next morning it rang again, and although she reached for it promptly, again she got a dial tone. The third morning she realized what it was: Casey had learned to duplicate the ring faultlessly.

Casey ate fruit, vegetables, chicken, egg yolks, pasta and whole-grain breads as well as parrot feed. One day, carrying a piece of melon to him, Pat had it slip from her hands and squash on the floor. "*#@&," she said. Casey eyed her. "Forget you heard that," she ordered hastily. "I didn't say it. I never say it. And I wouldn't have now if I hadn't just mopped the floor." Casey kept his beak shut and Pat relaxed.

Later that day a real estate agent arrived to go over some business papers with her. They were deep in discussion when Casey yelled from the den, "*#@&!"

Both women acted as though they'd heard nothing.

Liking the sibilance, Casey tried it again. "*#@&!" he shouted. "*#@&! *#@&! *#@&! *#@&!"

Pat, caught between humiliation and laughter, put her hand on her guest's arm. "Helen, it's sweet of you to pretend, but we both know you haven't suddenly gone deaf." They broke down in giggles and Casey ordered from the den, "Don't poo on the rug!"

"Oh, you bad bird," Pat scolded after the agent left. "She's going to think I go around all day saying four-letter words."

"What a mess," Casey said.

"You're darned right," Pat told him, reaching into his cage for the cup that hung there.

"How's your water?"

"Oh, dear, don't start saying that now. You really will ruin my reputation."

At work in the kitchen, Pat let Casey out of his cage, where he patrolled the counter and watched for a chance to snatch a lettuce leaf or vegetable peel. He'd sidle to the edge of the counter and drop his prize on the floor, then peek at her and say, "Did you do that?"

His favorite perch in the kitchen was the faucet in the sink; his favorite occupation, trying to remove the washer at the end of it. Once, to tease him, Pat held a handful of water over his head. Casey ceased his attack on the washer and swiveled his head to look at her. "What's the matter with you?" he demanded sharply.

If he disappeared from the kitchen and Pat heard him say, "Oh, you bad bird! You want to go back in your cage?" she knew to come running, that Casey was pecking at either the cane backs of her dining room chairs or the wallpaper in the foyer. In desperation, she had strips of clear plastic installed on the corners in the foyer, but still Casey found fresh places to attack.

"Is it worth it?" her son asked when he came to visit. "The front hall is beginning to look like bomb damage."

"Listen," Pat said, "give me my choice between a perfect, lonely house and a tacky, happy one, and I'll take the tacky one any day. As a matter of fact, I'd be so devastated to lose Casey that I've been teaching him his phone number in case I ever forget and leave a window or door open."

With a bit of prompting, Casey repeated the number. Pat's son listened solemnly, then advised the bird, "Just be sure you don't fly out of your area code, Casey."

One thing she could do to limit the damage, Pat decided, was to have Casey's claws clipped. On the drive to the vet's office, Casey rode silently in a carrying case beside her on the front seat until they were almost there, when suddenly he had a thought. "Where's my purse?" he demanded.

"What, you forgot your purse, you bad bird?" Pat joked. "You mean, I'm going to have to pay the doctor?"

To trim Casey's claws without getting bitten, the vet wrapped him tightly in a towel, turned him on his back, and handed him to an assistant to hold while he went to work. Helplessly Casey looked over at Pat and repeated a phrase she used when sympathizing with him. "Oh, the poor baby," he said piteously.

Occasions like this make Pat wonder if Casey knows the meaning of the words he's saying. On the whole, she's inclined to believe he simply connects certain phrases with certain actions, but sometimes the words are so apropos that she can't be sure. Recently a guest lingered on and on, standing talking in the doorway, until finally Casey called out impatiently, "Night-night!" When introduced on a different evening to a guest who had spent two hours talking nonstop about himself, Casey looked him up and down and delivered his opinion: "What a mess!"

When Pat wants him to learn something, however, Casey can be maddeningly mum. For her first Christmas back on her feet, Pat invited her children and grandchildren to a family dinner and hatched a scheme of teaching Casey to sing "Jingle Bell Rock." "It'll be your contribution to the festivities," she told him.

"Where's my glasses?"

"Never mind that. Just listen to me." But as often as Pat coached him, singing "Jingle bell, jingle bell, jingle bell rock" as she danced around the kitchen, the bird simply looked at her with a distinct air of wonder at her foolishness and said, "Wow!"

A week before Christmas Pat gave up. "All right, you stubborn creature, forget it. You probably can't carry a tune anyway."

Taking a beakful of seeds, Casey shook his head and flung

them in a radius around his cage, cocked his head and listened to them rain on the floor. "Did you do that?" he demanded in Pat's voice. "Shame on you, you bad bird!"

On Christmas day he belched for the grandchildren and said, "That's gross," and once, almost plaintively, he inquired, "What's going on around here?" amid the noise of laughter and packages being ripped open, but all through dinner he was silent. When it was time for dessert, Pat turned the lights down and touched a match to the plum pudding. The brandy blazed up. At that moment, with impeccable timing, Casey burst into "Jingle bell, jingle bell, jingle bell rock!"

With her health so much improved, Pat decided on a three-week European vacation. "You'll be all right," she told Casey. "You can stay with Annie and the kids."

"Phew," said Casey, which was what Annie said when she cleaned the bottom of his cage of the bits of food he'd discarded. "Ouch," he added, which was what he used to scare the family's golden retriever when the dog put his nose too close to the cage.

Annie laughed. "The dog has a lot more trouble with an animal who talks than you have with him," she told Casey.

The day Pat was due back, Annie returned Casey so he'd be there when Pat got out of the taxi from the airport. "Hi, Casey!" Pat called as she unlocked the door. There was no answer from the den. "Holy smokes, it's cold out there!" she shouted. Still no answer. Pat dropped her coat and hurried into the den. Casey glared at her. "Hey, aren't you glad to see me?" The bird moved to the far side of the cage. "Come on, Casey, don't be angry at me," Pat urged. "What do you say, shall we do the dishes?" She opened the door of the cage and held out her hand. Casey dropped to the bottom of the cage and huddled there.

In the morning Pat tried again. And the next day, and the next. Casey refused to speak. But finally, on the fifth day after Pat's return, he consented to climb on her wrist and be carried to the living room. When she sat down in the easy chair, he shifted uneasily and seemed about to fly away. "Please, Casey," Pat said softly. "I know I was away a long time, but you've got to forgive me."

Tentatively Casey took a few steps up her arm. But then he moved back to her knee and revolved uncertainly. "Were you frightened I wasn't ever coming back? Is that it?" Pat asked quietly. "Darling Casey, bonding goes two ways. I belong to you just as much as you belong to me." Casey cocked his head. "I'll never not come back if I can help it."

Step by step, Casey moved up her arm. Slowly Pat crooked her elbow. After a few moments Casey nestled down with his head on her shoulder. Pat stroked his head, smoothing his feathers with her forefinger. Finally Casey spoke.

"I love you, Pat Myers," he said.

★ ★ ★ ★ ★

Sister Smog and the Windshield Viper

In the Hermitage of Christ the King in Sebastopol, California, Sister Michael of God turned on the radio. She did this once a day to get the news, which she then passed on to the tiny community of contemplative nuns living in solitude, each in her own wooden hut, on ten acres of a tree-covered hillside.

It was the huts Sister Michael was thinking of as she listened. The community had exhausted its resources to pay for the cutting down of some dead trees that were threatening to fall on the huts, and now there was a new threat. Termites were gnawing away at the huts' foundations. Where would the nuns find the $1,000 needed to have the buildings termite-proofed?

The news ended and Sister Michael was reaching for the dial when her ear was caught by an announcement. Station KABL, San Francisco, in honor of the upcoming St. Patrick's Day, was sponsoring a snake race for charitable organizations. "First prize is two thousand dollars!" the announcer said. Sister Michael snapped to attention. Her eyes rolled heavenward. "Oh, no, Lord, I'm half Irish," she protested. "You can't really expect me to have anything to do with snakes." But just in case He did, she sent for an entry blank.

When the form arrived, Sister Michael reluctantly filled it out. Name of entrant? If she put down "Sister Michael of God," that would really commit her. Yet her initials, S.M.O.G., would look silly. So she compromised: "Sister Smog." Name of snake? *Goodness,* she thought with a snort, *does the snake really have to have a name? Well, in that case…* "Windshield Viper," she wrote.

Sister Michael mailed the form, a safe enough act, she thought, since Sebastopol was fifty miles from San Francisco and she had no way of getting there. But then friends of the Hermitage offered to drive her. On St. Patrick's Day, she prayed all the way to the city for a flat tire, to no avail. They arrived at Crown-Zellerbach Plaza at noon, just as the Irish band struck up. "Snakes alive," muttered Sister Michael, "I'm in for it."

When she confessed to her neighbor in the registration line that she was as nervous as an early Christian martyr on her way into Rome's Colosseum, the man tried to reassure her. "There's only one thing you got to remember," he said. "Don't hold the snake too tight. I did that last year and it turned around and bit me."

"I'll remember," Sister said weakly. She had no intention of holding the snake too tight. Or too loose. Or, for that matter, holding it at all.

At the registration table she was given a wooden dowel ("You can rap the table, Sister, but not the snake"), a piece of cardboard ("In case the snake starts going the wrong way"), a green paper derby ("To get you in the St. Patrick's Day spirit") and instructions to choose a snake from the supply in the green garbage can.

With the derby perched on top of her headgear, Sister Michael edged toward the snake-filled can. Withdrawing a shoe box from under her habit, she held it out to the man in charge. "You know more about snakes than I do," she said ingratiatingly. "Would you choose a fast one and put it in the box for me, please?"

The man calmly reached in and came up with twenty inches of thrashing gopher snake, which he popped into the shoe box. "Hey, what've you got in there?" he said as Sister Michael clapped the lid on.

"A hot water bottle. I heard that snakes like to be warm."

The man hooted. "You'll put him to sleep. Either that or you'll cook him."

The race was to be run in preliminary heats, semifinals and then the final. Every once in a while, as she waited for her heat to be called, Sister gently shook the box. No signs of life came from within. Should she try to peek in? The snake might be coiled, waiting to strike. Should she try to get the hot water bottle out? By now, if he was still alive, the snake probably considered the box his cave and would defend it fiercely.

"In lane number four," the loudspeaker boomed, "Sister Smog racing Windshield Viper!" Laughter, followed by a loud cheer, came from a Catholic Youth Organization gang. Sister waved her derby and advanced to the eighteen-foot-long racing table. Gingerly she snatched the lid from the box and shook Windshield Viper out into lane four.

The snake lay as loosely tangled and motionless as an old piece of rope. Sister Michael tried to see if his eyes were open, but she could locate only his tail, not his head. "Oh, dear, what have I done to you?" she murmured miserably.

It was one thing to be afraid of the snake, quite another to have roasted him alive. The announcer's voice came over the loudspeaker: "On your mark...get set!" Hastily Sister drew a vial of holy water from under her habit. "Please be all right. Please don't be dead," she whispered, and sprinkled the holy water on the snake's tail.

Windshield Viper shot into the air like a broken mainspring as the starting gun went off. Was it the cold holy water after the warm hot water bottle? The Viper was halfway to the finish line when he landed. The CYO group cheered wildly.

"Windshield Viper in the lead!" The announcer was calling the race. "Snake Hips coming up fast in lane six! Eve in lane two disqualified for jumping lanes! Here comes Star and Garter in three! There goes Star and Garter in three! Wrong way! Monty Python in lane one still in the starting gate!"

Windshield Viper rose for a look over the partition between lanes. Sister Smog blocked his view with the piece of cardboard. The Viper stuck out his tongue and waggled it at her. Snake Hips passed. Sister banged frantically on the table with her dowel. "Feel the vibes, Viper!" she shouted. "Get moving with the vibes!"

"It's Windshield Viper coming up fast! Windshield Viper takes the lead! And the winner is... Windshield Viper by a length!"

Sister ran around the table. Windshield Viper was sliding off the end. She grabbed him and slid him into the box, on top of the hot water bottle. Her CYO partisans were celebrating the victory. She doffed her derby, blew them a kiss and retired to the sidelines to catch her breath.

Some moments later she said to herself: "Did I do that? Did I really do that? Bare-handed, I picked up a snake?" She sat down heavily.

She tried to remember how the Viper had felt. Not cold,

not clammy, not slimy. Dry and clean to the touch. She sniffed her hand; there was just the trace of an autumn smell, of dried leaves. It wasn't at all what she'd expected. In fact, it was rather nice.

Poor thing, she thought. *I probably scared him half to death with the holy water. No wonder he stuck his tongue out at me.* Another thought occurred to her. *Maybe he's as frightened of nuns as I am of snakes. Particularly overweight nuns. Particularly overweight nuns wearing derby hats and called Sister Smog. If he's the Viper to me, I could be the S.S. to him.*

Their semifinal heat was called. Sweeping the lid off the shoe box with a flourish, Sister Smog poured Windshield Viper out on the table. He lay as inert as before. But this time she saw his eye. It was open. It was turquoise!

"On your mark…get set!" Out came the holy water. A dash on his tail and… "It's Windshield Viper off to another flying start!"

"Go, Viper, go!" the CYO group yelled. "Yeah, Smog! Yeah, Viper!"

Sister drummed on the table. The Viper curled and slithered, curled and slithered. Sister screamed encouragement. The Viper pressed on. They were a team; Sister was certain of it. The Viper knew what he had to do, and he did it. Sister ran around the table and caught him at the finish line. The cheers from the CYO group were deafening. They'd won the semifinal heat!

Sister picked the Viper up tenderly. He winked at her with one turquoise eye and tried to curl around her arm. "Now, now," she said, "you did great, but none of that." She caught his tail, straightened him out, admired the design of yellow stripes on his back and the way his basic brown shaded into creamy white on his underside, then popped him back in the shoe box. "You warm up for the finals," she told him, "while I scout the competition."

A snake named Max appeared to be the swiftest in the remaining semifinal races. His handler, Sister noticed, blew on the back of his neck, and with each puff, Max straightened and glided forward. It was legal, it was effective, and she must remember to do it.

It was time for the finals. "In lane five, Sister Smog and Windshield Viper!" Under cover of the cheers, as she slid the Viper out on the starting line, she whispered, "Go, Viper, go." He appeared to be asleep. She leaned closer. His eyes were closed. But his mouth...yes, she was sure of it—his mouth was curled in a smile. She had a feeling he knew they were going to win.

"On your mark!" A dash of the holy water and Windshield Viper was off! But she'd been too eager. He'd jumped the gun. She had to bring him back. He flicked his tongue at her. "I don't blame you. What a dope I am. But please, please, remember the termites."

"On your mark...get set!" This time the Viper wasn't startled by the water. "Go, Viper, go!" Sister screamed. He thought about it. "Go, Viper, go!" the CYO kids yelled. He curled up. "Go, Viper, go!" He felt Sister's hot breath on his neck, uncoiled and took a long glide forward. She beat on the table. "Catch the vibes!" He slid sideways. Sister huffed and puffed. He darted forward, then stopped to listen to the sound of a distant drumming. "Please, W.V.!" Another long glide. And another. He rose and surveyed the finish line. "Go, Viper, go!"

"They're neck and neck! Max and Windshield Viper! They're coming down the home stretch! It's Max! It's Windshield Viper! It's Max! They're at the finish line! And the winner by a nose is... Max! Second, Windshield Viper. Third..."

Sister went around the table and picked up Windshield

Viper. He flicked his tongue at her. "You're right. I deserve it. If I hadn't been so clumsy, you'd have won."

A hand caught her sleeve. "Congratulations, Sister. Come over here. Here they are, folks, Sister Smog and the Windshield Viper! Winner of one thousand dollars!"

"What?"

"Second prize, Sister. You've won a thousand dollars."

"Hey, W.V., did you hear that? Enough for the termites!" A turquoise eye flashed. "Oh, you smart snake, you knew it all the time."

When the TV interview was finished, the CYO kids crowded around Sister Smog. "How did you dare hold the snake?" one girl asked.

"Well, I found out he's like all God's creatures," Sister said. "He likes to be treated warmly."

"Why did you call him Windshield Viper? Weren't you afraid he'd just go side to side?"

"Oh, I never thought of that. Maybe I should have called him Julius Squeezer—he came, he saw, he conquered."

With the $1,000 check safely tucked in her habit, Sister returned Viper to the man who had picked him out. "I don't want anything to happen to him," she said.

"Nothing will. They're all going back to the nature preserve where I caught them."

As she reached into the shoe box, Sister Michael said, "Thanks, Viper, for teaching me about snakes. I promise not to be afraid of them anymore if you promise not to be afraid of nuns in green derby hats."

As Windshield Viper slid into the garbage can, his mouth curved in a smile. Sister Michael of God saw it quite clearly.

★ ★ ★ ★ ★

A Swan Called Porcelain

The eggs had hatched that morning. Ethel Russell watched from her house through binoculars as the mother swan took the newborn cygnets for a brief swim, then signaled them to follow her back to the nest. The muddy bank was slippery, but the babies straggled up it safely—all except the last. That little one slid helplessly back into the water. Struggling, the cygnet tried again. And slid back again. Through the glasses, Ethel could see the baby's beak open and close as she cheeped for help, but the wind was too strong for the mother swan to hear her cries. She was growing weaker. When she skidded into the water a third time, she stayed there. She was going to die.

Ethel dashed to the garage for her husband's long-handled fishing net and raced to the pond. Duke, the father of the baby swans, came charging toward her, defending the nest. Ethel scooped up the cygnet and ran, dodging those outstretched wings with the sharp "elbows" powerful enough to break a person's leg. When Duke judged her route, he went back to eating eelgrass. Ethel circled, trying to sneak close enough to deposit the baby in the nest. This time Duchess joined Duke on the attack. No one, not even Ethel, who often fed the swans, was allowed near the nest. After one more try, Ethel gave up and carried the little puff of pearly gray back to the house.

She knew it was unfair to imprint a wild creature on humans, but in the circumstances she had no choice, and secretly she was thrilled. Ever since her husband, Frank, had retired and they moved from Ohio to the shores of Chesapeake Bay, she had been fascinated by swans. To see the great white bodies of wild swans surging across the sky, to see the porcelain perfection of pinioned swans floating on neighborhood ponds, was a source of joy to her. Frank, knowing this, had had a pond dug on their property and had bought Duke and Duchess for her. Ethel loved seeing them and longed to know them firsthand. Now it seemed fate was about to grant her wish—if she could keep the baby alive.

She had the little cygnet wrapped in a Turkish towel in her lap when Frank came home. Even before she finished telling Frank the story, he was cradling the pretty creature in his big hands, admiring her bright brown eyes and dark bill and feet. "Ethel," he teased, "I think you've just become a mother." Retorting that, if so, this made him a father, Ethel put Frank to work finding a box and lining it with shredded newspaper. When he had suspended a twenty-five-watt bulb above it for heat and rigged up a water jar and feeding station, they settled the cygnet into it. Already Ethel was imagining her grown, so she had the answer when Frank asked what they should name the swan. "Porcelain," she said. "She will be as beautiful as porcelain."

If Frank and Ethel made odd-looking parents for a swan, Porcey, as they quickly came to call her, didn't seem to notice. She accepted them happily, breaking into cheerful *peep-peep*s at the merest glimpse of either of them and following as close as a feathered shadow when they took her for walks in the yard. The only time she seemed disappointed in them was when they didn't join her in the laundry tub for the twice-a-day swim she loved.

Her attachment to Ethel and Frank quickly raised the question of what to do with Porcey when they took a long-planned trip to Michigan to visit Ethel's parents. On the day they intended to start, Porcey would be just thirty days old. It was Frank who suggested that they take Porcey with them. It was Ethel who insisted on a trial run to see how the swan would react to the car.

Cautiously they settled her between them on the front seat in a hat box lined with disposable diapers. Frank eased the car out of the driveway. Porcey gossiped with Ethel. The car picked up speed. Ethel fed Porcey tufts of grass. She and Frank exchanged a congratulatory look just at the moment Porcey spied a car coming toward them. The cygnet dived for the bottom of the hat box. When next the small creature dared to peek above the rim of the box, another car was coming. She dived again. But finally she grew bolder, and a moment came when she held her ground and, with a graceful sweep of her neck, indicated to the oncoming car that it was to go around them.

So went the trip to Michigan, with Porcey between Ethel and Frank imperiously directing traffic, and eating when they ate, sipping water from a thermos and napping. In late afternoon they stopped at a motel surrounded by lawns, and Ethel went in to register. A sign on the desk decreed No Pets.

"Does that apply to birds?" Ethel asked. The owner, perhaps envisioning a canary in a cage, assured her it was all right to take a bird into the room. Even so, Ethel put the lid on the hat box until they had Porcey safely inside and had filled the bathtub for her swim. The cygnet swam and drank, drank and swam, then ducked her head under and beat the water into great sprays of droplets. Hastily Ethel pulled the shower curtain shut. After this workout, with the bathtub drained and filled with newspapers, Porcey settled down and slept until morning.

She awakened the Russells at daybreak with her chirping. After she'd had another swim, Ethel took her out on the lawn, believing it was too early for anyone else to be up. Suddenly around the corner of the building came the proprietor. He stopped in his tracks at the sight of a woman in a negligee and a swan airing her wings on his lawn. He said not a word, just slowly shook his head as though it falls to the lot of a motel keeper to see the darnedest things.

When the Russells arrived in Michigan, they told Ethel's mother that someone was waiting in the car to meet her. "Oh, dear," she wailed, "wait till I powder my nose."

"Never mind," Frank told her smilingly. "She'll love you just as you are." And Porcey did, enjoying every moment of her stay, including an almost endless stream of visitors as news spread of a handsome, perfectly behaved cygnet who liked to sit in people's laps.

Back home, Frank built an enclosure in the garage for Porcey to spend her nights in, fenced in the yard off the patio and sank a watering trough level with the ground, complete with running water so it would always be fresh. Mornings Porcey greeted Ethel at the garage door and they walked together to the yard. If a leaf, a twig or a scrap of paper was there that had not been there the day before, Porcey stood stock-still until Ethel picked it up.

One evening she refused to enter the garage. "What is it, Porcey?" Ethel asked. "What's the matter?" The swan looked up into her face, then back into the dim depths of the garage. Ethel followed the direction of her gaze but saw nothing. "Show me." Porcey looked into her face again and back at the same spot. Not until it moved did Ethel spot the tiny mouse cowering in a corner.

For her birthday that year, Frank gave Ethel an organ. Her playing left a great deal to be desired, but not as far as Porcey was concerned. At ten o'clock every morning the swan marched across the patio and rapped smartly on the glass door. "Come to listen, have you?" Ethel would say, spreading a piece of plastic for her to sit on, not yet having realized that swans are automatically housebroken, taking care of elimination in the water, not on land. Porcey settled on the plastic, crowding so close that Ethel had to be careful not to kick her as she reached for the pedals.

At one o'clock, following the strict routine she had fashioned for herself, as swans are wont to do, Porcey rapped again on the patio door, this time to be let out for a swim in her pool. Although she could see her siblings playing at the same time over in the pond, Porcey never paid the slightest attention to them. She was far more interested in the big ball she bounced from one end of the pool to the other.

When her swim was over, Porcey undertook the daily scrupulous care of her feathers, preening them, removing broken ones and, with the serrated edge of her beak, carefully cleaning soiled ones. As well as serving as brush and comb, a beak is many things to a swan: spoon, sieve, hammer, weapon and all-purpose tool. It is also the means by which swans express their feelings of fondness. Sometimes, in a rush of affection, Porcey would lean all her weight against Ethel and run her beak in long, stroking caresses up and down her back. "Yes, Porcey," Ethel would say as she stroked the swan's back in turn, "I know you love me, and I love you."

One night at a dinner party Porcey caressed a guest she had taken a particular fancy to, giving him such a turn that he dropped his wineglass. Probably she should not have been at the party at all, but the swan loved company, bobbing her head ceremoniously and making little greeting sounds to each person in turn. When she had made the rounds of the guests, she settled on a red velvet pillow, where, with her glistening white feathers and coral beak, she sat like a snow queen until it came time for her to display her talents.

Ethel had taught her to pluck a blade of grass from her lips, which the swan did so deftly and gently that her beak did not graze Ethel's mouth. Frank built on this ability to enlist the swan's aid in his magic tricks. He fanned a deck of cards and, upon command, Porcey plucked out just one and handed it back to him. If he pretended to drop one of his props, she quickly retrieved it and returned it to him. When he suggested that Porcey whisper a number to him, she stretched her neck to its fullest, stood on tiptoe and made little sounds in his ear, and when he asked her for a hug at the end of his act, she spread her wings and gently enfolded him.

The only people Porcey did not care for were deliverymen. Like all swans, Porcey was strongly territorial, and she had only to catch sight of someone on her property to come charging, wings outspread, talons at the ready. The Russells became resigned to searching the shrubbery at the end of the drive for laundry bundles and UPS parcels hastily flung by rapidly departing drivers.

One employee of Frank's was Porcey's particular enemy. Napping on her cushion one morning, she heard his voice at the front door a flight above. In a flash, she was up the stairs and had driven her beak through the screen door before Ethel could stop her. Only after Frank had dismissed the man for an unrelated cause did they learn that the man had once teased Porcey with an electric prod and she had neither forgiven nor forgotten.

But with Ethel and Frank, of course, because she had been less than twenty-four hours old when she came to live with them, Porcey was nothing but affectionate, well behaved and companionable. While they read or watched television in the evening, she often napped on the floor between them, and when she considered it her bedtime, she went and stood by the patio door. They'd let her out, and the three of them would walk together across the lawn to the garage.

In the spring of her second year, on a night of a full moon, Porcey moved from their side. She stopped at the edge of the lawn, lifted her head to the sky and called. "She's calling for a mate," Frank said. "It's time for her to leave us."

"Oh, Frank, how can we let her go?" Ethel cried. But just as parents know that however much they love their children, they must free them to live lives of their own, so Ethel knew that Frank was right. Swans have a life span of twenty to thirty years, and Porcey deserved to have in those decades the dear companionship that she and Frank shared.

The next afternoon Ethel led Porcey to the pond, and the swan glided along behind her as she rowed to a cove at the far end and set up a feeding station there. "Stay, Porcey, stay," Ethel told her, and as though she understood she was on her own now, the swan began a probing exploration of the shores of her cove. Ethel hoped that gradually the other swans would accept Porcey and let her join them, but day after day they drove her away. It became apparent that if Porcey was to have a mate, Frank and Ethel would have to find him for her.

An ad in a game magazine brought word of a fine two-year-old in Cleveland. The Russells made arrangements for him to be shipped, and when they brought him home from the airport, Porcey welcomed him excitedly to her cove. Watching them play and splash together, Frank and Ethel felt rather like parents of the bride.

Alas, they had congratulated themselves too soon. Within a day Porcey was rudely driving the newcomer from the water. When it became evident that this was no passing tiff, the Russells tried again with a bird from Indiana. Purposely they made their visits to the cove less frequent, thinking it might be jealousy that made Porcey difficult. Again all was well at first, but on the fourth day they found Indiana sitting gloomily on the bank while Porcey patrolled her domain triumphantly. Obviously this suitor had been rejected, too.

When the birdman came to pinion that season's offspring of Duke and Duchess (a simple and bloodless procedure if done early, pinioning is the removal of the second joint of one wing to prevent the bird from flying), Ethel and Frank told him of their sad failure as matchmakers. Mr. Miller excused himself. When he returned, he was apologetic. "It's my fault, not Porcey's," he said. Since it takes an expert to tell a male swan from a female, he had sexed Porcey at six months of age and confirmed the Russells' supposition that the cygnet was a female. "Not so," he now said. "She is a he."

A phone call to a breeder in Rhode Island turned up a four-year-old female who had lost her mate. Because swans mate for life, this time it would be a question not only of whether Porcey would accept the newcomer but also of whether the newcomer would accept a new mate. Only because she was young did it seem worth a try. Again Ethel and Frank drove the eighty miles to the airport to meet a plane with a crated swan aboard.

It was dark when they got back home and released the lovely, quiet bird into the water. Soon she was out of sight, but Frank and Ethel lingered by the pond's edge, his arm around her waist, her head resting on his shoulder. The night was warm, the breeze was soft and moonlight made a shimmering path the length of the pond.

Frank's grasp tightened. "Look," he whispered. Into the moonlight glided the two silver swans, as beautiful as porcelain on a mirrored lake. The breeze swung them gently toward each other. As they touched, Porcey lightly ran his beak up and down the newcomer's neck. A moment later the female returned his caress.

Ethel thinks of it often—that moment, that night. Now that Frank is gone, she looks at Porcey and remembers how happy she and Frank were, and she is glad for Porcey that he has found that sweet closeness she and Frank shared. She asks for the little cygnet grown into a swan only that he will be able to keep it as long and lovingly as they did.

★ ★ ★ ★ ★

An Experiment in Love

The dog discovered them, four newborn kittens abandoned in tall grass beside the road. When Livy returned from her walk carrying the tiny creatures in the palm of her hand, Steve, her husband, ordered, "Get those mice out of here." He was equally adamant when Livy showed him they were kittens. "No more animals," he said firmly. Steve had already been saddled with Livy's dog and three cats, and he was not used to a houseful of pets.

"I won't keep them," Livy promised. "Just until they're old enough to be on their own." Steve looked dubious. "Word of honor," Livy assured him, never dreaming how much she would come to regret that promise.

She made a warm nest for the babies by ripping up an old blue blanket and lining a wicker basket with it. Then she went to a nearby pet store to get advice about feeding them. "You can't raise kittens that young," the storekeeper warned her, but Livy decided to buy a set of toy nursing bottles for dolls and try. She warmed milk and she and the kittens struggled through several false starts until the kittens got the hang of it and drank avidly.

Two hours later they woke and set up an insistent chorus of soft little cries to be fed again. And every two hours after that. Four times in the night Livy crawled out of bed to warm their milk, and in the morning she congratulated herself that they were looking just a little bit stronger, a little bit bigger.

But by afternoon her pleasure had turned to pessimism. The kittens' intake was fine, but there was no outgo. Their little bellies were stretched tight as drums. Livy called everyone she could think of who might know what to do, but nobody had a suggestion. Hanging up after the last fruitless inquiry, she looked at the kittens sadly. So the storekeeper was right after all: she was not going to be able to save them. She picked up one of the kittens and began to rub its taut tummy in commiseration. Suddenly her hand was drenched. She picked up another kitten and rubbed its tummy. The same thing happened. Did a mother cat, after her kittens had nursed, give them a good rough washing? From then on, so did Livy, and the kittens thrived.

Steve, reporting on their progress to the people in his office, came home one evening with word that his secretary had offered to adopt Peaches, Livy's favorite because of her lovely soft coloring. As though it were Peaches's fault that she would soon be leaving her, Livy found herself picking up Peaches less often and making her wait her turn for the bottle instead of feeding her first. Idly she wondered if it would affect Peaches's personality no longer to be treated as special. Then the thought turned itself around. Suppose she gave one of the kittens extra amounts of mothering? Suppose she held and cuddled and talked to it more? Would it grow up to be any different from its siblings? She decided it would be an interesting experiment.

She chose the most unpromising of the kittens as her subject. This was a little black one Steve called Bat Cat because he was so homely with his dull fur, squashed porcine face and little folded flaps of skin for ears. The runt of the litter, Bat Cat was always on the bottom of the kitten heap, the last to be picked up, the last to be fed, the one who got the least attention.

Livy gave the tiny creature a new name—Boston, short for Boston Blackie—and repeated it softly over and over while she held him for his bottle. If he still seemed hungry after he finished one bottle, she gave him a second, and a third, as much as he wanted until, blissfully full, he fell asleep. Then she tucked him into her sweater so that he slept against her beating heart while she worked at her desk. When he woke, she snuffled his small body with her warm breath and talked to him before putting him back in the basket to play with his siblings.

The effect on the kitten was immediate. His newly opened eyes, which, like the others', had been vague and unfocused, became alert, and he studied Livy's face with interest. Quickly he learned his name, and when Livy spoke it, he clambered over the folds of the blue blanket as fast as his unsteady little legs could carry him to her. Now when he was in the sleeping heap of kittens, no longer did he passively accept the bottom spot; sweetly but determinedly he wriggled out from under and nested himself on top. Was it that, sensing himself valued, Boston began to value himself?

He was the first of the kittens to discover he could purr, the first to make endearingly clumsy attempts to wash himself, the first to undertake the adventure of climbing out of the wicker basket. When the others, exhausted from their tumbling play, fell asleep, he climbed over the side of the basket and searched for Livy. Finding her, he struggled to sit up on his haunches and held out his front paws in a plea to be picked up. Unable to resist, Livy lifted the tiny body gently, turned him on his back and nuzzled the star-shaped sprinkling of white hairs on his tummy. After a moment his small paws reached up to pat her cheek and his bright eyes searched hers as he listened to the words she murmured.

Even Boston's looks changed. His fur, from being rusty and rough, grew sleek and shiny. At first the luster was just on his head, but gradually the glossiness moved down his entire body until little Boston gleamed from the tip of his nose to the tip of his tail. Though never beautiful, he became so alert and merry, so trusting and affectionate, that the mere sight of him was a delight. Obviously Livy's experiment in love was an unqualified success, except for one large drawback: in giving Boston so much love, Livy had come to care deeply about him in return.

Secretly she hoped Steve would also be captured by Boston's charm. While he did agree that the extra attention given Boston had had a fascinating effect, Steve's interest was mainly academic. And, unfortunately, Boston was not always tactful. If Steve picked him up, his head swiveled to look for Livy.

As he grew, Boston became ever more responsive, watching until he learned the meaning of each move Livy made. Did she think of starting dinner? He was on his way to the kitchen. Did she think of going outside? He was at the door. One day he made a throaty sound midway between a purr and a miaow. "Yes, little Boss," Livy responded, "I know you're there," and from then on he quickly learned to produce the sound at will. With Livy offering interpretations, such as "Yes, I expect you do want your supper now," and "I'm glad to see you, too, Boss," he added more sounds, specific sounds that meant "supper" and "hello" and "how are you?" until he had a vocabulary of more than thirty "words."

Livy never walked in a room without his volunteering, "Hello." She never said, "How are you, little Boss?" without him answering. In fact, as long as she would talk to him, he would reply, which caused a problem when Livy was on the telephone. Since no one else was present, Boston assumed the words were meant for him and answered so enthusiastically that often Livy had trouble carrying on the human conversation.

After dinner, Boston liked to sit on Livy's shoulder and watch the soap bubbles pop while she washed the dishes. He was in his usual spot one evening when Steve walked in and heard the two of them "talking." "You're going to miss him when he goes," Steve said.

Livy wheeled from the sink. "Oh, Steve..."

Steve looked steadily back. Livy saw from his expression that this was a test between them. Would she keep her word to him or did she value a little black kitten more than his wishes? Steve had had trouble learning to trust, and Livy realized she dare not jeopardize the confidence she had worked so hard to gain. "Yes," she said as evenly as she could. "Yes, I am going to miss him."

Peaches and the ginger-colored cat went to new homes, and soon after their departure, Steve came home with word that someone in his office had recently lost a cat and might be willing to adopt both Boston and Striper. She was coming to inspect the kittens that night. When the doorbell rang, Livy snatched up one of the adult cats, a magnificent tortoiseshell Persian, arranged her among the cushions on the couch and provided a pinch of catnip to keep her there. The woman thought the kittens were cute, but her eyes kept straying to the Persian. She left saying she wouldn't decide just now about the kittens, not until she'd looked into the possibility of getting a purebred.

But Livy had no countermove when Steve came home with word of a church bazaar that was requesting kittens to be donated for sale at a pet table. It was obvious that these were to be Livy's last days with Boston. Now when she cradled him in her arms, it was often tears on her cheeks that he patted. "Oh, little Boss, it's going to be so empty without you," she would tell him, and his eyes would narrow with the effort to understand her distress.

The day before Boston and Striper were to go to the fair, a friend of Steve's secretary said she would like one of the kittens for her six-year-old son and they would come that evening to choose between Boston and Striper. Livy's heart contracted when the little boy, looking like a miniature football player, stormed through the door. How could such a tiny creature as Boston survive the roughness of his hands in play? Marching up to the kittens, the boy grabbed his choice around the stomach with both hands and announced, "His name is Grady and he's mine." He had chosen Striper.

So Boston would go alone to the church fair. Steve called at noon the next day to remind Livy that a description of his age, sex and food preferences was to go with him. "I've already typed it up," Livy said. Wary that she might have worded it in such a way that no one would want Boston, Steve asked her to read it to him. It included this final note: "Boston has been hand-raised with an unusual amount of loving attention, which has made him extraordinarily intelligent and responsive. He is gentle, perfectly behaved, loves all games, likes to ride in the car, has a large vocabulary and is a devoted companion. Please treat him with the great affection he will give you."

Steve was silent for a moment. "You've made him sound like an exceptional creature," he said.

"He is," Livy said, and hung up.

She was in the kitchen getting dinner that night when Steve came home. Boston went to the door to greet him, but Livy couldn't; she was fighting too hard not to cry. There was a long delay before Steve joined her. When he did, he was carrying Boston, who had a big red ribbon tied around his neck. Silently Steve held out an envelope. Inside was a Christmas card, and written on it was: "It's only November, but let's give ourselves a Christmas present."

"If you can be big enough to let him go," Steve said with love and understanding in his eyes, "I can be big enough to let him stay."

Livy reached out to hug Steve through her happy tears, and Boston, wriggling to get to her, slipped through Steve's hands. As the kitten struck the floor, he screamed terribly. One of his hind legs stuck out at an angle. Thinking he had dislocated his hip, Livy gave the leg a sharp yank. Boston screamed again, tried to run and collapsed.

His leg was broken, but the vet had even sadder news for them. Boston was suffering from an inborn defect in calcium absorption. Kittens with this problem could sometimes be saved by injections of calcium, and if they survived to adulthood, the condition tended to correct itself. But there was no guarantee the treatment would work and the cost of the injections would mount up. Did they want to have him put down instead?

Quickly Livy said, "I'll pay for the injections."

"Nonsense," said Steve. "He's our cat." And he told the vet to do what he could to save Boston.

The vet marveled at little Boston's disposition. Even though Bossie knew he was in the office for his daily injection, he greeted the doctor cheerfully and crept into Livy's arms to be comforted only when the ordeal was over. His leg healed quickly, although he walked with a funny little swing of his hip, but three weeks after the last injection, he took a tumble and it was obvious the other hind leg was broken. This time the vet did not even ask if he should try to save him. Ten more injections and Boston was racing around as nimbly as ever, the stiff-legged swing of his rump even more pronounced but not handicapping. Little Boston's calcium deficiency made him a very expensive Christmas present, but he was over it.

It is said that when a child is born into the world, the first years of his or her life are taken up with finding answers to the most basic of questions: "Is it a good and benign world? Can the people in it be trusted? Am I loved?" If a little kitten can also be curious about such things, the special love given Boston answered all his questions with a resounding yes.

It showed in his favorite activity, which was to fly across the back lawn, leap at a tree and scramble ten or fifteen feet up it. Then he would call. Livy would answer, and he would call again until Livy spotted his tiny body clinging to a branch. "What's the matter, Boss?" she would say. "Can't you get down?" He would admit he couldn't. The first time it happened, Steve went for a ladder while Livy stood under the tree, arms outstretched to catch the teetering cat. He did fall, and Livy caught him. But had he fallen or jumped? Livy wasn't sure. The next time he was stuck, Livy held out her arms and said, "Jump, Boss," and he did, instantly, with absolute confidence, right into her arms. And every time after that.

On the first warm day of summer that year, Livy put her kayak in the river that bordered their land and paddled upstream. Boston followed worriedly along the bank, calling to her, and when he came to an opening in the underbrush, he scrambled down the bank and out on a rock. There he stood, his front paws in the water, his whole body leaning so yearningly forward that Livy was afraid he was going to launch himself into the stream. She steered the kayak in beside him, picked him up and put him in her lap. He sat pressed against her, his eyes wide, an occasional involuntary shudder running through him, while she paddled upstream and then turned the kayak and drifted down on the current. Boston did not move or make a sound. The current carried them in toward the bank. They were still six feet away from it when, without warning, Boston catapulted himself in a black streaking arc from boat to shore, landing without a fraction of an inch to spare. His calculation of the distance he could jump had been exact. Then he turned and spoke anxiously to Livy until she, too, was safely back on dry land.

Another time she heard worry in his voice was early one morning when she was awakened by his talking through the crack under the bedroom door. At first she told him to go back to sleep, that it was not yet breakfast time, but he spoke so insistently that she got up to see what was troubling him. Instead of rushing into the room to leap on the bed for his morning loving, he turned and hurried halfway downstairs, then stopped to look back at Livy and spoke again. Verifying at each step that Livy was following, he led her downstairs and into the living room. As she entered, there was a whirring sound and the three older cats flashed to the top of the couch. They were in pursuit of a starling that had come down the chimney in the night. Livy shouted, distracting the cats.

The bird flew to the top of the curtain—and finally out of one of the windows Livy opened.

Although Boston also saved another bird's life in the same way—by coming to fetch her in the garden and leading her to where a blue jay was immobilized by a stick wedged in its beak—Boston was not the nonhunter these incidents would suggest. He loved to stalk flies and wasps, instinctively knowing that the one could be swatted with impunity but the other only with lightning-fast caution, and the Persian introduced him to the excitement of mouse hunting. She cornered one in the cellar one day and allowed Boston to share in its capture. The next thing Livy knew, he was vomiting violently and up came the remains of the mouse.

Having observed that, Livy was not concerned when, on an evening in July, she went out to pick lettuce in the back garden and found Boston crouched over the remains of a rabbit. "Good heavens, Bossie," she said, "however did you catch that?" He looked at her, glassy-eyed from overeating, his stomach round as a barrel, and she assumed that the rabbit, like the mouse, would soon be coming up. But it stayed down and the next morning Boston was back to normal size.

A few days later he began to seem listless. Livy felt his ears and they were cool, his nose and it was moist, and decided that it was only some minor indisposition. But the next afternoon when he did not greet Livy at the door and she found him sitting hunched in a corner, she gathered him up and set out for the vet's. On the way there she remembered the rabbit. Boston was too small to catch a healthy rabbit. Perhaps it had already been dead when he found it. A nearby railroad had recently sprayed a defoliant....

The vet scolded Livy for assuming that a cat's nose and ears are reliable indicators of his health. Boston had a fever of 105 degrees and was severely dehydrated. What was needed was to get as much food and medicine into him as possible. Livy stopped at a supermarket to get the liver, baby food and milk the vet had suggested and an eyedropper to feed him with if he did not eat voluntarily. Back home, she went around to the passenger side of the car and lifted him in her arms. He cried out, stiffened, his spine arched and it was over. Little Boston was dead.

Livy could not believe it. For eleven months she and Boston had been so close. They had talked so clearly. How could she not have known he was so ill? Steve tried to comfort her, but his own eyes were clouded with tears as they buried the tiny black body, now featherlight, under the tree he had loved to jump from. When the last trowelful of dirt was in place and they had transplanted myrtle to cover his grave, Steve stood looking down at the spot where Boston lay. Finally he said, "You were right. He was a truly remarkable small creature."

Months later, when the ache of missing Boston had eased enough to let Livy think back on her experiment, she decided to visit the other kittens, now grown. Peaches was sweet and bland. Ginger was sharp and unfriendly. Striper spent most of his time hiding under furniture. Only Boston had been unique in his intelligence and affectionate, outgoing nature. That love has unmatched power to nurture, to bless, to make cheerful and whole, Livy's experiment had demonstrated. But it was little Boston who proved that when you give love freely, you get something quite extraordinary in return.

★ ★ ★ ★ ★

Goose Steps

"You've got a sick goose over there," Gene Fleming remarked to his sister-in-law as they walked toward his car. He had stopped by Billee Schuck's farm in Harvard, Nebraska, to pick up some ducklings for his pond and noticed a goose who kept toppling over.

Billee didn't even look around. "Naw, that's Andy," she said. "He was born without feet."

With the ducklings stowed in his pickup, Fleming went over to take a look at the handicapped goose. "You're a gutsy fella," he said as Andy, his wings flapping wildly, tried to run away. The gray goose looked like a little boy on his first pair of stilts. His legs, thin as twigs, ended in callused knobs the size of silver dollars. The only way Andy could stay upright was to run as fast as he could until his momentum pitched him forward on his breast. He fell now, and Gene reached out to smooth his feathers. Because geese tend to be peevish creatures, Gene expected to get his hand sharply nipped, but Andy was quiet under his touch.

Gene kept thinking about the crippled goose as he headed

home to his own ninety-one-acre spread in Hastings. Had there been an appeal in those shoe-button eyes as Andy lay forlornly on the ground, his breast caked with mud? Gene thought about how he was a Shriner and Shriners are dedicated to helping crippled children. "That goose is just as helpless as a little child," he told himself. "I ought to be able to do something for him."

He put his inventive mind to work, just as he had years before on another occasion. That time his sympathy had gone out to cows tormented by insect bites, and he set about inventing a device they could rub against to scratch themselves and get a dose of insecticide and soothing oil on the itching spot. He called it the Rol-Oyl Cattle Oiler, and his company, the Fleming Manufacturing Co. of Hastings, Nebraska, had by that time made and sold more than four hundred thousand of them.

As soon as he got back to Hastings, Gene called his sister-in-law. "Billee," he said, "how about I take that footless goose off your hands? He'll be better off swimming in my pond than tryin' to walk on those sticks of his."

Billee Schuck refused. "I'm saving him for Thanksgiving dinner," she said. "Besides, even though he can't mate because he can't stand up, Polly is his wife and I'm not going to separate them."

"I'll take Polly, too," Gene proposed. Still his sister-in-law said no. Finally Gene offered to trade two blue-eyed Pomeranian geese for them. Telling him he was crazy to trade valuable geese for a gray one without feet, Billee accepted the offer.

Gene fetched Andy and Polly and turned them loose in his pond. Polly sailed gracefully off. Andy, struggling to follow her, worked his footless stilts as fast as an eggbeater but succeeded only in churning up silt. Gene lifted him out of the pond. "Okay, young fella," he said, "let's see what we can figure out for you."

Gene had his back to the pond while he was examining Andy's stilts and didn't see Polly climb out. She rushed at him and grabbed his pants, tugging furiously. "It's okay, Polly. I'm gonna help him if I can," Gene assured her. But Polly was determined to defend Andy. "Exile for you, my girl," Gene decreed. "You're gonna have to stay out of the way until I get your old man on his feet." He knew from Billee Schuck that Polly had spent weeks the previous spring sitting on eggs that never hatched and had finally taken to mothering a clutch of ducklings. "Just you be patient," he told her as he shooed her into a shed. "With a little bit of luck, I'll fix you up a proper husband."

Shoes, Gene decided. Andy needed some sort of shoes. Gene went into town and bought a pair of white leather baby shoes, size zero. Andy was deceptively patient while Gene slipped them over his knobs, laced them and tied a bow. Then the goose leaned over, untied the bows with his beak and pulled his legs free. Gene got some glue and glued the bows to the shoes. Andy fell into the pond, kicked one shoe off and, paddling with the other, swam in a circle until Gene caught him.

Bit by bit, experimenting as he went, Gene worked out what was needed. On his left foot Andy had a bit of a heel, but there was none on his right foot, and his right leg was cocked. Gene placed sponge rubber toward the outside of the right shoe and at the top of the shoe on the left side so that both soles would rest flat on the ground. More sponge rubber went in the toes of the shoes. He cut the back of the right shoe so the cocked leg would fit in and punched small holes into the soles so that water would drain out.

In the meantime Andy's life was being made miserable by two Chinese white geese who considered it their job to patrol the farmyard. Their hearing was acute and their honks so loud that they scared away coyotes, raccoons and possums wishing to dine on duckling, but they also felt that a goose who could not strut was an interloper and attacked Andy, pecking at his legs and wings and sending him cowering into corners. "Never mind, Andy," Gene told him. "One of these days you'll show 'em."

When the shoes were ready, Gene drew little white socks over Andy's knobs, laced the greatly adapted shoes snugly around his ankles and glued the bows. He set Andy on his feet. The goose sank to the ground helplessly. He seemed to think he had mud on his legs, and for three days kicked backward trying to shake the shoes off. Unable to rid himself of them, he lay on his breast and pushed himself along the ground with the tips of the shoes. Gene debated getting him a skateboard, but he decided first to have a go at trying to teach Andy to walk.

He buckled a dog harness around the goose's body and dangled him from a leash like a puppet on a string. "You've got toes now, Andy. Lean into them and take a step." Over and over he bounced Andy on his new feet. "Come on, Andy, you can walk if you think you can. All it takes is believing you can."

Three hours went by. Still Gene was patient. "You can do it, Andy. I know you can." Suddenly Andy took a baby step. It wasn't more than four inches, but it was a step. "That's it, Andy!" Gene exulted. "You've got it. Do it again. Lean into your toes. And again. Good boy! You're walking!"

Staggering like a fat baby in diapers, Andy inched around the farmyard. Gene unhooked the leash. Andy teetered but stayed upright. He looked at Gene. "You've done it," Gene congratulated him, and as though he understood, Andy stretched his neck and, lifting his head high, honked exultantly. He was six inches taller than he had ever been before.

Because he never had reason to use them, Andy's ankles were stiff and his walk tended to resemble a drunken stagger. But he stayed on his feet, and after several days of practice he was strutting around the farmyard. Gene released Polly from the shed to come and look at her mate. She stalked directly to Andy and stared at his new white feet. "What do you think, Polly?" Gene asked her.

She gave a shake of her head and flounced away as if to say, *He's a silly goose.* Suddenly there was a terrific honking. The two Chinese whites were bearing down on Polly and Andy. With a flurry of feathers, Polly fled into the pond, but Andy stood his ground. Rising on the toes of his new shoes, he beat the air with his wings and intimidated the Chinese geese into retreat. Then he marched to the pond and launched himself into the water. With his legs stretched out behind him, kicking his "feet" in unison, Andy propelled himself forward like a paddle-wheel steamer. Quickly he outdistanced Polly, then turned and proudly swam circles around her.

The principle of the shoes was a success, but the shoes themselves were worn out in a month. Since they cost $12.99 a pair and the life expectancy of a goose is thirty years, Gene figured it would cost him close to $5,000 to keep Andy on his feet unless he could come up with a substitute. He went to town again and this time returned with a pair of Nike sneakers. They worked perfectly and proved much more durable.

Word got around Hastings that Gene Fleming was buying

baby shoes for a goose. The local paper carried a picture of Andy standing tall in his sneakers, and a teacher asked Gene if he would bring Andy to school to show the children. "Unless," she said, knowing the temperament of geese, "you think he'll snap at them."

"Not Andy," Gene said confidently. "He likes people." Gene set about fashioning a carrier in which Andy could travel comfortably with his head out, bought him a new red harness and leash, made a tape recording of Polly honking and off they went to the school.

Andy strutted back and forth in front of the class, showing off how well he could walk, and when Gene played the tape of Polly's voice, he lifted his head and honked joyously. The children loved it, and Andy did not mind at all when they crowded around and petted him.

The visit was such a success that Gene took Andy to every grammar school in Hastings and began answering requests from neighboring towns. "We don't often get a chance to do something really big for our fellow creatures, human or animal," Gene told the children. "But keep your eyes open for the little things you can do, because sometimes little things can make an awfully big difference. Like the difference shoes have made for Andy."

The letters Gene gets from the children after Andy visits suggest they understand. "If I find anything that's hurt," one little boy wrote, "I'll try to fix him like you fixed Andy." But Gene cherishes most a February card from a girl in the second grade. "Andy's my valentine," she printed on a big red heart. "But I love Mr. Fleming because he gave Andy goose steps."

"It's a funny thing how blessings come in disguise, isn't it, Andy?" Gene sometimes muses as he drives home with the goose on the seat beside him. "What seems like the worst thing that could've happened, like your being born without feet, turns out to be the best. What other goose gets to wear sneakers and go to school and be made an honorary member of the chamber of commerce and have the Eagles give him a birthday party?" He reaches out to smooth Andy's feathers where the carrier has ruffled them, and Andy gently catches Gene's sleeve in his beak to give it a tweak. Is that a wink or a blink of Andy's shoe-button eyes? Gene is never quite sure, but just in case, he always winks back.

The Dog Who Healed
a Family

What led up to the catastrophe was this. The Dykhouse family was watching a cable TV show about hard-to-adopt children, and a little boy with a crooked Jimmy Stewart grin limped into their affections. "Why couldn't we take him?" proposed eleven-year-old Julee Dykhouse.

"Hey, yeah, that'd be cool," Steve, fourteen, agreed. "I'd have a guy to play with."

"It'd be like bookends," Sherry, who was a serious thirteen, said. She was referring to the fact that Steve had been adopted as a baby, and if a younger boy was added to the family, he and Steve would flank the two natural daughters. "What do you think, Mom? Dad?"

Sharon and Don Dykhouse had been pretending to read the newspaper, but they, too, had felt the tug of the little boy. They looked at each other. In their fieldstone house there was enough room. In their ninety acres of Wisconsin fields and woods there was enough room. In their hearts there was enough room. The next day Sharon traveled to the city and the adoption agency. But in the delay between the taping of the TV show and its airing, the lame boy had already gone to a family.

So that was the end of that generous idea. Except that some weeks later a photo of another eight-year-old boy arrived from the agency. *Yes,* thought Sharon, responding to the vulnerability the lad was trying to disguise by the straightness of his slight body and the protective way his arms sheltered two little girls, one on either side of him. Even when she read the letter that came with the picture and learned the girls were his sisters and the adoption agency stipulated that the three children must be kept together, Sharon still thought, *Yes.*

"If you can manage three more, so can I," was Don's cheerful response to the snapshot. His veterinary practice was large enough to support them.

He and Sharon looked at the letter from the agency again. Timothy, eight, Claire, five, and Laurie, four, they read, were the children of a college graduate who had emerged from a severe automobile accident with her looks intact but with her brain so damaged that right and wrong were no longer meaningful to her and she went with any man who paid for drinks and supplied drugs. Thus the children had unknown fathers and an unpredictable, frequently forgetful mother. When she disappeared for days, Timothy took care of the little girls as best he could, feeding them whatever he could find in the house, washing and dressing them, and when his mother brought a strange man home, he tried to protect the crying baby from being hit—or worse.

The day their mother forgot them on a street corner in five-degree weather was the day the child welfare authorities discovered their situation and began checking on them.

When they visited and found the girls covered with bruises, they placed the children in foster homes. But the youngsters were so unhappy at being separated—and so difficult to handle in their unhappiness—that now the agency was seeking an adoptive home for the three together.

Sharon and Don held a family conference with Steve, Sherry and Julee. Again Sherry commented on the symmetry: a boy and two girls, just like they were. Feeling good about the decision, all agreed that Tim and Claire and Laurie should come to them.

It was a disaster.

Timothy, at eight, was a little old man who had never learned to play. Weighted down with responsibility, he was cautious, rigid, pessimistic and humorless. When Steve tried to teach him to throw a ball, he displayed the aptitude and interest of a wooden Indian, and when the girls tried to engage him in games of tag, he tripped over his own feet and scurried back inside the house. The Dykhouse children quickly concluded he was about as much fun to have around as an undertaker.

Claire, on the other hand, never stopped smiling. The smile was as bland and unvarying as though it were painted on a doll, and she smiled it no matter what was said or done to her. The only thing she was absolutely positive about was that her favorite color was black, and she spent much of her time jabbing a black crayon into scraps of paper and secreting the scraps around the house. She alternated this behavior with hitting herself on the nose until the blood flowed in twin rivers and then smearing the blood on the walls.

One afternoon when Sharon Dykhouse tried to head off this behavior by proposing a doll's tea party with the blue luster cups her daughters loved, four-year-old Laurie had a temper tantrum and upended the table. Laurie's temper tantrums came four and five times a day. Often, during them, she flew at her sister and raked Claire's face with her fingernails, and one terrible day she stabbed her with the pointed end of a compass. Sharon pleaded with Claire to defend herself, at least until Sharon could come to her aid, but Claire only smiled her bland smile.

Every evening when Don came home, Laurie suffered a panic attack, screaming and weeping for minutes at a time. She was terrified of men and would not let Don come near her, nor would she allow Sharon to comfort her; she went rigid at any attempt to touch her, however gently.

Peace and comity leaked out of the house like air from a punctured tire. The old and new threesomes of children shunned each other, and the older children became progressively more alienated even from their parents because of the presence of this difficult trio. Sharon sought professional help. She took the new children for diagnosis and treatment, engaged in play therapy with them at home and tried, sometimes forcibly, to make them let her cuddle them. But the children could not trust, nor relax, nor believe their world had become better and kinder in any meaningful way.

One day when open warfare had erupted and Sharon felt she was at the end of her rope and ready to be hung from it, the telephone rang. It was Don calling from his office. "Put the kids in the car and come on down."

"What for?"

"You'll see," Don said, and hung up.

Sharon's voice was so irritable as she ordered the kids into the car that none dared object. So it was that all six children stormed into the veterinary clinic's waiting room, alarming a large, black, silky-haired dog who leaped to her feet and erupted into deep-chested barks in defense of her owners and their baby.

Alerted by the noise, Don emerged from his examining room. "These people are moving to the city," he told Sharon, introducing her to the young couple. "Their dog is a good watchdog and loves children, but they can't have her in the city and they can't find anyone to take her, so they've brought her here to be put down."

"Oh, no!" Julee, an even more passionate animal lover than her parents, protested. "Daddy, you can't! Mom, can't we take her?"

Sharon bit her lip so she wouldn't comment about the trouble they were in because of the last time Julee had proposed an adoption. She glared at Don for putting her on the spot in front of the children and the young couple.

"She's only a year old, and a strong, healthy dog," Don said, defending himself. "But it's up to you."

Rage flooded Sharon. Sure, Don wanted the dog because her silky fur was like Rusty's, the favorite companion of his teenage years. And sure, he'd known that Julee would fall in love with the dog because she looked like Blackie, their Labrador who had been stolen months before. But why hadn't he given some thought to her position? She was desperately trying to hold this family together, and the last thing she needed was one more frightened and displaced creature to contend with.

"Keep her in the kennel and we'll see," Sharon ground out between stiff lips, and marched the children back out to the car.

Driving home, Sharon waited for the pleas to start. Not from the little kids—they were afraid of dogs, just as they were afraid of everything else. But even Julee said nothing.

Suddenly Sharon realized what her children were thinking: she would have said yes to the dog if it hadn't been for the newcomers, so now the Dykhouse children had one more reason to resent the little kids. When they arrived home, Sharon called Don and said to bring the dog home, that they would try her out.

"What's her name?" she asked before she hung up.

"Shaneen."

"If she's as dumb as her name, she's not staying."

That night, all night long, untempted by the blanket she could have curled up on inside the snug doghouse, Shaneen stretched to the length of her chain and howled. In the morning Julee said numbly, "We can't keep her, I guess."

"Go bring her in," Sharon said. "Let's see if that stops her barking."

The dog huddled in a corner of the kitchen while the children raced to get ready for school. When all were gone except Laurie, Sharon knelt and looked across the room at Shaneen.

"Come here," she said.

The dog wagged the tip of her tail timidly and promptly wet the floor.

"Bad dog! Bad dog!" Laurie screamed. "Go away!"

Sharon caught the child's upraised arm before she could strike the dog. "Not bad," Sharon corrected quietly. "Frightened. She doesn't know us. She doesn't know if we'll be kind to her." She sat on the floor and spoke quietly. "Shaneen... Shaneen, it's all right. This is your home now. We'll never hurt you. We'll love you and take care of you. You'll be all right, I promise you."

The dog bellied across the vinyl tiles until she was close enough to sniff Sharon's hand. As Laurie looked on, Shaneen sighed thankfully and laid her head in Sharon's lap. Laurie reached out and touched her. The dog's tail thumped lightly. Sharon held her breath. Had Laurie known the message was for her, too? Laurie buried her face in Shaneen's silky ruff, and Sharon shifted her arm to enfold the child as well as the dog. The child didn't pull away. It was the first bit of contact she had allowed.

Later that day Laurie had a temper tantrum and threw herself on the floor kicking and screaming. Shaneen looked on from a distance, then seized a corner of her blanket, dragged it across the floor, dropped it on Laurie and wagged her tail hopefully. The child was so startled she stopped screaming.

"I think she's offering to play tug-of-war with you," Sharon said.

Laurie screwed up her face to resume screaming. Shaneen nosed the blanket closer. Laurie grasped a corner of it. Shaneen pounced on the opposite corner. Laurie pulled. Shaneen planted her back feet and tugged. The dog was stronger, but her paws couldn't get a purchase on the waxed floor. Shouting with laughter, Laurie dragged Shaneen around the kitchen until both fell in a tumbling heap.

That evening when Don Dykhouse came home and Laurie's hysterics began, Shaneen's barking almost drowned her out. "Hey, I saved your life," Don told the dog, but Shaneen had been trained to guard the young couple's baby, and Sharon had to take her by the collar, hold her and talk to her before Don could come into the house. After several nights of this, Laurie's hysterics stopped, as though observing the dog's fuss over nothing made her own seem silly, too.

One evening Don Dykhouse, pondering Timothy's inability to play, brought home the simplest toy he could find, a water pistol. Shaneen was lingering near as Don showed Tim how to fill it and squeeze the trigger. As the water arced through the air, the dog made a tremendous leap and tried to catch it. Tim crowed with amusement. He grabbed the pistol and fired it. Shaneen leaped again, and again. Don left the two of them playing happily together.

As well as loving water, Shaneen liked to fetch, and Steve obliged by throwing sticks for her to find and bring back. When Steve wasn't there, Shaneen dropped a stick at Tim's feet and wagged her tail hopefully, but Tim's attempts to throw the stick failed as it fell to the ground a few feet away, so one day he asked Steve to teach him how. They started with a tennis ball. Shaneen retrieved it when Tim threw it in a wayward direction, but as he got better, she began to jump for the ball and the game evolved into keep-away, with Tim and Steve throwing to each other and Shaneen in the middle trying to intercept the ball. Now, when supper was over, instead of disappearing, Steve began saying to Tim, "Come on, let's go outside and play with Shaneen."

At thirteen, Sherry was too dignified to romp and wrestle with the dog as the boys did. Intensely jealous of her privacy, she was suffering, as Sharon remarked to Don, from adolescent megrims. Shaneen seemed to sense this, and if she could nose Sherry's door open, she entered softly and laid her chin on the bed, not intruding but gazing at Sherry quietly until Sherry roused herself and called the dog to her for a hug.

The umpteenth time Sherry found black crayoned scraps among her most treasured possessions she screamed at Claire, "Don't you dare ever come in my room again! You're gross!"

For the first time Claire's smile faltered. She looked bewildered and hid in a corner. When Sharon went to see if she could persuade the girl to talk to her, she found her sobbing into Shaneen's ruff. "At least you like me," she whispered to the dog. Never before had the child let herself cry. From then on, whenever she was upset, it was Shaneen she turned to for comforting.

"It's as if we'd found the most wonderful nursemaid who knows when each child is troubled and just what that child needs," Sharon marveled to Don. "She senses when to be playful and when to be quiet, when to roughhouse and when to romp." She wanted to add that Shaneen was clear, as clear as a Wisconsin lake, and through her the poor, damaged children were learning that it was safe to trust, but she was afraid Don would think that fanciful.

"If she's so smart," Don grumbled, "why does she still treat me like the enemy? I saved her life and she won't even let me pet her."

One afternoon when Sharon was baking, Laurie and Claire and Tim hung over the counter waiting to lick the icing bowl. Laurie suddenly asked, "Is Shaneen foster or adopted?"

"Oh, adopted," Sharon told her. "Adopted means we're not just looking after her. She's ours. She's family."

"Even if she's bad, you won't send her away?"

"Never."

"You won't hurt her?"

"Never."

Claire said, "We're adopted."

"Yes," Sharon said. "Yes, you're adopted."

The children were silent until Laurie said, "I'll tell you what. After we've iced the cakes and the big kids come home, let's have a tea party with the pretty cups."

"Not me," said Tim. "Shaneen and me and Steve are going bear hunting in the woods."

Later, when Sharon was getting the blue luster teacups from the cupboard, she glanced out the window. The boys and the dog were running across the meadow and Tim was doing giant leaps. It crossed Sharon's mind that she had never seen a more carefree-looking boy.

On an evening soon after that, Sharon and Don took the six kids to the roller rink. All of them entered a limbo contest, but one by one they fell as they tried to slither under the ever-lower bar—all except Claire. "Hey, look at clunky Claire go," Sherry said as it became apparent the little girl had a chance to win. Quickly Sherry organized their bleacher row into a cheering section. "Go, Claire, go!" they chanted. Claire flushed, then grinned and waved. Cheered on by the encouraging shouts, she kept going until she was the last one left standing.

Sharon thought it was winning the trophy that made Claire's closed face suddenly look open and radiant, but when they got back to the house, she heard Claire shouting for Shaneen as she raced to be the first through the door. The dog instantly caught the child's excitement and leaped and barked as Claire delightedly told her, "They cheered for me, Shaneen! I've got friends! I've got friends!"

Often in the evenings the children would lounge on the floor in front of the fire, and always in their midst was Shaneen. Her favorite treat was popcorn, and she turned from one child to another to have a piece thrown in the air for her to catch and gobble down.

It was as though the kids were the spokes of a wheel, Sharon thought, watching them, and Shaneen, at the hub, linked them together. Through loving her, they were learning to love each other.

"Hey, kids, that's enough popcorn for the dog," Don cautioned them. He spoke her name. "Shaneen…"

She still came to him with some reluctance. But as the kids quieted and lay looking at the fire with their heads pillowed on each other, and as Don's fingers gently explored the tender spot behind her ears where she liked to be scratched, Shaneen settled herself closer and tucked her head into the crook between his neck and shoulder. Moments later Laurie nuzzled her way in between Sharon and Don and rested her head on Don's other shoulder.

Sharon and Don smiled at each other over the child's head. "She's made us a family," Don said softly.

"Thank you, Shaneen," Sharon said.

★ ★ ★ ★ ★

A Deer Asks for Help

The dog saw the deer first. Dropping into a crouch, he gathered himself to spring and run. This alerted Alison Millard, and she tightened her grip on the leash, pulling it taut to signal Topper that he was not to chase the deer.

She looked up, expecting to spot the white tail of the deer as it bounded off through the woods. To her surprise, the doe was standing perfectly still at the edge of the path about twenty yards ahead. It was half concealed in underbrush, but its forequarters were in the open and its head was turned toward Alison and the dog. It was staring fixedly in their direction.

It's hurt, Alison thought. *It's dazed.* She had seen that same stare on a deer grazed by a car on a nearby mountain road. For minute after minute the deer had stood unmoving in the middle of the road until an impatient motorist honked. Then, with a sudden shake of its head, the deer had come to its senses and leaped away into a field.

Alison clapped her hands sharply, expecting the same thing to happen now. Instead, the deer turned to look toward the path ahead, then back at Alison. The deer's eyes, Alison realized, were not blank, unseeing. They were focused, and there was something in them of a question. Or was it an appeal? Again, the deer turned its head just enough to indicate the path ahead before its steady gaze went back to Alison.

Alison had the clear impression the deer was asking her to follow it. *How strange,* she thought. *That sort of thing only happens in fairy tales.* The doe signaled again with a turn of its head to look along the path, then took a long look back at Alison. Alison hesitated. Should she follow? *What can happen?* she asked herself. *This isn't a bear or coyote. The deer isn't going to hurt me.* She tied Topper's leash to a tree and said, "Stay," quietly but firmly.

She started down the path toward the deer. When she was a dozen steps away, the deer moved off the path into the woods. Staying a bit ahead, it moved through the woods parallel to the path, turning its head every few steps to check that Alison was following. Alison, because she and Topper often walked this way, knew the path and knew that it passed a cottage tucked into the woods at the end of a long lane.

They were coming to it now. Alison could see the white picket fence in front of it. The doe stopped at the edge of the woods where the trees thinned out and waited until Alison drew even. When their eyes met, the doe shifted her gaze to the picket fence. Back to Alison. Back to the fence.

The fence was not high, only three feet or so. A deer could easily vault over it. Why was the doe staring at it and seeming to will Alison to look at it, too?

Alison stepped free of the woods. She moved closer to the fence and ran her eye along it. Now she understood. Trapped between two of the pickets was a tiny fawn a few days old.

It was easy to guess what had happened. The mother had

jumped the fence, and the fawn, too small to make the leap, had tried to run between two pickets and become wedged midway through. The doe had probably nosed the fawn and rumbled encouragingly in its throat as the fawn struggled, but the struggling had only wedged the baby more firmly, and there was nothing the mother could do to free it. So it had done the next best, but surprising, thing: when it heard Alison and Topper coming through the woods, the deer risked its own safety and asked for help.

The fawn panicked as Alison came near, kicking and thrashing. Alison knelt and caught its hindquarters to hold the tiny creature still. Her voice and touch were soothing, and when the fawn had quieted, she set to work tugging with all her strength at first one, then the other of the imprisoning pickets. There was no give to either; the wood was new and strong, the fence stoutly made. She found a sturdy stick and tried to wedge the pickets open an inch. They didn't move. Could she work a nail loose? She threw all her weight into the effort. Nothing budged.

If only she had a tool—a saw or crowbar or hammer. The couple who lived in the cottage were away all day at work. The house would be locked and Alison couldn't imagine breaking in to get a tool even on an errand of mercy. To walk to her own house to fetch a crowbar would take too long; the deer might well have abandoned the baby by the time she got back. She wondered if a passing car might have some sort of tool that could serve to pry a picket loose. She decided to walk out to the road.

She looked toward the woods, trying to pick out the silhouette of the deer against the pattern of trees. "I'll be back," she called toward the woods. "I'm going for help. I'll be back." Did the doe hear her? Was she still there? Would she understand? Alison kept looking over her shoulder as she started up the lane, searching for the slightest movement, but the woods were still and silent.

On the road it was long minutes before she heard a car coming, and then it was not a neighbor or a workman in a pickup, as she hoped, but a stranger, a man in aviator sunglasses driving a sleek black convertible. The man resettled the tweed cap on his silver-streaked hair as Alison hurried through an explanation of why she had stopped him. "A fawn?" he said, his voice rising. "You stopped me for a fawn?"

"I thought if you had a jack…"

"Changing a tire is not something I do."

"The handle of a jack. To use as a lever." Alison indicated the lane. "It's just down there…."

The man scowled. "I've got an appointment. But okay, I'll take a look. Get in."

Get in a car with a man she'd never seen before and drive into the woods? Alison hesitated. The man's gloved hand drummed on the steering wheel. Alison thought about the risk the deer had taken to get help for her fawn. She got in the car.

At the house, the man left the motor running and strode toward the fence. "The jack?" Alison called after him. He didn't reply. Alison saw with alarm that the fawn's head was now hanging limply. She hurried through a gate in the fence and sank down to brace its head in her lap.

"Piece of cake," the man announced, surveying the situation. As Alison had done, he grabbed a picket and pulled. He jerked it, rattled it, yanked it. He pushed the picket on the near side of the fawn and pulled the one on the far side. He rocked the fence. He picked up the stick Alison had used, threaded it between the two pickets and yanked. The stick broke. Irritably he stepped back and set himself to kick, then looked down at his Italian-made shoes and thought better of it. He looked around. "What can I use?"

"If you have a tire iron in the car…" Alison started, but the man was already heading for a cairn of rocks at the side of the lane. He returned with the biggest one he could hold in one hand. "Stay out of the way," he ordered Alison. She assumed he was going to try to pound a picket loose. Instead, he took aim and crashed the rock into the center of one of the pickets holding the fawn fast. The picket fractured. Two more swift, hard blows broke it in half. Alison grabbed the bottom half and wrenched it aside. Her hands went under the fawn. She cradled it, speaking softly as she lifted it into her arms.

The man tossed the rock toward the woods. "That does it, right?"

"Yes. Thank you. Thank you very much."

"Made a mess of the fence."

"I'll get a carpenter to fix it," Alison said. "I know you're in a hurry…."

"Right." The man started for his car, then turned back and gestured at the fawn. "Is it going to be all right? What are you going to do with it?"

"I'm hoping its mother is still in the woods there."

The man reached into his pocket and held out a business card. "Let me know how it turns out," he said over his shoulder. "It's kind of a pretty little thing."

"I will. Thank you again."

Alison waited until the car was out of sight. Carrying the fawn, she went through the gate and knelt on the grass at the edge of the woods. When the drumbeat of the fawn's heart had slowed, she set the small creature on the grass, testing if its legs would hold it. The fawn, swaying, lifted its head and let out a small, seeking bleat. After a while, it bleated again, a little louder, a little panicky. There came from the woods a snort, a quick release of air through flaring nostrils, not close, but the fawn heard it and took a trembling step. Another. Another. Then it was bounding into the woods.

Alison collected the broken pieces of picket, wrote a note for the owners of the house, and headed for the path to liberate Topper and resume their walk. When she got home, she would call the number on the business card and leave a message that the story had a happy ending. The fawn was back with its mother.

★ ★ ★ ★ ★

Where's Bubba?

In Texas brush country near the Mexican border, Buddy Thorne, an ex-rodeo rider, was on his way to hunt rattlesnakes with a friend of his when the men spotted two small creatures. They were about the size of rabbits and they stood swaying unsteadily in the middle of the dusty track. "What are they?" wondered Buddy as he jammed on the brakes to keep from running over them.

As the men leaped from the pickup, the babies came tottering toward them. So young that one still had the umbilical cord attached, they were crawling with fleas and gaunt with starvation. "They're javelinas!" Buddy exclaimed, pronouncing it "havelina" in the Spanish way. He dropped to his knees beside one. "Hey there, Bubba. You're really in bad shape, aren't you? Where's yo' mama?"

As a surveyor for a power company, Buddy had occasionally come upon small numbers of the miniature wild pigs foraging for cactus roots. Mild-mannered creatures, javelinas were so loyal to the pack that if a hunter shot one, the others stayed by it even at risk to their own lives. That's what made it so unusual that these two babies were on their own.

"They don't have a chance," Buddy said. "If they haven't starved to death by nightfall, the coyotes will get 'em." The babies nuzzled his boots hungrily. Buddy hesitated. "Oh, heck," he said, sweeping them up in his arms, "we can't just leave 'em here to die."

At a general store, the men bought flea powder, canned milk and nursing bottles, then cleaned and fed the tiny animals. Although the babies gained strength from the feeding, they were far too young to survive on their own. Again Buddy pondered what to do. Perhaps it was his own war experience, when severely wounded in combat he had prayed for rescue, that made him reluctant to abandon these creatures. "What d'ya say you take that one," he suggested to his companion, "and I'll look after Bubba here?"

Buddy wasn't sure what his wife, Patsy, and two teenage daughters would say when he arrived home in Corpus Christi with a baby javelina. But he needn't have worried. The minute he turned back the flap of his jacket and Bubba's trusting brown eyes peered out, they fell in love with the small creature. "Milk," Patsy decreed. "Warm milk right now. Kids, where's that old doll carriage of yours?"

While Patsy heated the milk, the girls settled Bubba in a nest of blankets in the doll carriage with a teddy bear to keep him company. That night they got up every two hours to feed him. The next day, and for many weeks thereafter, they wheeled him around in the carriage and carried him in their arms, talking and playing with him.

Bubba thrived on the love and attention. Soon he was romping with the girls and lying on the floor watching television with them. After graduating to solid food, he fell into the habit of pattering into Buddy and Patsy's room at six in the morning and tugging at the sheet. He didn't jump on the bed—one scolding taught him not to do that—but if pulling the sheet off didn't wake Buddy, the javelina butted the mattress until Buddy laughed and rolled out of bed to get him his breakfast.

After eating, Bubba joined the girls while they brushed their teeth. One morning, to tease him, they put a dollop of toothpaste on his nose. Relishing the taste, from then on Bubba sat beside them every morning while they scrubbed his tusks with a toothbrush of his own and allowed him to swallow the foam.

When it took just twenty-four hours to paper-train Bubba, Buddy pronounced him to be smarter than any dog or horse he'd ever known. Indeed, the day the family came home to find the television set on and Bubba sitting in front of it watching the screen, he declared Bubba to be a prodigy among animals. But when it never happened again, the family reluctantly concluded that Bubba had hit the on button accidentally.

The Thorne daughters were raising a lamb as a 4-H project, and when Bubba was six months old, he joined Kirby in a small shed in the backyard where there was hay to snuggle into and a heat lamp for chilly nights. The javelina and the lamb rapidly became fast friends, tirelessly playing a game in which Kirby butted Bubba and Bubba lumbered around the yard in pursuit of Kirby. A neighbor's dog, envying the fun, learned to jump the four-foot fence and join in.

Every morning Buddy cooked an extra portion of his own breakfast of bacon and eggs and toast for Bubba; in the evening when she was making dinner, Patsy also made a plate for Bubba, whether it was steak and vegetables, spaghetti or pork chops. If the family stopped at a fast-food place, a takeout order of fried chicken went home with them for Bubba.

Chewing slowly and reflectively, Bubba munched his way through supper, then stood at the back door waiting for dessert. If, by any chance, someone forgot to bring it, Bubba would still be standing there patiently at midnight. He loved ice cream and would open his mouth wide for one of the girls to feed it to him spoonful by blissful spoonful. For beer, too, he happily waited for a swallow to be poured down his throat. But his absolute favorite was chocolate.

"You're a chocoholic," Buddy accused him. "Why are you sniffing my pockets? What d'ya think's in there? Ah, you found 'em, didya?" And Buddy would laugh and pull out the chocolate malt balls he always carried as a treat for Bubba.

A neighbor in her eighties, knowing the javelina's weakness, often leaned over the fence and shared chocolate chip cookies with him. One night Bubba repaid her kindness by scaring off an intruder trying to jimmy her back door. Repeatedly throwing himself against the fence, Bubba made such a racket that the burglar ran out from under his cap in his haste to get away.

Ordinarily, however, Bubba was the most peaceable of creatures. Neighborhood children stopped on their way home from school to pet him. If Patsy laid a hand on his back and instructed him to lie down, he complied immediately. "When we were playing and he grabbed my arm in his mouth," Buddy remembers, "all I had to do was say 'ouch' and he let go." And when the games were over, Bubba liked nothing better than to lie with his head in a lap, having his ears scratched and falling asleep in his contentment.

Thinking back, Buddy says, "I'm sure other families have loved an animal like we loved Bubba. But I'm darned if I know of any."

"He was like one of our kids," Patsy adds. "We didn't do

anything that we didn't think of Bubba." Her voice breaks and tears fill her eyes as she remembers the events of six months before.

Bubba had been with them ten years when a family from Kansas moved into the neighborhood. One day the young mother peered across several backyards, spotted Bubba and imagined he was a wild boar, a beast capable of charging through fences and attacking her children. She raced inside and called the city's Animal Control Department, which in turn notified the Texas Parks and Wildlife Department.

The first the Thornes knew of the complaint was when two wildlife agents appeared at their door asking to see their license to keep a wild animal. "But Bubba isn't a wild animal," Buddy explained. "He's always lived here." He described the circumstances under which he had found Bubba and brought him home to save his life.

"Doesn't matter," said the agents, insisting that a javelina, any javelina, is a wild animal and must be returned to the wild.

"But Bubba would die in the wild," Buddy protested. "He can't eat cactus roots and fight off coyotes. He doesn't know how."

Nevertheless, the agents said, it was the law.

"At least give me twenty-four hours," Buddy begged. "I've got a friend with a ranch. I'll take him there."

He and the agents were arguing the point when Patsy arrived home. Learning that the men intended to take Bubba, she burst into tears. "I wish I had a shotgun," she sobbed into Buddy's shoulder.

The agents, choosing to interpret her remark as a threat, marched through the house into the backyard. Bubba ran to greet them. Backing off, the men shot him with a tranquilizer gun.

Bewildered, Bubba struggled to reach Buddy. As Buddy knelt to gather him in his arms, Bubba lost consciousness.

The agents wrote out a summons for keeping a wild animal, dragged Bubba to their truck and drove off.

"If only I'd followed them," says Buddy. But he wanted to calm Patsy and he assumed the agents would hold Bubba for twenty-four hours, as was customary, before taking any action. The next morning, however, when he went to the Wildlife Department to argue again to be allowed to take Bubba to his friend's ranch, he was told the agents had tranquilized Bubba a second time, transferred him to the trunk of a car and driven into the country, where they had left him by the side of the road.

"Where?" Buddy pleaded. "Tell me where."

The agents refused. Buddy, indignant at their handling of the situation and frightened for Bubba's life, went to the newspapers. Radio and television reporters picked up the story. Suddenly Bubba was a *cause célèbre.* "High-handed," "insensitive," "bureaucratic foul-up," trumpeted editorials. "Pignapping," claimed callers to radio talk shows. Buddy and Patsy were interviewed on the nightly news. T-shirts with WHERE'S BUBBA? appeared as if by magic, and stickers with BRING BUBBA BACK and BUBBA CALL HOME sprouted on car bumpers all over town.

A week later, when Buddy and Patsy appeared in court on the misdemeanor charge of keeping a wild animal, the courtroom was filled with reporters, TV cameras and spectators; members of the Humane Society picketed outside. The Thornes' lawyer introduced into evidence snapshots of Bubba eating ice cream, standing on his hind legs to kiss Patsy and wearing a party hat. "Now, I ask you," the lawyer said to the presiding justice, "is a javelina who attends a New Year's Eve party a wild animal?"

"He is," insisted the Wildlife Department. The court ruled that although javelinas are wild animals, Bubba himself obviously was not. But the wildlife authorities still refused to tell where they had released the animal, and the court did not have the power to force them to reveal the information. Patsy and Buddy immediately filed suit in a higher court.

One week had already passed, and it would be three more before their suit could be heard. Desperately afraid that Bubba couldn't make it on his own that long, the Thornes spent every free moment combing country roads for him. People everywhere were also on the lookout. Calls came daily saying that a javelina had been spotted eating at a trough with domestic pigs, a friendly javelina had approached a party of picnickers, a javelina had been spotted hiding in a culvert. Buddy and Patsy drove hundreds of miles, sometimes getting up in the middle of the night when a report of a sighting came. But as many times as they shouted his name and searched and called again, no Bubba came trotting out of the brush to lay his weary head in their laps.

Interviewed repeatedly by the media, Buddy leaned over backward to be fair. "The last thing I want," he said, "is for people to hear how wonderful Bubba was and then go shoot a javelina so they can take her baby. Or take in an owl or a raccoon or any other animal to keep as a pet. Wild animals really do belong in the wild."

"But what if someone finds an injured or abandoned animal like you did?" he was asked.

"They should take it to a wildlife rehabilitator who is trained to care for an animal in such a way that it can be released back into the wild," Buddy answered. If he had it to do over, Buddy said, that's what he would do with Bubba. "But I didn't know then that rehabilitators existed," he said, "and I did what I thought was right at the time. My quarrel with the Wildlife Department now is the heartless way they've gone about this. If the authorities really cared about the animal, they wouldn't have left Bubba by the side of the road to starve."

The higher court agreed and ordered the Wildlife Department to supply the Thornes with a map showing where Bubba had been released. A volunteer pilot was standing by to make an air search. Hundreds more volunteers were poised to make a sweep on the ground. Buddy had posted a $1,500 bond against possible damage to private property by the searchers. Everything was in readiness for the moment the map would be turned over.

Instead of providing a map, the Wildlife Department filed an appeal.

Buddy and Patsy kept asking themselves why. The Wildlife Department must realize they were dooming Bubba by seeking this further delay. Was he already dead, killed by the second tranquilizing injection? Was that why the Wildlife Department was stonewalling? The Thornes were never to know the answer.

In April, four months later, the Wildlife Department lost the appeal and finally handed over the map. No searchers were on hand then to help look for Bubba. No one believed he was still alive. But Buddy and Patsy hoped against hope.

They drove to the spot marked on the map. It was empty country. There was nothing as far as the eye could see—no house or barn Bubba might have gone to for refuge. It was useless for the Thornes even to get out of the car. But they did. Buddy stood with his arm around Patsy as they looked off to the far horizon. Finally Patsy said, "Is it because we loved Bubba so much that I feel he's still alive out there somewhere?"

Buddy nodded. "Maybe that's what love means," he said after a while. "You stay alive in the hearts of the people who loved you long after you're gone."

It is unlikely that the Thornes will ever know the end of Bubba's story. But because of Bubba and the outcry over his treatment, the Texas Parks and Wildlife Department has changed their policy. Now owners are allowed to place a wild animal who has become a pet in a location of their choice or, alternatively, to turn it over to a wildlife rehabilitation center, to be released only when and if it can survive in the wild. So, in one sense, Bubba's story does have an ending after all—a happy ending for other animals who, for one reason or another, have come in out of the wild.

★ ★ ★ ★ ★

Woman (and Dog)
to the Rescue

The lady always wears a beeper on her belt or carries it in her pocketbook. A backpack and duffel bag are packed and ready in the bottom of her closet. On a moment's notice Caroline Hebard dons orange coveralls, buckles an orange vest on Aly, her German shepherd, and sets out for wherever in the world the two of them are needed.

Such a call came on a November day. Within forty-eight hours this slightly built woman with an elegant cut to her blond hair had left her husband and children far behind in their home in Bernardsville, New Jersey, and was crawling through collapsed buildings with the stench of death all about her in earthquake-ravaged Soviet Armenia.

"I've never seen such devastation," Hebard says. "Towns eighty to ninety-nine percent destroyed. Schools, factories, apartment buildings—everything flattened, pancaked. Leninakan, where we were, was a city of death—coffins stacked on street corners, piled in fields. And cold. Bitter, bitter cold. That's why we had so few live finds."

"Live finds" is how Caroline Hebard and the other vol-unteer members of the USAID disaster response team speak of still-breathing people they and their search dogs locate trapped under tons of rubble. Hebard tells of one such find in Leninakan: "A father pleaded with us to return to a build-ing we'd already searched. Grief does funny things to people's senses, but he was so insistent he'd heard sounds that finally we went with him."

Searching is such a team effort that Hebard cannot now remember if she was the handler who located a way into the debris, gave Aly the order "Go find" and crawled in right behind him. In any event, one of the search dogs, with his handler on his heels, picked and squirmed his way through the rubble, tracking scents that drifted like smoke through cracks and crevices in the collapsed building. When the dog alerted, signaling a live find, a second dog and handler went in because the search component of the team never calls in the rescue component unless two dogs indicate a find; time is too precious to waste digging in an area only to come up empty-handed.

The second dog confirmed a live find. The rescue team went to work with cutting and lifting tools, and hours later an eleven-year-old girl, buried for four days alongside the dead bodies of her grandmother and brothers and sisters, was dug out from under masses of smashed concrete, miraculously unhurt except for broken ribs.

Hebard didn't witness the reunion of father and daughter, however, because as soon as the area of the find had been marked with orange tape, the search team moved on, rac-ing to locate as many people as possible while there was still hope of getting them out alive. The searchers went for long stretches without sleep or food. Even the dogs shared in the sense of urgency, and Hebard had to coax Aly to eat and rest for fear he would drop with exhaustion.

The stamina of both dogs and handlers is severely tested in such chaotic emergencies as the Armenian earthquake, and Hebard sees to it that Aly stays in top-notch condition. His thick tan and black coat gleams with health; his brown eyes snap with interest and intelligence. Even for a German shepherd, Aly is a large dog, perhaps because he was imported from Germany, where breeding standards are rigorous. But despite his serious size and deep-chested bark, Aly, when not on duty, is a warm and friendly creature who greets a visitor with such a variety of gleeful rumblings he seems about to burst into speech.

Traveling on a search mission with Hebard, Aly attracts toddlers in airports who pull his tail and try to climb on his broad back, which he not only tolerates but appears to enjoy. By prior arrangement with the airlines, he travels in the passenger section with Hebard because, like all highly trained search dogs, he is much too valuable to be put at risk of a drop in temperature or pressure in the baggage compartment. Also, were he to be left in a crate on the tarmac to await loading, the fumes from the jet engines would render his keen sense of smell inoperative for at least twenty-four hours, which is time that cannot be lost in search and rescue work.

When they go into action, Hebard at a reed-slim five feet six inches and 105 pounds would seem no match for Aly in endurance. Yet she manages well on little sleep and keeps going day and night in circumstances that would floor a sinewy man. The daughter of a British diplomat, Hebard grew up in Chile, Venezuela, Argentina, Switzerland, Portugal, Turkey and Bahrain and speaks the languages of these countries, which is immensely helpful in international rescue operations.

In this and other ways, her life seems to have been almost uniquely molded to fit her for search and rescue work. As a teenager, when her father was posted to the British embassy in Washington, Caroline's hobby was exploring caves in the Virginia mountains. Then later, as a graduate student at Stanford University in California, she added rock climbing and wilderness backpacking to her interests. Because of her skill at rope techniques and at finding her way with map and compass, Caroline became someone called upon to join search parties when hikers disappeared in the High Sierra or climbers met with an accident.

She married a physicist who shared her love of wilderness, and they have four children. While they were living in California, she acquired two German shepherds. One, bred in Germany, had been trained in tracking, obedience and protection work, and Caroline thought it might be useful to understand Zibo's capabilities. Joining a group of law-enforcement officers being trained by an exacting instructor, also from Germany, she quickly displayed a special aptitude at handling dogs. When her husband's work brought the family east, one of the first things Caroline did was join a local unit of the American Rescue Dog Association.

Members of the association respond to situations in this country as varied as a missing child, a drowned white-water rafter or a police request to track a suspected murder victim. One of Caroline and Zibo's first searches took place in a small town in Virginia where the police asked for help in finding a senile old man who had wandered off and been missing for several days.

They were deep in the woods and Zibo was sniffing the air with interest when a radio message called off the search because of a severe thunderstorm alert. The next morning, although assigned elsewhere, Caroline said she had a feeling about where they'd been. She and Zibo retraced their steps, and Zibo, picking up a scent, ranged ahead of her. In minutes, he came racing back through the woods and snatched up a stick in his mouth, tail wagging madly.

Caroline followed him to a clearing but saw nothing. "Here?" she asked Zibo. "Where?" He put the stick down and nosed at the trunk of a tree. Stepping around it, Caroline saw that it was hollow, and inside, on a bed of leaves, lay the old man, suffering from exposure but alive.

Caroline radioed back for transport, and while they waited for it to arrive, she praised Zibo and threw the stick for him to fetch as his reward for a job well done. All the dogs are trained not to bark when they find someone lost in the woods for fear their sudden appearance will be totally unnerving to an already badly frightened person. Thus Zibo's signal to Caroline of mission accomplished is to bring her a stick, indicating he is about to earn his reward of having her play with him.

Training a dog to search starts when he is very young. "A puppy," says Caroline, "begins bonding to his owner immediately, so his instinct if his owner hides is to go looking for him. By increasing the distances, the dog learns to track, and by not letting him see the direction his owner has gone in, he learns to search." Caroline's preference is for German shepherds, but any working breed—that is, hunting or herding dogs—can be trained for search and rescue work. On the international team there are a Labrador, a giant schnauzer, a golden retriever, a rottweiler, a Doberman, an Australian cattle dog and two Newfoundlands.

"Each dog is different," Caroline notes, "and you have to observe him closely to learn whether you're being too tough and discouraging him or giving him too much praise and

making him lazy." Hebard doesn't believe in harsh training and feels that women make particularly good handlers,
"perhaps because our experience of raising children gives us
patience and consistency." She observes, "Praise, reward and
affection are what motivate a dog. For every ounce of correction, you should give nine ounces of love." As she says this,
her hand reaches out to stroke Aly, and he takes a step closer
to lean against her.

For a basic wilderness search, a year's training is required
for both handlers and dogs. Twice a month they go through a
daylong training session in a simulated disaster situation, and
every three months there is a full weekend of training and
evaluation. After basic training, the dog is taken to shopping
centers to accustom him to noise and crowds. He learns to
respond to hand signals as well as voice commands because
he will often be working in high-noise situations, with bull-
dozers, cranes and power tools going full blast.

Each dog develops his own body language. When Aly
scents a find, if the person is alive, he pricks his ears forward,
wags his tail enthusiastically and digs at the rubble. If the
person is close to death, he whines and moves his tail slowly,
apparently basing his estimate on the scent of hormones such
as adrenaline that the body gives off. If it is a dead find, Aly
lets his tail droop dispiritedly.

Aly, who is six years old, will work until he is ten, by which
time Hebard will have another dog trained and ready. Although Aly has a kennel and run outside that he shares with
two other German shepherds, one retired from search work,
he sleeps in the house in inclement weather. When the Hebard children come home from school, they play with him,
and when dog and children are tired from wrestling and run-

ning, they stretch out on the floor of the family room, the children using Aly as a pillow while they watch TV.

The closest bond, though, is between Caroline Hebard and Aly, for they have gone through many dangers together—the threat of aftershocks in earthquakes, shifting debris in a pancaked building and mud slides following a flood. No dog is ever sent into an emergency situation alone. Hebard, wearing orange coveralls for visibility, a hard hat with a miner's lamp, boots, work gloves and often a mask to filter out dust, goes into the chaos close behind Aly, sometimes wriggling through jackstraw heaps of bricks and beams, sometimes deposited by the bucket of a crane on top of a mountain of crashed concrete.

"Concrete makes dust when it crumbles," Hebard observes, "and in the Bridgeport, Connecticut, office building collapse, it was raining. The dust turned to a slippery mud, and there we were, trying to climb around this massive mess of slabs tilted every which way. It was a hairy situation." As well as agility and stamina, searching for victims takes courage, which Hebard does not mention. What she does say is, "You can't be claustrophobic, and you've got to have a strong stomach. Sometimes a severed arm or leg is sticking out of the rubble. Sometimes you have to crawl right over a dead body."

In a flood disaster in Johnstown, Pennsylvania, Hebard, who was pregnant at the time, was assigned to search a trailer park buried in mud. "The reek of death was unimaginable," she comments, adding wryly, "It gave me a whole new definition of morning sickness." Later in that pregnancy and for several months afterward, she did not go on missions. Nor will she go now if one of her children is ill, a graduation is coming up or an important family occasion is planned. Family concerns come first, but her husband and children are extremely proud and supportive of her work, and she is fortunate to have a live-in housekeeper to keep the house running smoothly when she is away.

Why does Hebard do search and rescue work? "It takes a lot of dedication," she admits. "It's heartrending work. But also it's an adrenaline high full of drama, excitement and intense involvement. You're a highly trained professional, doing a job few people can do. There's great camaraderie among the team members—in freezing cold Russia, we put an American flag and a sign in front of our tents saying, 'Welcome to the Leninakan Hilton.'"

Hebard, who has a drawerful of awards, including a commendation from the Mexican government, has had advanced Red Cross training in first aid and CPR and is herself certified to train emergency medical technicians. Her most recent course was in critical incident stress debriefing. "We watch our team members closely for signs that they are being stressed by being exposed to so much death. When people stop communicating, become short-tempered, stop eating or sleeping, we deal with it right away by talking it out before it becomes a full-blown problem."

The work is entirely voluntary; there is no pay involved, and each person supplies his or her own equipment, which can run to considerable expense. Team members must have a special radio costing several hundred dollars, a beeper, a sleeping bag, a portable stove, boots, and so on. Lately the Alpo Corporation has been helping by paying for some of the equipment, underwriting airfares within the United States and sponsoring a national training seminar.

The best, most highly trained of the handlers and dogs are recommended by their local search and rescue units for the USAID disaster response team, which is co-directed by Hebard and Bill Dotson of Virginia and is under the auspices of the Office of Foreign Disaster Assistance (OFDA) of the State Department. Six of the eight handlers available to go to Armenia happened to be women, the majority of them women with jobs. Members of the team make advance arrangements with their employers to leave at a moment's notice when their services are needed.

Engineers and firefighters specially trained at extricating people from collapsed buildings are also part of the team, as are physicians skilled in treating trauma. Altogether the team numbers about thirty people and is self-sufficient in everything except ground transportation and fuel. Food for the team is military rations supplied by the U.S. government; food for the dogs is a high-energy puppy ration supplied by Alpo.

Transport is arranged by the OFDA and is by the fastest means available, whether military, commercial or chartered plane. "In the El Salvador earthquake," Hebard remembers, "we got in quick and saved thirty-seven people in a matter of hours.

"The thing of it is," she goes on with a touch of regret in her voice, "the local people have rescued the victims who can be seen or heard by the time we get there. We find people who haven't been detected, and alas, that means a great deal of our work is body finds, not live finds."

The generally poor odds make an experience such as rescuing twelve children lost on the Appalachian Trail that much more rewarding. It was late at night and the temperature had dived to ten degrees when Aly and Hebard set out with Park Service rangers to hunt for the little band. There was no question of waiting for daybreak, for people can die of exposure quite quickly. "Anyway," says Hebard, "I'd rather search at night. Scent travels farther and people tend to stay put, so it is easier to find them."

Out on the trail, Caroline spotted footprints in a muddy patch that had frozen. That told her the direction the children had gone, and she instructed Aly to use a tracking mode, nose to the ground, rather than a scenting mode, nose in the air. Miles later the trail crossed a road, and a ranger said, "Okay, now all we have to figure out is whether they turned north or south on the road."

"Neither," said Caroline, watching Aly. "They continued on the trail." Sure enough, two miles farther on, Aly began wagging his tail enthusiastically. Rounding a bend in the trail, they came upon the huddled children, desperately cold and badly frightened but otherwise all right. Even at two in the morning, Aly got his reward of playing with a stick, as well as a hug from Hebard and quickly whispered words of praise.

Caroline's face lights up as she tells this story. It is infinitely more satisfying to find twelve children alive than, for example, frozen bodies in Leninakan or the drowned bodies of people swept downstream in the Schoharie Creek Bridge disaster on the New York Thruway. But whatever the catastrophe, the lady and her dog are mission-ready at all times to go anywhere in the world to give the help they are uniquely qualified to provide.

★ ★ ★ ★ ★

How Do You Spank a Duck?

They were the two dirtiest ducks Kay Sherwood had ever seen. Large and white with warty red faces, they were sipping water from a mud puddle in the hay field across the road from her house, and every time they raised their heads to let the water slide down their throats, the mud flowed down their necks like lava. Kay had gone out in her front garden to cut June roses for the dinner table, and when the ducks caught sight of her, they decided to see if she would feed them and came waddling across the road. She shooed them away. Keen about gardening, the last thing Kay wanted was to have two flat-footed ducks trampling her flower beds.

The next morning as she was getting breakfast she glanced out the window. The ducks were in her raspberry patch, snapping up the reddest, ripest berries. Grabbing a saucepan and a slotted spoon to bang it with, Kay hurried out the back door making a terrific clatter. The ducks rushed a dozen steps off, decided she was bluffing and plodded resolutely back to the raspberry patch. Kay whistled for her dog. Barking furiously, the dog retreated steadily across the lawn as the ducks

advanced on him, hissing and bobbing their heads menac-
ingly. Obviously Kay would have to use strategy, not force,
to rid herself of the ducks. She fetched a box of saltines from
the house. Scattering broken crackers as she went, she en-
ticed the ducks around the house, across the road and back
to the hay field.

That taught the pair of them a lesson. Unfortunately, the
lesson was not to stay out of the raspberry patch but to make
a feint toward it so Kay would rush out of the kitchen door
with crackers for them. Kay had to concede they had won
that round, but she was determined not to be lured into making friends with them. Nor would she by any means allow
them to settle down in the daylily bed just because they had
decided it was a shady spot from which to keep sharp eyes
fixed on the back stoop for her appearance.

The only problem was…how do you spank a duck?

The ducks took up residence in the daylily bed, and whenever Kay came out of the house, they rose majestically and
came waddling toward her as fast as they could slap one
webbed foot down in front of the other. Watching them approach one day, almost tumbling in their haste but with something about them as stately as dowagers, Kay laughed at how
much they looked like two venerable great-aunts of hers. The
ducks had won another round; they now had names—Phyllis and Annie.

But which was to be Annie, which Phyllis? There was not
a wart's worth of difference in their scarlet beaks, their tiny
brilliant eyes, their overall size and shape. All Kay was really
sure of was that one was always perceptibly muddier than the
other, so she became Dirty Annie. And Phyllis shortly became
Philip when, abandoning the pretense that she wasn't growing ridiculously fond of her presumptuous guests, Kay reached

out to stroke Dirty Annie's feathered neck. Philip stopped eating, fixed her with a sharp look, and hissed. "Ah, she's yours, is she?" Kay said, suddenly realizing that, of course, they were a pair.

Once aware of that, Kay began noticing how their behavior differed. Philip always took the lead in their excursions across the road, through the fields and down to the river, while Dirty Annie was quicker to go to people. It was she who stood on Kay's feet to reach a cracker in her hand. It was she who followed close behind when Kay picked raspberries and gave her jeans a sharp tweak when Kay was slow to share the berries with them. It was she who ate the quarter pound of Brie cheese Kay put out on the terrace table when guests were coming for a drink; Kay knew it was Annie because Annie was wearing the wrapper around her neck like a ruff. And it was Annie who flapped up on that same low terrace table, skidded across its tiled top and plumped herself down in Kay's lap for her afternoon nap—which made Kay forgive her all her other transgressions.

The better Kay got to know the ducks, the more paradoxical she found them. They had wings but never flew. They had webbed feet but never swam (Philip went in the river to bathe once a day, but Dirty Annie seldom went near the water). They were inseparable but seemed quite willing to seriously wound each other over a cracker. They were ducks but they did not quack. They were defenseless but afraid of nothing. They were fiercely independent but followed Kay everywhere.

During the day their greatest pleasure was to have her weed the garden. As she worked along a row, they kept a sharp eye out, and when she uncovered a bug or beetle, they snapped it up. When she uncovered a worm, all three of them pounced,

Kay to save it for the good of the garden, the ducks to pull it wriggling from the earth. Seldom did Kay win; often did she get her knuckles sharply rapped for interfering.

Although their days were spent at Kay's house, Annie and Philip slept at night in a hollow on the riverbank. In the morning they crossed the road, circled the house and patrolled at the foot of the kitchen steps until breakfast was forthcoming. In the late afternoon they crossed to go to the river for Philip's bath, then returned to the house at dinnertime. For reasons Kay never fathomed, they considered that supper, unlike breakfast, came via the front door, and they waited at the bottom of the porch steps for it to appear. If it was delayed, Dirty Annie tried to climb the steps, slapping a webbed foot on the edge and falling on her face as her foot slipped off. Finally, with a great flailing of wings, she would manage to scramble up, whereupon she would march to the screen door, rap sternly upon it with her beak and peer beady-eyed into the dark interior until Kay appeared with slices of bread and a handful of lettuce leaves.

Their routine was so unvarying that Kay began to worry when one twilight came with no sign of them. She walked down the road calling their names. Finally she spotted a patch of white and hurried toward it, dreading to find that one or both had been hit by a car. Dirty Annie was standing on the riverbank by herself. When she saw Kay, she began to bob her head—her distress signal. Kay ran to her. Then she saw Philip. He was in the river, close to the far bank. As Kay hesitated, he gave a mighty thrash of his wings and sank down exhausted. He was drowning.

Kay plunged into the river, clothes, shoes, wristwatch and all, and half waded, half swam across. Reaching Philip, she snatched him up in her arms. And she saw what had happened. He wasn't just entangled in submerged branches, as she had supposed. One webbed foot was held fast in the jagged jaws of a muskrat trap.

As soon as she freed him, Philip paddled straight across to Dirty Annie. Face-to-face on the bank, they bobbed their heads at each other over and over, quite as though Philip was expressing his relief at being rescued and Dirty Annie was scolding, *I told you not to go near the water.*

Not long after that, it was Philip's turn to come to the rescue of Dirty Annie. Late one night Kay went out on the porch to call the dog. What answered her call was a puppy, a Siberian husky, obviously lost and ecstatic at finding someone to take him in. In the morning when Kay went out to feed the ducks, the puppy tumbled through the door behind her and was after the ducks before she could stop him. Philip scattered one way, Dirty Annie another.

The puppy, barking madly, cornered Dirty Annie. Philip halted, registered Dirty Annie's plight and waddled hastily back. For an instant he wavered, eyeing the wriggling, noisy puppy, then made up his mind. With a huge flap of his wings, he leaped on the puppy's back and pecked at his head. The puppy, yelping, ran. Philip balanced on his back as long as he could, and when he fell off, he spread his wings and gave chase on tiptoe.

Kay thought Philip's near drowning might have made him afraid of the river, but as the summer grew oppressively hot and she took to floating on the river on an air mattress with the dog swimming beside her, Philip joined them, paddling in lazy circles around the drifting mattress. Every so often there would be a rustling on the bank and Dirty Annie's head came poking through the tall weeds to peer at their progress, but nothing would entice her into the water.

As August rounded into September, increasingly Kay fretted about Dirty Annie and Philip and the coming winter. Soon she would be coming to the country only on weekends. Had they become dependent on her feeding them? Could they survive on their own? She decided not to risk it. She would put them in the car and take them to the village. People fed a flock of wild ducks by the river there, and Dirty Annie and Philip could join the flock and be sure of enough to eat.

One fine morning she filled a pie plate with bits of bread and tucked two pillowcases under her arm. As soon as the ducks were busy eating, she tried to slip a pillowcase over Annie's head. Annie squawked in alarm. Philip rushed at Kay, beak at the ready. Kay abandoned that plan. She got planks, fashioned a ramp into the car and spread bread crumbs on it. The ducks rapped on the planks with their bills and snapped up the crumbs as they rolled down. Kay's last idea was to place a whole loaf of bread in the car, with the door invitingly open. Dirty Annie and Philip, their heads bobbing, consulted each other and went off to sleep in the daylilies.

Well, she was going to Maine. They'd be on their own for ten days, and she'd see how they fared for that length of time. It was nighttime when she arrived back. She walked down to the river and there they were, asleep in their usual spot, their feathers gleaming whitely in the dark.

The next morning the ducks appeared at the kitchen door for their breakfast at the usual time. Kay hurried out to feed them, and just as always, Dirty Annie stood on her feet in her eagerness to get more than her share. Just as always, they supervised a last weeding of the garden. And just as always, Annie flopped in Kay's lap for her afternoon nap. Looking down at the beautiful tracery of feathers on her neck, Kay wondered for the thousandth time that summer why she had never heard or read of what wonderful companions ducks make. Philip and Dirty Annie were as intelligent as any animal, with the advantage of having extraordinarily acute vision and hearing—nothing, inside the house or out, escaped their notice. And they were as friendly as the dog while being equally as good watchdogs since they stood up and flapped their wings at the first sign of anyone's approach.

Because they had fared so well through Kay's ten-day absence, she was not concerned about leaving them the next week when she returned to the city, and she did not check that their whiteness was there in the dark when she arrived back late Friday night. She let the dog out Saturday morning, thinking this would signal them to come for breakfast. But nine o'clock came and went and the ducks did not appear. At ten Kay went looking for them. They weren't in the field. They weren't on the riverbank.

Twice more that day she searched, and along about twilight she spotted them. They were far down the road. When she got within earshot she called their names. They did not turn their heads. When she drew close, they moved uneasily. She held out a cracker and they backed away. They were afraid of her.

All day Sunday and again the following weekend Kay watched and hoped, but they did not come to the house. She took food to them twice a day, but they would not eat from her hand nor let her get near. Not wanting to add to their obvious distress, she put the food on the ground and went away.

Each time she passed their former sleeping place on the riverbank, she reminded herself she must collect the litter left by fishermen. Finally she remembered to bring a garbage bag, and after collecting soda cans, sandwich wrappers and bait containers, she moved on a few steps to where white feathers were caught in the tangled grass. The ducks' nest was filled with broken glass. Green beer bottles, difficult to see among the grass, had been smashed and scattered there. She had to fetch gloves and a rake before she could be sure the area was clear.

That night Philip and Dirty Annie were back in their nest. As soon as they were over their fright, they would be friends again, Kay was sure. But the following weekend, to her horror, she arrived to find the front yard full of feathers. The feathers were not the down the ducks customarily shed but large wing and tail feathers. A fox? Raccoon? Car?

She was searching for their bodies when a car stopped. "Looking for the ducks?" a neighbor asked. "A lady who lives on the mountain road has them in her garage because some kids pulled out most of their feathers."

Several times Kay went up the mountain to see how Philip and Annie were faring, but there was never anyone home and two large German shepherds kept her from going near the garage. Then one day in the spring, when she reopened her house after the winter, she was driving along the mountain road and saw the woman who had sheltered the ducks raking her front lawn. Kay stopped and asked if she still had the ducks.

"They got out a few weeks ago," the woman said, "but the kids have seen them back in the woods." She led the way through a field and into a stand of trees where a little creek ran. And there was Dirty Annie. Kay called, and Annie came to her. "You want her back?" the woman asked. "I'll get my husband to bring her down."

Kay spent that day and the next searching for Philip but found no trace of him. When Dirty Annie arrived in a big cardboard box, Kay carried her to the back of her land, on the riverbank but away from the road, hoping she'd find a place to nest there out of sight of passersby.

Released from the box, Annie, shifting nervously from one foot to the other, eyed the river. Suddenly making up her mind, she launched herself awkwardly into the air and splashed down in the river, where she proceeded to take an energetic bath. Clearly, a winter without washing had been too much even for Dirty Annie. When she was snow-white again, she climbed out on the bank and for the next two hours, while Kay came and went in her search for Philip, she preened her feathers.

When all was in order, Annie stood gazing at the river. Kay offered her some crackers. She snapped them up absently. Then, as though she had arrived at a decision, she again catapulted herself into the water. The current caught her and swept her downstream. Over the rocks she went, under the bridge, until, paddling strongly now, she came to the spot where she and Philip had nested the previous summer. She climbed out on the bank and settled into the hollow.

There she stayed. Kay ached for her aloneness without Philip and sometimes wondered if Annie blamed her for it, because her old cheerfulness was gone. When Kay took food to her, she marched in ever-tightening circles around her and pecked at Kay's feet. And one day she charged her. When she was quite certain she had driven her off, she made her way into a thicket beside the hollow and, fluffing her feathers, settled down carefully. Kay crept close enough to peer through the bushes. Dirty Annie was sitting on a new nest.

Kay had given up hope that Philip was still alive. But now her heart lifted. Dirty Annie would raise their ducklings, and one day in June Kay would look up from her gardening and there would be Dirty Annie marching across the road. Her ducklings, single file behind her, would be hurrying to keep up. Kay had no doubt they would head straight for her raspberries. Next time she went to the store, she must remember to lay in a good supply of crackers.

★ ★ ★ ★ ★

Connie and the Dog

When Connie Carey was a child, what she wanted most in the world was a dog. But her parents wouldn't hear of it. "A dog in the city? Never!" her mother decreed. "Out of the question!" her father confirmed. They were loving parents, however, so Connie did not give up hope. She kept the subject alive, and the day her smiling father came home early and announced he had a wonderful surprise, Connie let out a whoop of joy.

"A puppy!" she yelled, racing out in the hall to look for it. "Where is it? Is it all mine? Can I name it?"

"Come back here," her father ordered. "You've been told over and over, no dog."

"But you said you had a wonderful surprise."

"I do. You have a baby brother."

"Oh."

The load of disappointment in that single syllable became a running joke in the family, and Connie still sends her brother birthday cards teasingly reminding him that she would have preferred a dog.

Why didn't Connie get a dog when she was grown and making her own decisions? Well, first there was college, then graduate school, then years of teaching abroad. But finally she was living in a country house and she asked her friend Pat to go with her to choose a dog at the local ASPCA.

She was drawn to an aged, spindly-legged apricot poodle who shook with nerves, but Connie accepted Pat's word as an experienced dog owner that a black puppy with three white socks and a white tip to his tail was a better bet. "Look at his head," Pat urged. "It's beautifully shaped, and he has the coloring of a border collie. He'll be smart." So the black and white puppy was adopted and christened Charlie, and Connie got a book from the library about the training of dogs.

After a while she acquired two more books, for she didn't seem to be making much headway with Charlie. He was an exuberant, sweet-natured pup who was happy to cooperate for the length of his very short attention span; after that, he danced around her just out of reach, barking a cheerful song of defiance. When Pat witnessed this noisy fandango, after she stopped laughing she offered to take over because she was the one who knew how to handle dogs.

Charlie somehow mistook Pat's patient instruction as offers to play, and she couldn't make him behave any better than Connie could. It appeared she had been wrong in predicting his intelligence and had quite failed to spot his streak of willfulness. In desperation, Connie hired a trainer to come to the house.

The trainer, a broad, flat lady with iron-gray hair, arrived with three Pomeranians marching in formation at her heels. At a word from her, all three dogs leaped straight in the air, executed a 180-degree turn, came down facing in the opposite direction and stood at attention. Obviously, Charlie was about to meet his match.

He thought so, too. *"Achtung!"* the trainer snapped. "Heel!" Charlie dutifully placed himself on her left and marched beside her, up and down, out and back, wheeling smartly at the turns. "Charlie knows," the lady announced. "Now you." She handed the leash to Connie. *"Nein!* Not right! Not right!" After twenty minutes of shouted scolding, Connie, bathed in sweat and humiliation, turned the leash over to Pat. Now it was Pat's turn to have scorn heaped on her head.

"Nothing wrong with Herr Charlie," the trainer announced as the dog once again obeyed her every order to sit, lie down, roll over and speak. She pocketed her $75 fee and marched her Pomeranians out the door, muttering darkly, "The owner. Always the owner."

As soon as she left, Charlie affably denied working knowledge of how to do a single one of the desirable things he had done for the trainer. While he danced and barked, Connie looked at Pat. "Be careful what you wish for," she quoted wryly. "You may get it. All my life I wanted a dog, and now there's nothing I want less."

But she and Charlie rubbed along together until the day she came home to find that the dog not only had mistaken one of her shoes for a rawhide bone but had ripped the leather cover off a prized family Bible. Connie marched to the phone, dialed the ASPCA, and stated her intention to return a dog that had come from there. "All right," the attendant said, "but you'll have to wait until we have room for him. We'll call you as soon as we can take him."

Although Connie still claims that Charlie understood her end of this conversation, it was undoubtedly just coincidence, plus the fact he was about to turn a year old, that he began mending his wild ways. Overnight he started paying attention when spoken to, soon was behaving so well on walks that he could be let off the leash to run in the fields, responded immediately to a whistle, chewed only his own food and was so impeccably housebroken that to be outdoors was not enough; he had to be outdoors at what he considered a sufficiently tactful distance from the house. Most touching of all, he fell in love with Connie. From being just another object in his world, she became his world. He did not voluntarily let her out of his sight, and now his funny dance was used not to defy her but to express his delight when she came home to him.

As their companionship deepened, Connie wondered what she would say when the call came from the ASPCA. Then one day it dawned on her that it was never going to come, that the ASPCA knew dogs and people and a thing or two about the love between them and how it grows.

"Isn't he beautiful?" Connie remarked to Pat as Charlie moved into being full grown, with a plumed tail, silky fur and that handsome head. "I mean, besides being a great companion, he's a delight to look at."

"Be careful what you wish for," Pat teased. "You may get it."

"Yes, I know I said that." Connie was silent for a moment, thinking. "The thing of it is, sometimes it takes quite a while before you realize you really have gotten what you wanted after all."

★ ★ ★ ★ ★

The Owl Release

G uests who excuse themselves at Frances and Ben Robert-
son's house are apt to be gone quite a while, waylaid by
a fascinating sight. The way to the powder room is through
a hall that has French doors to a terrace across one side. Beyond the terrace is an expanse of lawn rimmed by woods,
and in the center of the lawn is a feeding station, a roofed but
open-sided summerhouse sheltering bins of corn and grain.

During the day, ducks and Canada geese advance on the
bins in a stately waddle, while at night raccoons, possums,
skunks, deer and an occasional fox feed there, undeterred by
the floodlighting that allows them to be seen from the house.

On a winter night, as Mindy Schiffman passed through
the darkened hallway, she glimpsed a largish shape against
the snow, and on her way back from the powder room, she
picked up a pair of the binoculars the Robertsons kept on a
table in the hall and focused them on the shape. It was, as
she had assumed, a deer, a small doe not a great deal larger
than a hound.

Another turn of the focusing dial brought the doe's head so

sharply close that she seemed only two or three feet in front of Mindy. Mindy smiled at the longing she felt to reach out and stroke the doe's sleek neck and was lowering the glasses when her attention was arrested by a dark mass near the doe's shoulder.

It was globular, the size of a grapefruit, a part of her yet hanging on her like some sucking creature. It was a mass of dried, blackened blood and fur and skin, a macabre snowball that had struck but not fallen. It was her flesh ripped and churned by bullets.

She's got a chance, Mindy thought. *If nothing reopens the wound, she'll make it.* She moved the glasses down the doe's length, and cried out. The doe's hind leg on the opposite side had been shot away. There was nothing below the knee joint; the leg ended in midair in another coagulated mass.

As though she had heard Mindy's cry, the doe turned her head toward the house and Mindy met her eyes in the glasses. Mindy had nursed her beloved Persian cat when she was broken by a car, held her springer spaniel while he died, and been struck at seeing only acceptance in their eyes. It was she who had railed against their pain, as she was railing now.

Frances came into the hallway and, reading Mindy's face, picked up another pair of glasses. When she saw what Mindy had seen, she lowered them and turned away to fumble for a handkerchief. When she turned back, she said, "The poor thing can't dig in the snow for food with that damaged front leg. She'll only starve to death if we let her go on like this."

While Frances went to speak to Ben, Mindy stayed on in the shadowy hallway, reluctant to return to the candlelight and laughter of the dining room. She thought of a line from *Hamlet,* "I must be cruel only to be kind," and wished it were a world in which paradox did not reign, in which it was possible simply to be kind in order to be kind.

Sometimes it is, of course. In this same house, six months earlier, twenty guests had listened to a powerful, rough-clad man talk joyously of his work with injured raptors. Broken-winged and broken-legged hawks, eagles and owls hurt in encounters with wires, cars or guns are brought to Len Soucy from all over the Northeast, and he, in his compound on the edge of the Great Swamp near Morristown, New Jersey, sets about mending them. When they become strong again at the broken places, he makes a ceremony of releasing the birds, inviting people who support his work to share in his delight at restoring them to the wild.

On a night when a full moon had risen over the pond in front of the Robertsons' house, Len Soucy led the way outside to where a stack of crates waited. In the light of flaming torches, he reached into a crate and brought forth a red-shouldered hawk in his gauntleted hand. "Who wants to release him?" he asked.

A boy of eleven or twelve volunteered, putting Mindy to shame, for she was afraid of the wicked glance and the curved talons of the hawk. One by one, as Len Soucy brought out the raptors, a guest stepped forward, donned a gauntlet and, grasping a raptor by the legs, held it aloft and released it into the night sky. But Mindy hung back, happy to leave the experience to others.

Finally there was one bird left, a great horned owl, the largest of the raptors and the fiercest looking. Len Soucy cautiously reached into the crate and grasped the creature's legs. His eyes went around the circle. "Who hasn't released one? You haven't," he said, singling out Mindy. His assistant handed her a gauntlet. Reluctantly Mindy slipped it on and, following instructions, placed her hand over Len's, her forefinger between the owl's legs, and closed her hand gently but firmly around the legs. Len withdrew his hand and stepped back.

Mindy moved outside the circle of light, facing the pond. There was only the darkness of the night sky and the moon-light on the water and the great horned owl. The owl at the end of her outstretched arm was…as light as a feather! That beetle-browed, glaring creature well over a foot tall weighed only ounces in her hand. His bones were hollow, his bulk was air, his being as fragile as thistledown in the wind. The power was all hers.

She raised the great bird high. "Go," she exulted. "Go and be free!" She tossed him at the moon. He spread his wings and soared.

Frances came back. "Ben's called the deputy who patrols for us during the hunting season," she said. "He'll be here in a few minutes."

Ben joined them. He swore softly as he looked through the glasses. "A doe, that's illegal. Hunting on private property, that's illegal. That's why she got away. The hunter was afraid to go after her for fear we'd spot him."

They heard the deputy's car coming up the long drive. The deer heard it, too, and raised her head sharply. "Don't run, don't run," Ben pleaded quietly. "It's better this way." The deputy cut his lights and motor and coasted in. The doe went back to eating. But she was wary now and kept lifting her head to listen. Somewhere out there was a man preparing to kill her. Her eyes turned to the house, and again it seemed, in the intimate glasses, that she was looking into their eyes, asking the fathomless question, *Why?*

Why? they echoed silently.

Because there are two factions in the world: the protectors

and the destroyers. This night the destroyers had forced Mindy and Frances and Ben over to their side. What might bring the destroyers over to their side? If not a doe's eyes, what?

The sound was like the crack of a whip. The deer leaped. The gallant creature tried to run on three legs. Five bounds toward the safety of the woods. Her wounded front leg crumpled. She somersaulted to the ground. She twitched and lay still.

Her right to live on this beautiful earth had been taken from her. All Mindy could hope now was that they had released her spirit. "Go," Mindy whispered. "Go and be free."

★ ★ ★ ★ ★

The Good Shepherd

L ana Crawford sat numbly at the kitchen table. Her life in Klamath Falls, Oregon, once so happy, lay in ruins. Her marriage was over and the yellow house she loved had a For Sale sign in the front yard.

Reaching to stroke the German shepherd at her feet brought fresh tears to Lana's eyes. This special animal had been Jeremy's dearest friend and companion in the final days of her teenage son's life. "Oh, Grizzly," she moaned softly, "what will you and I do now? How do we go on?"

Two years earlier Jeremy, a running back and karate practitioner, had been unable to get up after being tackled in a football game. X-rays of his pelvis revealed bone cancer, and the teenager, once muscular and tan, grew pale and hollow-cheeked as he fought for his life.

Lana gave up her job as a music teacher to care for him, and his older sister, Susanne, traveled often from her home in Seattle to spend as much time as possible with him. They tried hard to keep him cheerful and optimistic, and Jeremy struggled valiantly against his pain and exhaustion. Trying to think of something that would please him and knowing that he had always had a special fondness for German shepherds, on a day between chemo treatments Lana suggested to Jeremy that they visit a kennel specializing in the breed. As they sat on a bench in the sun outside the dog runs with Ella Brown, the kennel owner, a litter of puppies tumbled and played at their feet. One of the puppies came to Jeremy. Jeremy picked him up and held him in his arms. "He's so beautiful," Jeremy said. "But why is he whimpering, Ella? Doesn't he like me?"

"That's his way of talking," Ella Brown explained. "Every once in a while there'll be one special dog in a litter who's a talker. That special dog deserves to go to a special person who will understand and cherish him. I think that might be you, Jeremy. Why don't you take him home and see if I'm right that you two belong together?"

Jeremy named the puppy Grizzly, and Ella was right: boy and dog quickly became inseparable. Jeremy understood all the small sounds Grizzly made in his throat, and Grizzly became attuned to the shades of meaning in Jeremy's voice, face and gestures. On days Jeremy was feeling well enough, they took long drives in Jeremy's little pickup or he threw his football in long spiral passes and Grizzly raced to jump and intercept it. On the not-good days, Jeremy dozed in bed and Grizzly lay quietly beside him, his body pressed close.

Grizzly could sense when it was pain keeping Jeremy in bed and when it was discouragement. When it was discouragement, Grizzly nosed Jeremy's hand and woofled deep in his throat until Jeremy began to talk to him, confiding his fear that he would never get well. As Jeremy's condition worsened, Lana spent the nights on the floor beside his bed. Grizzly tucked himself in beside her, and the two of them dozed through the long hours. Once when Jeremy woke up, he said to his mother, "If I don't make it, I want you to have Grizzly. Maybe there'll be some way the two of you can help other kids."

In the days following Jeremy's death, Lana lay in bed, unable to face life without her son. One afternoon she heard Grizzly nose open her closet door. A moment later he laid one of her running shoes on her pillow. He fetched its mate and began woofing encouragingly. The dog took her sleeve in his mouth and gently tugged. "I can't, Grizzly," Lana told him. But each day Grizzly tried again, until a day came when Lana followed him and they walked around the block. Each day after that he led her farther, and Lana began to grow strong again.

In the fall they came upon a park where boys were playing football. One of them was as tall and blond as Jeremy, and Lana remembered the promise she had made to her son. At age thirty-eight, she decided to move to Utah and enroll in the university there to take courses in psychology. As part of the fieldwork for her degree, Lana proposed that she take Grizzly to visit patients on the pediatric floor at the University of Utah Health Sciences Center.

She was nervous as a nurse led them to the room of a boy with cystic fibrosis. The boy was crying as a technician drew blood and hooked him up to an IV. The nurse asked the boy if he would like to meet Grizzly. His eyes widened. "A dog! Come here, Grizzly." The needles were forgotten as the boy talked to Grizzly and Grizzly responded with his soft, muffled woofs. "He's answering me! Can I take him for a walk?" Down the hall they went, IV pole and all.

Soon Lana and Grizzly were going to the hospital for weekly visits, and Grizzly seemed to know exactly how to respond to each ill child, whether to romp or lie with his head in a lap, to allow his ears to be pulled or nuzzle the child's ear and make her giggle, to woofle or give tiny, teasing barks. Lana could not explain his intuition except to say that Grizzly, through having loved Jeremy, seemed to understand his purpose in life to be to respond to pain and fear and need.

One day they visited a seventeen-year-old boy in the oncology unit. The severely depressed boy, who was losing his vision and muscular control, looked devastatingly like Jeremy. "This is Grizzly, the good shepherd," Lana said, telling herself that if she could get through this, she could get through anything. Grizzly was as shaken as she was, she saw, but when the boy asked for Grizzly to come up on the bed beside him, the dog hesitated only briefly before climbing up on the draw sheet the nurse spread and inching between the tubes to lie beside the boy. There he stayed, never moving, until the boy fell asleep.

As Lana was asked to go to different children's facilities with Grizzly, she became aware that the need for animal-assisted therapy was greater than she and Grizzly could meet alone. She formed a nonprofit organization, the Good Shepherd Association, to train handlers and their animals to work in therapeutic settings, and the association soon became an affiliate of the worldwide Delta Society, a volunteer, nonprofit society providing animal-assisted therapy.

At a center for emotionally troubled children, Lana and Grizzly met Tammy, an unkempt eleven-year-old who had been in and out of fourteen foster homes and centers, displayed extreme mood swings and fought with other children. She refused to say a word to Lana and paid no attention to Grizzly until, midway through the hour, Grizzly stood up, walked out into the hallway and began his gentle woofing talk. "What's he doing?" Tammy demanded.

"Maybe he's asking you to come out in the hall," Lana suggested.

Tammy tossed her head contemptuously, snatched up a doll and twisted its legs until she tore them off. But as Grizzly continued to talk, curiosity got the better of her and she edged out the door. Lana rose to intervene in case Tammy intended to hurt Grizzly, but Grizzly's quiet woofle went on, and soon Lana heard Tammy's voice soften as she whispered to Grizzly: "I'm scared. I'm lonely. Nobody wants me. Nobody likes me."

For two years Lana and Grizzly visited the troubled girl every other week. When Tammy was rough, Grizzly moved away with quiet dignity. When she was sad, he lay beside her and woofed with understanding. Tammy would not or could not tell her therapist what was troubling her, but she confided in Grizzly in such a way that the therapist overheard her and thus was able to help her.

Tammy still threw tantrums, but never around Grizzly. "His love seems to calm her," her therapist told Lana. "For the first time she's found a creature she can trust, and her behavior in general is beginning to improve."

Someone at the center happened to remark that Grizzly's eyes did not look quite right, which led Lana to take him to a veterinarian to be examined. It was thus she learned Grizzly had long been blind, probably, the doctor said, as a result of a blow to the head. Lana's thoughts leaped back to the night Jeremy died and Grizzly ran out of the house directly into the side of a passing car. Ever since then, she realized, Grizzly must have been seeing with his heart, not his eyes.

Recently Lana and Grizzly were honored guests at a dinner honoring volunteers at the children's center. After a program of songs by the children's chorus, Tammy stepped forward.

Once slovenly, with unwashed hair and broken fingernails, she was now well groomed and no longer slouched but stood proudly as she thanked Lana and Grizzly for all they had done for her and the others, the difference the two of them together had made in the children's lives.

When it was Lana's turn to speak, she said: "Once there was a special boy named Jeremy and he had a special dog named Grizzly. Jeremy had to leave us, but before he did, he asked Grizzly and me to try to find a way to help other children. Jeremy would be so pleased tonight to know we've succeeded and that his good shepherd has been your good shepherd, too."

★ ★ ★ ★ ★

Saving Trouper

The baby raccoon, no bigger than a drowned kitten, was sprawled facedown in a puddle in the road. Pat Kelso-Condos, an animal control officer in West Orange, New Jersey, stopped her van to collect the body. She could guess what must have happened: recent heavy rains had caused flash flooding in the area and a mother raccoon decided to move her litter to a safer place; this little one fell behind and the mother abandoned him to save the others.

"Poor thing," Pat murmured as she bent to pick him up. She had a soft spot in her heart for raccoons. Because rabies was present in the area, local residents killed every one they saw, and Pat, understanding the slaughter but knowing much of it was needless, felt protective toward them.

With a towel covering her hand she grasped the tiny creature. A shudder ran through his body. "Hey, you're still alive," she said, marveling as water streamed from his fur and he drew a rasping breath. She rubbed him with the towel and gently wiped away the mucus welling from his eyes and nose. A rumbling sound started in the baby's throat. Raccoons can purr like a cat, and Pat realized that was what this small creature was trying to do. He opened his eyes and looked up at her. If he'd spoken aloud, his plea couldn't have been clearer: *Please help me.*

Pat, a former veterinary technician, made an educated guess about the baby's condition—not rabies but probably distemper and certainly pneumonia. The breath gurgling through the fluid in his lungs sounded like a child blowing bubbles in a glass of milk. Pat guessed he might live minutes, a few hours at most.

The town had no facility for boarding wild animals. Pat's orders were to trap and release the healthy ones in a suitable area and destroy the ill and badly injured. But the appeal in this little one's eyes made her hesitate. She decided to take him home with her. There she dried him with a hair dryer, force-fed him a tiny bit of formula and laid him in a nest of towels under a heat lamp. At midnight she succeeded in getting a few more drops of formula into him. In the morning he was still alive.

"You're a trouper," she told him, impressed that as small and ill as he was, the baby was keeping up the battle to breathe. "If you're going to fight so hard to live, I've got to try to get you some help."

Many veterinarians are averse to treating wild animals, but Dr. Sharri Hill of the Animal Emergency Group in West Caldwell, New Jersey, was as touched by the little creature as Pat had been. She administered antibiotics and subcutaneous fluid and gave Pat a supply of both so she could continue to doctor the infant on her own. With her pen poised to fill out a chart, Dr. Hill paused at the first line. "What'll I put down for a name?"

"Trouper," said Pat, "because he's such a gutsy little fellow."

"Gutsy or not, I'm afraid his chances of making it are zero to none," the vet warned. "Raccoons very seldom survive distemper."

"Yes, I know," Pat said. "But I don't want to give up until he does."

Pat decided to ask her friends at the Wildlife Way Station in a nearby town if they would take him, because it was likely they would be able to do more for him than she could. She had to wait until evening to make the call because the two animal rehabilitators who had founded the facility worked at other jobs during the day, Andrea Abramson as director of the East Campus of Kean College, Freda Remmers as a teacher of communications at the college. When Pat reached Andrea, she described Trouper and his condition.

Andrea listened, then explained their situation. That day a possum hit by a car had been taken by the driver to the nearest vet. The vet had gotten hold of Freda, who stood by and pulled thirteen babies from the mother's pouch as the vet euthanized the severely injured mother. This meant that Andrea and Freda had thirteen infant possums who had to be bottle-fed every two hours. "Not only that," Andrea said, "but Boomer's back."

Pat remembered Boomer, who'd been everybody's favorite because even for a raccoon he was unusually smart. He'd learned to open a sliding glass door by watching Andrea and Freda do it, and he was great at tracking down treats hidden in their pockets. Months after he'd been released to the wild, he returned one brilliant moonlit night and his booming voice rang out. Freda and Andrea stepped outside, and there Boomer stood, a female raccoon beside him. "Look at that," Freda whispered. "He's brought his girl home to meet his mothers."

But this time he'd come back for help. He called to them, and when they went out, they saw that one of his front legs was bloody and mangled, the bone broken in several places. Raccoons can be vicious and Boomer was obviously in great pain, but they didn't need their thick leather gauntlets to pick him up because he remembered how they'd cared for him before and he trusted them utterly.

They took him to veterinarian Barry Orange, who opened the leg from paw to shoulder to piece the smashed bone back together, using wires and pins to hold it in place. So many stitches were needed to close the leg up again that Boomer looked like a sewing machine had run over him. The leg couldn't be put in a cast because Boomer, like any self-respecting raccoon, would have gone right to work to chew it off.

"So," Andrea finished her story, "Freda and I are taking turns sitting up with him during the night to distract him if he starts pulling at the stitches. Luckily, we can do that and feed the possum babies at the same time. But it doesn't sound like your little fellow is going to make it anyway, so if you could keep him, it would really be a help."

In the next days mucus continued to pour from Trouper's nose and eyes. Wheezing and rattling, he struggled to suck in air and grew ever thinner and more dehydrated. But still he clung to life. Pat put tiny dabs of Nutri-Cal on her finger and waited patiently until Trouper could summon the strength to lick them off. She kept him wrapped in a blanket, and he told her by his efforts to purr that he liked her to hold him.

After four days, Pat picked up another raccoon, and her partner also brought one in. Since distemper is highly contagious and she had no facilities for isolating Trouper, she felt that now she had to take him to the Wildlife Way Station.

With her husband driving and Pat keeping the tiny bundle warm inside her coat, they delivered Trouper to Andrea and Freda.

"I've seen dish mops with more life in them," Andrea commented when they handed him over. "You do know his chances are about one percent?"

"That's better than zero, which is what they were the last time I asked."

Andrea and Freda put Trouper in a cat carrier that was half on, half off a heating pad so he could have warmth if he needed it or crawl to the other side if it grew too hot for him. They started him on antibiotic injections and every four hours filled a syringe with hydrating fluid and Esbilac, a puppy milk replacement, and dripped it, drop by painstaking drop, into his mouth.

Even two rooms away and with the doors closed, Trouper's labored breathing was audible. The vet prescribed a bronchodilator. They crushed the pill and put it in the Esbilac. Trouper refused to swallow. They put it in Nutri-Cal, which he liked, but he refused to lick that. The only way they could get the pill into him was to put it in a pill popper, shoot it into the back of his mouth and hold his jaws closed until the pill went down his throat.

Every two hours either Freda or Andrea held the little dab of fur by the hind legs, turned him upside down and thumped him on his back and chest. The mucus poured out. They wiped it away with tissues. Soon his nose was raw. They coated the tissues with aloe vera. After every thumping session, as weak as he was, Trouper opened his eyes to look for his treat of Nutri-Cal.

Every evening Pat called to ask how Trouper was. Every evening the answer was the same: "He's still alive. Just." But after three weeks Andrea thought she detected a slight improvement. She put a dab of Nutri-Cal in a dish and set the dish near Trouper. He lifted his head and sniffed. Wobbling from side to side, he inched his way out of the towel-lined bowl that was his nest and licked the dish clean. That night when Pat called, Andrea said, "I think maybe your baby is going to win his fight."

"I knew he was a trouper!" Pat cried.

Soon, whenever Freda or Andrea came into the room, Trouper tottered to the door of the carrier and waited expectantly to be picked up, thumped, held and fed. Ordinarily the rehabilitators took pains to keep the animals from bonding with them, but with Trouper needing so much attention, they had no choice but to handle him. And handling led to fondling since he obviously loved having his ears scratched and responded with loud purrs when they talked to him.

After six weeks of treatment Trouper's breathing became less labored and his fur began to develop a sheen. He was kept on antibiotics for two more weeks to make sure the pneumonia had truly cleared, but then the little raccoon developed asthma. Again the rehabilitators despaired of his life until they noticed that the attacks occurred mainly when Andrea entered the room. It had been Andrea who had provided most of the two months of almost hourly handling that Trouper required, which meant that, as far as Trouper was concerned, Andrea was his mother, and when he saw her, he became so excited that he wheezed and choked.

As wrenching as it was to give up handling and petting the affectionate creature, it was clearly time to begin weaning him from human contact. They gave him a stuffed animal, which he took into his nest and slept with. As he became stronger, he began playing with it, challenging it to fight and giving it ferocious shakes. He was practicing the moves needed to survive in the wild, just as a baby raccoon would do with his littermates. When he wasn't pouncing on the plush toy, he talked to it, developing the vocalizations raccoons use to communicate with each other.

As it happened, another young raccoon also without a family arrived at the Wildlife Way Station about this time. Rocky had been an illegal family pet and needed to be trained for survival before he could be released; otherwise, it was likely that he would walk up to humans expecting to be petted and might instead be clubbed because people would assume he was attacking. After he had been quarantined sufficiently long for Andrea and Freda to be certain he was healthy, he and Trouper were moved together to an outdoor cage. The cage was as big as a walk-in closet and had wire mesh sides, a clip lock on the door because raccoons are clever enough to open any ordinary latch and a nesting box high up in a corner. Their first encounter was noisy as the two of them threatened each other with violence, but when their territorial disputes had been settled, they quickly became fast friends. Now each had a live partner to practice getting along with in the wild.

Because raccoons are nocturnal, Trouper and Rocky slept in their nesting box through the days. They roused enough to peek out when Freda stepped into the cage to clean it and bring them food, but then their bright, inquisitive faces vanished from the hole and they returned to their napping. When it was Andrea, however, Trouper swung out of the box onto a high shelf and walked along it until he was beside her and could lean forward to have his ears scratched.

But she never held him, fondled him or called him by name anymore. It tugged at her heart, but both she and Freda had worked hard to save his life, and she wanted Trouper to have every chance at surviving when he was released into the wild.

Is it worth going to the lengths they did just to save the life of an animal? Is it worth the considerable expense? Andrea and Freda support the Wildlife Way Station with their salaries from the college. It was their time and money that went into the training required to become licensed wildlife rehabilitators, their time and money that goes into saving the lives of some three hundred squirrels, rabbits, woodchucks, skunks and raccoons each year. Why do they do it?

They do it because they believe that all life on this planet is an interconnected web, and when they come upon a rent in that web, they want to do what they can to mend it. And they do it for the sake of a day like one the following spring when they took Trouper and Rocky some miles away to the property of friends where there were woods and fields and streams.

They set the animal carrier down at the edge of the woods, unbolted the door and crossed the field, back to where they'd left the car. Freda got in the driver's seat but Andrea continued to stand there, looking back at the carrier. After a while, Rocky nosed open the door, surveyed the field, tested to see if he really was free and made a dash for the woods. Trouper, half in, half out of the carrier, watched him go, then slowly turned this way and that, his eyes searching the field back and forth, back and forth. He took two steps out of the carrier, just enough to look over the top of it, and was looking there when Andrea, the width of the field away, brushed a gnat away. The movement caught Trouper's eye. He moved free of the carrier, sat up on his haunches and fixed his eyes on Andrea. Andrea ducked out of sight behind the car, and still he watched. Minute after minute went by.

"Get in the car," Freda told her. "Trouper's not going to move as long as you're here."

Reluctantly Andrea agreed. She moved back into view, stood for a moment, then waved goodbye.

They were told later by the friends whose property it was that twice Rocky reappeared and called to Trouper, but not until more than an hour had passed did Trouper turn and follow him into the woods.

★ ★ ★ ★ ★

The Pig Who Loved People

The phone rang at Bette and Don Atty's house in Johnstown, New York. A friend was calling to ask if they'd like to have a miniature pig.

"His name is Lord Bacon. He's four months old, and he's smarter than any dog," the friend told Don. "He loves people, and with Bette at home all the time I thought she might like company."

For a year Don had stood by helplessly as his wife struggled with agoraphobia, a fear of open spaces and crowds, apparently triggered by stress at work. Even after Bette had quit her job and was working at home as a freelance accountant, she suffered an incapacitating attack of anxiety just from going to the local mall. She never left the house now unless Don was with her.

Bette, when Don relayed the friend's offer to give them the pig, shook her head. "Think about it a minute," Don urged. "It might be good for you to have a pet."

Bette recalled reading in one of the many psychology books she had consulted about her condition that caring for another creature strengthens a person's inner being. But could a pig help her nerves?

"All right," she said reluctantly. "I guess a farmer will take him if we have to get rid of him."

Lord Bacon was fourteen inches high and twenty-four inches long, weighed forty-five pounds and was shaped like a root beer keg on stilts, they discovered when he arrived. Don laughed when he saw him: "That snout looks like he ran into a wall doing ninety!" Bette remarked, "I've got an old hairbrush with better-looking bristles than his."

The cage was opened and Lord Bacon trotted out wagging his tail. He looked around and headed for Bette. She knelt to greet him. He heaved himself up on his hind legs, laid his head on her shoulder and kissed her on the cheek with his leathery snout. For the first time in a long time Bette smiled.

The pig bustled about, exploring the house. He sat up on his broad bottom and begged for a treat. He gently chewed on Don's beard when Don put him on his lap. When Don or Bette whistled, the pig came to them, and when it was bedtime, he tried to follow them upstairs. With his potbelly he couldn't negotiate the steps, and Bette made up a bed for him in the kitchen, then sat on the floor and stroked him. "It's all right, Lord Bacon. We'll be here in the morning," she promised.

The next morning, instead of dreading having to face another day, Bette was eager to see her new pet. Lord Bacon scrambled to greet her and rubbed against her leg, which was like being massaged with a scouring pad. From then on, Bette was destined always to have a red rash of affection on her leg.

After breakfast the pig followed Bette into the home office, where she prepared tax returns, and settled down beside her desk. Bette found that when she grew edgy, if she reached down and petted Lord Bacon and said a few words, it made her feel calmer. When it was clear that the office was where the pig would be spending his days, Don brought home a doggie bed to put next to Bette's desk. Lord Bacon looked it over and decided that, with some alteration, it would do nicely. He planted his hoofs, ripped open the tartan pillow, pulled out the stuffing and then crawled inside the cover, content.

In the evenings, when Bette and Don drew up their armchairs to watch television, the pig pushed a chair over with his snout, sat on the floor in front of it and watched the figures on the screen, his head bobbing from side to side. Because they soon discovered he disliked loud noises, they kept the sound turned low. In her office Bette's phone hung on a post beside the desk, and Lord Bacon figured out that it stopped ringing when Bette picked it up. If Bette wasn't there to answer it immediately, he yanked the receiver off the hook, stood over it and grunted into the mouthpiece.

I wonder what my clients must think, Bette thought, half amused but a little embarrassed by the possibility that her clients assumed it was she doing the grunting.

A client came to see her about his tax return and was so charmed by her pet that he asked to bring his children to meet him. Soon other children were stopping by to see Lord Bacon. Finding this to be too serious a name for such a friendly pig, the kids took to calling him Pigger. The name stuck, and Pigger he was from then on.

The first time several people crowded into her office, Bette felt herself growing tense. Soon realizing, however, that they were too fascinated by the pig to pay any attention to her, she relaxed and enjoyed the company.

"It's fun coming home from work now," Don told Bette. "The first thing you say is, 'Guess what Pigger did today. He pulled the blankets off the bed,' or whatever, and we get to laughing and it feels like when we were first married."

"It wasn't so funny this morning when he locked me out of the house," Bette grumbled, but not very seriously. Pigger, following Bette in and out of the house, had watched her close the door behind her, and the next time he went in he did the same. The only problem was, the door was on the latch and Bette was still outside. Luckily, a spare key was hidden in the backyard.

Pigger was a superb mimic, and Bette found he would imitate whatever she did. If she shook her head, Pigger would shake his. If she twirled, Pigger would twirl. Soon Bette was teaching tricks to her pig that few dogs are smart enough to learn. Her father tried to persuade her to bring Pigger to a senior citizens' gathering to entertain them. Bette demurred. "Pigger can run like the wind and feint like a soccer player," she said. "If he gets away from me, I won't be able to catch him, and I can't put him on a leash because he plants his feet and refuses to walk. I'd look pretty silly, wouldn't I, a grown lady dragging a pig?"

The next evening Don came home with a baby stroller. "What's that for?" Bette demanded.

"It's a pigmobile, so you can take Pigger to the seniors' meeting." He lifted Pigger into the stroller, and Pigger sat up in it, a blanket around his shoulders, a green visor on his head. As Don pushed him about, it was clear that Pigger loved it, so Bette agreed to take him to meet the seniors.

Her nerves tightened as she drove up to the building. She turned off the motor and sat in the car trembling. She stroked Pigger, seat-belted beside her, and felt calmer. *I've got to conquer my fears,* she told herself. *I can't spend the rest of my life being afraid*. She struggled out, settled Pigger in the pigmobile and wheeled him into the building.

The seniors were intrigued. "What is *that?*" they asked. Bette lifted Pigger to the floor. He immediately singled out the oldest woman in the place and trotted over to nuzzle her cheek. The seniors broke into laughter and crowded around to pet him. Bette answered their questions, at first haltingly, then with enthusiasm. She told the seniors that pigs are smarter than dogs and twice as clean: "Pigger loves it when I put him in the bathtub for a good scrub." To show off how smart he was, she called to Pigger and told him he was a handsome hog. Pigger strutted about proudly. Then she scolded him for being piggy. Pigger lowered his head in shame and, for good measure, let his tongue hang out. His audience laughed and cheered.

Word got around about the clever pig, and soon Bette and Pigger were going on what Don called their "pig gigs." At a nursing home, Bette wheeled Pigger from room to room to visit with the patients. In one room, an old woman was sitting staring at her hands clenched in her lap. Suddenly her head came up and her face cracked in the beginnings of a smile. She held out her hands, then wrapped her arms around herself. An aide whispered to Bette that the woman had not smiled, spoken or taken an interest in anything since her husband's death some months before. "What is it?" Bette asked. "Do you want to hug him?" As Bette picked up Pigger and held him so the old woman could pet him, Pigger stayed perfectly still, his ears cocked and his mouth drawn up in a grin.

On later visits, when Pigger came through the front door in his pigmobile, the call would go out: "Pigger's here!" A commotion would start in the halls—the squeak of wheelchairs, the *tap-tap* of walkers, the shuffle of slippered feet—as the residents hurried to talk to him and pet him. The more Bette saw of sick and helpless people, the more thoughts of her own illness faded away. "I used to hate myself," she told Don, "but now I'm beginning to thank God every day for being me. Pigger is making me well."

It occurred to Bette that Pigger could carry a message to schoolchildren, and she began to take him into classrooms. She invited the children to ask Pigger if he would ever take drugs. Pigger shook his head emphatically while grunting and snorting with disgust at the idea. Asked if he'd stay in school and study hard, Pigger bowed low and nodded solemnly. The kids wanted to know what Pigger liked to eat. "Dog biscuits, of course," Bette told them. "Also beans, corn, carrots, apples and Cheerios. But the two things Pigger loves best are popcorn and ice cream. At the Dairy Queen he gets his own dish of ice cream and eats it neatly from a spoon."

The kids' comments about Pigger ranged from "He feels like a pot scrubber" to "He has cute ears" to "He looks like my uncle." One little boy, hugging Pigger, said wistfully, "I wish you could come home with me. I know you'd love me." Bette had to grip Pigger's collar tightly to keep him from following the boy.

Sometimes Bette and Don would be shopping in the supermarket and from the next aisle a child's voice would ring out: "There's the pig's mother and father!" An embarrassed parent would be dragged over to be introduced to "the pig's family."

When strangers stopped, stared and inquired what Pigger was, Don answered, "To us, he's a pig, but to him, he's people." Occasionally he quoted Winston Churchill: "Dogs look up to us. Cats look down on us. Pigs treat us as equals." And Pigger would confirm this by grunting.

By the end of a year, Pigger and Bette had made ninety-five public appearances, and Bette was handling the occasions with poise and flair. In July, Pigger was invited to attend the annual Fulton County senior citizens' picnic. The day before was hot, and Bette opened the back door. "Why don't you go out and cool off in your pool, Pigger?" she suggested.

Pigger trotted into the yard and Bette went back to work. Something prompted her to check on him half an hour later. He was lying in his favorite napping spot in the shade of a barberry bush, but Bette thought he seemed unnaturally still. She went to him. He wasn't breathing.

Panic engulfed Bette and she began to wail. *No, I mustn't carry on. Pigger doesn't like loud noises.* She went in the house and called a friend to come be with her until Don got home. Then she knew she was going to make it.

Pigger had succumbed to a pulmonary aneurysm, but Bette has her own explanation of why he died. "Pigger had a heart so big, it burst with all the love in it." She goes on to say, "He not only helped me become my old self, he brightened so many other lives, too. He was a wonderful friend. There will never be another Pigger."

★ ★ ★ ★ ★

Afterword:

The Year of Pure Love

Why do people become devoted to an animal, sometimes with an intensity that is startling? The recent loss of a cat I held dear has made me ponder the reasons. Why did I love Bitty so much? Why do I mourn him so fiercely?

It was a year ago that I found him. A friend and I had gone for a walk on the mountain road, with my dog, Freebie, in the lead. Suddenly, with loud, glad cries, a kitten rushed from a roadside thicket and ran straight to Freebie. The dog was too surprised to bark or back off as the kitten reared up on his hind legs and butted Freebie's chin while uttering delighted sounds at having found company. Well nourished and neat, the kitten had obviously not been out in the winter cold long, which suggested he'd dashed, unnoticed, out a briefly opened door of one of the houses within walking distance. We picked him up and set about returning him to his owner.

"No," we were told at one house after another. "No, it's not our kitten. Thanks anyway."

When we'd run out of houses and with the twilight smelling of snow soon to fall, there was nothing to do but tuck the kitten into my down jacket and carry him home—not to keep, because I already had two cats, but to shelter until he could be taken to the Humane Society the next day. We were amused as we traveled down the mountain that the kitten, his head resting on the jacket's zipper, never stopped talking. His animated cries were not miaows and there was no note of distress in them. Indeed, they sounded like a joyous "wow," sometimes pronounced exuberantly, sometimes interrogatively, sometimes, as though he were a rock singer, broken into two or three syllables. He uttered these "wows" as he looked at whoever was speaking, quite as though he intended them as his contribution to the conversation.

At the house he kept up a running commentary as he met the resident cats, had some cold chicken for supper and explored the house. Even after I'd settled him in the kitchen in a towel-lined wicker basket on top of a chest, his head popped up whenever the volume of the conversation changed, and he added his cheerful opinion.

So endearing was his insistence on communicating that by morning the projected trip to the Humane Society had somehow become an excursion to the vet instead to check the kitten's health and sex preparatory to keeping him. Despite appearances and the kitten's young age, I had begun to believe that he was a female and in heat, else why was he so vocal? But the vet scotched this theory, pronouncing him male, about nine weeks old and in perfect condition, without a mite in his ear or a flea in his coat.

"So," I said as the kitten rode home beside me on the front seat, his paws neatly tucked under, "you're just a very talkative little bit of a cat."

"Wow-ow," he agreed cheerily.

After that, his name was Little Bit for a while; then it became Bitty.

I, who had always been partial to longhairs with plumed tails and pantalooned rumps, thought Bitty not ugly—it's a rare cat who is really ugly—but uninteresting-looking. He was a tabby, a domestic shorthair—a generic cat, as a friend described him—with stripes of darkness in his brindle coat, white paws and a rather too pointed face. In his favor was that he was spotless and his eyes were vigilant with love and interest in the world. He was not so much curious as participatory, eager to assist at all openings of doors, boxes, letters and grocery bags, and choosing always to sleep, if he had a choice, in arms or a lap, under bedcovers against a back or, in the absence of a human body, between Freebie's front paws.

He was never demanding, always equable, never frightened, always cheerful. Even when lugged around throughout an entire day by a visiting seven-year-old nephew, he did not complain. He played a number of invented games with Freebie, who adored him. He did not sharpen his claws on the furniture and sat on the velvet chairs only when I wasn't home. Whenever I walked into a room where he was asleep, he immediately roused himself to say hello, and no matter how tired he was from roaming in the fields, he welcomed being picked up and hugged. Affectionate, responsive, loving and communicative, he was the perfect cat.

At least I thought so, and when he disappeared, I was heartbroken. I had had guests for dinner one Saturday night, and he nipped through the door when they departed. It was the kind of night irresistible to a cat. A huge moon bathed the meadow across the way in white light and black shadows, so it was fruitless to try to call him back, and anyway, he often enough spent a night in the fields and in the morning was waiting on the front porch to be let in for breakfast.

But on Sunday morning he wasn't on the porch. I began calling and soon went looking for him. I searched up and down the road, in the first field across the road, in the second field, in the copse that separates them, along the broad path that once was a single-line railroad. I asked at the barn where thoroughbred trotters are stabled and at the houses within any conceivable distance. I searched and called and listened for his answering "wow-ow," growing more and more alarmed until my fear was like a great gray sack of feathers weighing down my back.

Chester, a cat I'd had before Bitty, had been savaged by a raccoon. Had Bitty met a similar fate? I hunted for him frantically. If only I could come upon him still alive, I would somehow manage to save him, I was sure. But after four days, when I gave up hope because the nights had turned bitter and he wouldn't have been able to survive in such cold, I longed to come across any clue to his fate. I dreaded finding a scrap of fur, a gnawed leg bone, a mangled body, but I could scarcely bear not knowing what had happened to him.

I didn't find a clue. It has been months now and still I grieve, still I cannot look out the front door without the foolish hope that a generic-looking cat will be sitting on the porch with his paws tucked under and that I will hear that inimitable voice say, "Wow?"

The depth of my pain has made me think about my year with Bitty. We never quarreled, never disagreed, never got on each other's nerves as people sometimes do. We had nothing to hold against each other, no residue of bitterness, no unhealed wounds. I had never scolded; he had never let me down. I had never been impatient; he had never pushed me away. It had been a year of pure love.

As I thought about this year of pure love, I wondered if it wasn't at least part of the reason an animal can become so important in one's life. Pure love is rare among humans. I have loved and been loved in my life, sometimes deeply, but never without reserve; there were always strings, caveats. I see now that that is almost inevitable in human love, and not only inevitable but desirable. A constant problem for every human being is to feel close enough to another to stave off fear of aloneness and distant enough from that same other to maintain the boundaries of the self. One must not engulf and must equally avoid being swallowed up.

But that's not a problem with an animal. It doesn't feel the least bit threatening to be boundlessly loved by a dog or cat, and the dog or cat is more than content to be boundlessly loved in return. It doesn't interfere with his individuality or autonomy. He'll go right on being an animal, his own animal, no matter how much affection is lavished on him. Thus, a human has carte blanche to love a pet at the top of his bent, just as fully, generously, wholeheartedly as he is capable of, and that is a superbly satisfying thing—to live out one's feelings without reserve.

Human love is, in Donald Barthelme's description, both "grisly and golden." How relaxing it is, then, to experience the simplicity of loving an animal. You don't have to worry that the love might not be returned fully enough or that it might be returned too fully. You can love a pet without worries about the quality of the love, without judgments, without agendas. It is, as it was with Bitty, pure love, a confirmation of one's capacity to love and a relief from the complications of human love.

Those complications—and so much else—one is always trying to put into words. Bitty had only his one word, "wow," the volume and resonance of which he varied to suit the situation, his need of the moment, and the feeling he wished to express. And again that very simplicity was relaxing. How good it is not to have to hunt for the right words, to communicate without the barrier of words. An aunt of mine had a passion for tiny babies, and I understand it now—the holding in your arms of a small, warm body, the conveying of love and reassurance by comforting, wordless sounds, the absolute being there for another living being.

There is, as well, the tactile pleasure of closeness. With Bitty sleeping in my lap while I read or watched television, I let my fingers wander in his fur and enjoyed the velvety feel. He would grow heavier and heavier as he sank into deep sleep, and that, too, would enlist my heart, for it spoke of profound trust. Bitty trusted as I don't suppose any person ever has or ever could. It didn't occur to him that I might hurt, frighten or reject him. He utterly assumed that I always wanted him in my lap, which I sometimes didn't, although I never let him know it, because I never wanted him to feel that his companionship, so freely offered, was not as freely welcomed.

Companionship—that is, I suppose, the single word most often used when people try to explain their attachment to a pet. The companionship has the inestimable value of being able to be bought and, although purchased, willingly given. Unless an animal is badly mistreated—and sometimes even then—its devotion can be counted on. A young man who walks with his dog on the road past my house often stops to chat if I am working in the garden, and while we talk, Lucy, his mongrel dog, never takes her eyes off his face. She listens so attentively to his tone of voice that she moves to his side when he starts to say goodbye. I don't know this man's story except that he lives alone in a house in the woods, and while I might wish for him some human companionship, I know he is safe in the world and connected because he has Lucy.

The acceptance of a person by an animal is unconditional. I have a ninety-year-old friend who recently had to have her ancient dog put down. Over her protests that she was a life-long dog person, I took her to the Humane Society to adopt a kitten. She picked out a friendly, orange-colored cat who immediately set about becoming as attached to a ninety-year-old as he would have to a nine-year-old. Animals have no preconceived notion of what an owner should look like or be like; they have no age or sex preferences. Whatever your looks, gifts or assets, or lack of them, "they ask no questions," as George Eliot noted, "they pass no criticisms." They accept the owner they get and, if treated kindly, are deliciously satisfied.

Incidentally, this erstwhile dog person claims the kitten has changed her life. When I telephone, she doesn't wait to hear what I've called about but starts right in: "I'm absolutely dotty about that kitten! He's wonderful! He follows me every-where. He talks to me." Her enthusiasm for life, which had dimmed, is once again bright, not just because of the kitten's companionship but because once more she has something that needs her. Erik Erikson described the mature stage of life as characterized by "generativity," the drive to nurture, protect and enable the small and the dependent. It is the need to be needed. We all experience it, and animals allow us to express it long after children are grown and gone.

The animal who is looked after returns the favor, not in kind, but by reminding us of some important truisms about life. One is to live in the present moment. We muse about yesterday—what was said or done or left undone—or the far yesterdays of roads taken or not taken, chances missed, loves lost. We think about tomorrow—plans, dates, hopes, worries. What we don't exist in, at least not nearly often enough, is *now*. We are always looking backward or forward, forgetting to notice this moment, this time, forgetting to enjoy *now*.

Bitty made me conscious of this. He would seek out and luxuriate in the one patch of sunlight on the kitchen floor, enjoying what the present had to offer to its fullest. Seeing him made me remind myself to "be here now"—feel the sun, taste the food, listen to the music, hear the words.

Animals put us in touch with the basics, with the natural world, which has little to do with get, spend, consume, throw away. They are a bridge to the natural world. Searching for Bitty in the field, I moved from the periphery, where I ordinarily walked, into the center. There I discovered in the stiff winter weeds an area laced with byways; some of the paths, as crooked as capillaries, ended in cul-de-sacs, some in piazzas of flattened grasses where deer bedded down, some in burrows from field mouse to woodchuck size. Was Bitty even now at the bottom of one of those burrows, dragged there by a creature bigger, stronger, more predatory than he?

Should I, foreseeing this might happen, have prevented Bitty from commuting between the human and animal worlds? I think not. As there is a dark side to nature, there is a dark side to human nature, a side that likes to control, dominate, lord it over the animals. They are in our power, and it is always tempting to exercise power when we have it. It is a temptation to be resisted. Just as much as is consonant with reasonable safety, I think an animal should be free to run, climb, stalk, bask, dig, wander—not if he lives in the city, obviously, but if his home is in a place where this is feasible. It is perfectly possible that I am wrong about this—many people would say so—but I have always felt that it is more to the point to be happy than to be safe. Life is risky, and you are most alive when you have the most at risk. People put themselves in jeopardy mountain climbing, speed racing or deep-sea diving for the extreme joy of surviving the dangers. Why shouldn't an animal have the same thrill?

I could not deny it to Bitty, who loved the wild. If I had it to do over again, would I still have the courage to let him roam free? Perhaps if I knew I was going to lose him after only a year, no. But there will be another kitten one day, and when he is old enough, I'll let him wander the fields if that is his pleasure because animals, like humans, need to follow their bliss if they are to get the deepest enjoyment from life and find the deepest meaning in it.

Friends knowing my grief over the loss of Bitty say, "That's why I don't have a pet anymore. It hurts too much when you lose it." It does hurt. But which is worse: the tragedy of a loss or the emptiness of having all that love inside you and nothing to give it to?

Having is best. Having had is second best. Never having had at all is less than a distant third; it doesn't place at all. If I had said "I cannot go through this hurt again" when Katie died or Chester was killed by the raccoon or Freebie had the stroke, I would have missed this year of pure love with Bitty.

"Tenderness and absolute trust and communication and truth: these things matter more and more as one grows older," writes a character in Iris Murdoch's novel *The Sea, the Sea.* I believe it to be so. I also believe these things are hard to find, except partially, in other people—and hard to bestow on other people, at least in the full, easy measure implied. As our bodies collect debits as we grow older, so do we collect psychological scar tissue, which gets in the way of tenderness and trust and communication and truth. But not in relation to an animal. I never said a cross word to Bitty, never ignored or made fun of him, never did not respond, never failed to be loving. Although only a cat, Bitty let me be the person I could have been unfailingly if life experience hadn't gotten in the way.

Am I exaggerating? Yes, a little. Perhaps a lot. Pets do not provide a full life, only make life fuller. However grisly relationships with other people may be, they are still golden and immensely necessary. An animal does not substitute for them, and I have not meant to imply that they do. I have only tried to explore why I and the people in the accounts in this book became so involved with an animal, went so far out of our way, cared so much.

We may belong to what has occasionally and derogatively been called "the mafia of animal lovers," but we have our reasons.

★ ★ ★ ★ ★

The Dog
with the
Old Soul

Introduction

"An animal anthology? Really? You?" new friends may ask upon hearing about this book project, looking around my well-ordered house, devoid of cat hair or a wet-dog smell. What gives? There are no bags of pet food in my garage. My newspaper is recycled promptly, never placed at the bottom of a birdcage. Older friends nod in understanding, though, since they knew the Airedale that lives on forever in my heart.

Animals take up residence in our hearts, sometimes consuming all available space and leaving no room for another dog, cat, horse or bird to be added to the mix. I love dogs, but I haven't had one myself in years. Just like some people have only one perfect love in their lives and, once it is over, don't feel the need to replace it, my dog Big Guy spoiled me as an owner. I delight in having others' pets around me, though, and I love to watch the affection and interaction between animals and people.

We are devoted to our animals, and they can be just as devoted to us. A recent news item touched everyone who stumbled upon it—the story of a man in China who passed away, leaving only a yellow dog behind. The dog refused to leave his grave, lying atop it day after day. Villagers brought the dog food and water, and one resident told reporters that the sight of the grieving dog "made my heart smile and cry."

The stories in *The Dog with the Old Soul* will also make your heart both smile and cry. There are stories of joy—the thrill of a new puppy, the excitement of a young girl's first horse show ribbon, the silliness of a room filled with cats. But life isn't always joyful, and there are stories of the comforting role that animals can play in our emotional lives. There are times in life when reaching down to pet a familiar fuzzy head can help ground us in a way nothing else can.

It is my hope that these stories touch you deeply, and that more than once while reading, you reach out and pull your pets in closer to you on the couch. Enjoy!

Jennifer Basye Sander

The Dog with the Old Soul

Finley Taylor

Sometimes people—or in my case, a dog—come into your life at just the right time.

Even before we were married, my husband and I talked about the dogs we would get someday. I wanted a Scottish terrier; he wanted a basset hound. Both of us liked both dogs, and neither of us minded which one we got first. We eventually decided that since bassets were known for being calm, low maintenance and child friendly—and since we were planning on having children soon—we'd get a basset first. Only problem was, for the first year and a half of our marriage we lived in a tiny apartment in Midtown.

When we moved to a larger home in 2009, it was time to start thinking about getting a dog. Well, actually, it was time to start thinking about having those children. Getting a dog was something we might push off till after the first baby was born, we thought. But the months went by and the pregnancy tests kept turning up negative.

The thought of including a different type of being, one

with four legs, as part of our family never was far from our thoughts. As much as we talked about baby names and family vacations and how we would *not* give our eight-year-old a cell phone, we also talked about hiking trips and strolls along the river and what we'd name our dog.

Three days after my twenty-seventh birthday, my husband sent me a seemingly innocuous photo from a local shelter's website of a perky-looking tricolored basset hound with intelligent, old-soul eyes. Her name was Chloe.

I work from home, so the squeal I let out fell on an otherwise silent house—a silence that over the months had developed a pitch of frustration, sadness and worry that became more palpable with each Facebook pregnancy announcement I saw. I called my husband and asked if he was game to go look at the pup with the world-heavy expression.

That night we stood outside the kennel of a loudly barking Chloe, who seemed to be conveying her frustration at being cooped up for so long, and at life for being a little rough on her as of late.

I didn't blame her. A kind but frazzled shelter employee told us this was the second time Chloe had been brought to the shelter.

Chloe let out a characteristic basset bark that rumbled deep in my bones, rattling loose feelings of compassion and a desire to care for another living being—feelings I'd lately been walling off in an act of self-preservation. My husband and I looked at each other. "Let's go home and sleep on it," I said.

When we told the front-desk clerk that we needed a night to ponder adopting Chloe, she said, "You know, a family adopted her and brought her back ten days later because she had a cut on her leg. A cut." The disdain in her voice stung my ears. It appeared this pup would not be given away again without the blessing of some very strong gatekeepers.

The next night we were back at the shelter, ready to adopt Chloe. My jangled thoughts and emotions zipped about my brain as if I were a kid in a bounce house. *Are we ready for this? Can we be good enough guardians for her? Our lives are about to change.*

"She's a very vocal dog," said a frazzled employee, this one with a platinum blond ponytail, while opening the kennel.

Chloe *aooof*fed nonstop out of impatience.

A cage that had not been cleaned out recently and a pen in which a matted microfleece blanket lay on the cold concrete were evidence of what the staff had already told us: the new shelter was struggling to survive, even as it tried to house a growing number of animals.

We were allowed to let this feverish canine out and to walk her, and she immediately put her nose to the ground with the loving familiarity of a mother tracing a finger over her child's face. Within minutes, our hearts were completely won over by a panting, slobbering, smelly tank of infectiously lovable dog.

"We'd like to adopt Chloe," we announced at the front desk.

"Adoptions ended a half hour ago," said the front desk person, who was a different woman than the night before. Her name tag read "Staci."

Crushed, we went home, nonetheless determined to be there right when the shelter opened the next day.

We arrived ten minutes before the shelter opened, and a coldness that didn't come from the damp December air enveloped me when I saw about a half dozen other people in front of us in line.

"Are they all here to adopt?" I whispered to my husband.

"You don't think someone here wants to adopt Chloe, do you?"

My husband gave me a look. "Well, we'd better hightail it to the front desk as soon as possible," he said.

When the front doors opened, we were the first to the desk. Staci, the woman who had turned us down the night before, was working again today. She smiled, pushing a lock of cocoa-brown hair out of her face. "You're here to adopt the basset hound."

We nodded like fools.

"I'll go get her." She rose to leave the desk, then turned to face us. "You know, she's very vocal."

We made assuring noises and stepped back when she sent a volunteer to get Chloe. A mother and two teenage girls came up to the desk. The mother said to an employee behind the desk—the one with the platinum blond ponytail who had allowed us to open Chloe's pen the night before—"We're here to adopt Chloe, the basset hound."

Our eyes went wide. *Wait, not* our *basset.*

"We were here last night," the mother explained, "and started to fill out paperwork, but they said we couldn't adopt her, because it was too late."

The blond employee, who had not heard our conversation a moment ago with Staci at the front desk, said, "Okay, I'll go get her."

My husband went up to Staci, who had just sent the volunteer to retrieve Chloe. "I don't want to cause a scene, but we just heard someone say they wanted to adopt the basset that you're getting for us."

Staci looked at us. "Oh." She got the attention of the blond employee, who came back to the desk and listened as Staci told our story.

"Yeah, I remember you," said the blond woman. "But this family did start the paperwork." They looked at each other, and then the blond woman hurried to the back, where the volunteer was supposedly getting "our" dog.

How could this happen?

We had tried twice to take Chloe home, we knew we were ready for her, and now our little addition might be ripped away from us before we even had a chance to have her. We looked at the other family discreetly. They looked nice enough, with their perfect white smiles and their matching sweatshirts with their private high school's name emblazoned on them. But she was supposed to be *our* dog.

Finally, the blond woman came back, holding the leash to Chloe, who was elated to be outside her kennel. We and the other family stood there awkwardly. The blond woman walked up to me and held out the leash. "Here you go," she said.

I looked at the leash in my hand. And smiled at it.

Twenty minutes later, after filling out enough paperwork to apply for a home loan, we walked out of the shelter the proud new guardians of a vocal, four-year-old basset hound, our hearts still stinging a bit at the image in our minds of the disappointed teenagers as they dejectedly walked past us to go home empty-handed. We never found out why the shelter chose us over the other family.

On the way to the car, we called our newest family member by the name we had chosen the night before, Bridgette—a name we felt encapsulated her unique, sweet yet spunky nature. We later found out that the name means "the exalted one" and "one who is strong and protective."

"Do you think she's happy to be out of there?" my husband asked, trying to get a look at her through the rearview window as he drove. I looked at the backseat, where Bridgette, with her long, thick body, flung herself onto her side like a breaching whale and breathed a contented sigh.

Four months later I was diagnosed with infertility, and we discovered that the only way we could have a biological family of our own was by in vitro fertilization. As I underwent testing and surgery, Bridgette was steadfast. And as I await a risky and uncertain treatment, she remains at my feet, showing a constancy that throws into sharp relief the actions of those in her previous life, those who had been entrusted with her care—a constancy that challenges me to return what she has given me. I stand at a threshold, facing an uncertain future of my own, and her old-soul eyes serve as a daily reminder of grace as I am brought through the doors of a temporary holding place that I hope will eventually lead me home.

★ ★ ★ ★ ★

Simon Says

Katherine Traci

November. Dark. Cold. I was driving home from a late-night writing workshop, a brutal night of fellow writers casually critiquing what was my own heart typed out neatly on the page. The exact same heart that had been trampled on by a liar three weeks prior. We'd gone to Venice to fall more deeply in love, cement it all in ancient stone. But no. Instead the medieval city was the scene of a modern breakup.

"Good plan, Kate," I scoffed to myself in my car, gripping the wheel and picturing what I should have done instead—pushed him into the dirty Grand Canal. I hadn't pushed him in. I'd gotten on the plane home like a good girl and flown back to an empty house, an empty heart. Tonight I'd hoped that writing it down and sharing it, letting others know how I felt, would help me heal. And maybe it would in the long run; but right then, alone, surrounded by strangers, empty and at a loss, I sat waiting to turn left onto the dark on-ramp, headed home. My head turned to follow a tiny cat that streaked across the road as it crossed my line of vision.

Feral, I thought as it headed toward the freeway. Odd behavior for any smart feral that lived in the area. I watched as what I now saw was a kitten run up the embankment toward a busy freeway overpass. It was almost 10:00 p.m. and the street was empty. I was tired…I was hungry…I was sad…I wanted to be home. The light changed. I stayed where I was.

Hmm, well timed on behalf of the cat, I thought. I had left class at the right second, had driven the right speed, had paused just long enough to turn at the exact moment that the little cat decided to sprint across six full lanes of the street in front of my truck.

Sighing, I felt the full weight of my own empty life hit me. If I couldn't push a man in a canal, at least I could rescue a kitty on the side of the road. I pulled over as far as possible onto the left shoulder and hit my hazards. There he was, hunkered down in the greenery far above me. I rolled down my window. I watched the kitten. The kitten watched me. I got out of the car.

I looked up the steep embankment at him. *Ice plant. Damn.* It was cold. I am a 911 dispatch operator. For me, hazards lurk everywhere, even in the safest of homes. A slippery shower, a frayed electrical cord. So many of the calls we take are the result of foolhardy behavior. This would fall easily into that category.

I have nothing to put a cat in. I don't even have a blanket. I have no idea what I am doing, I thought as I looked around. *And I'm mostly a dog girl. I'll go out of my way to rescue dogs. But a cat?* I shivered and tried to focus on a workable plan.

I decided to try and approach him. If he ran up toward the top of the embankment, I'd have to back off. I didn't want to be responsible for a cat on a busy freeway. I started up the steep embankment and the kitten didn't move. He blinked at me. He sat in the ice plant near the freeway on-ramp and slowly blinked his big teary eyes, open, shut, open. The light shone down from the streetlamp and his eyes glowed. Open. Shut.

I clutched at the fence along the embankment with one hand and made my way up the slippery ice plant. It was a good slope. My clumsiness well known, I tried to keep out of my head the images of me tumbling back down to the asphalt below.

I could hear the morning news in my head: "An unidentified woman tried to climb ice plant in an attempt to access the freeway for unknown reasons. She was unkempt and messy, and all evidence suggests she suffers from broken heart syndrome. The authorities have hesitated to confirm or deny this, and it is unknown at this time if this syndrome is related to last night's incident. She is in critical but stable condition today at the medical center, after falling twenty feet. Doctors say she fell sometime late last night and was not discovered until morning."

I was one foot away. I could touch him if I reached out. Should I take off my hoodie to grab him and wrap him up?

Nooo, I thought as I zipped the hoodie up further. *It's too cold.*

I pulled the hoodie's wrist cuffs down over my hands, minimal protection against claws at best, and stretched out toward him. I aimed for the back of his neck.

Cat scratch fever, cat scratch fever. . . cat scratch fever! My dad's voice reverberated in my head. Whether it was a warning or the lyrics to a song, I couldn't quite remember.

I reached out once…twice…three times. Each time the kitty turned his head around to look at my hand but didn't move.

Oh. I'm going to pick him up and he will be a bloody mess, badly injured, I thought, feeling sick to my stomach in addition to feeling cold. I could see only his tiny head. And those big blinking eyes.

Really, this was too absurd. Remember, I see potential danger everywhere. Yet there I was on a dark, cold night, perched on a slope of ice plant near a freeway overpass in the middle of a part of town you really shouldn't slow down in, let alone pull over and stop in. I was alone, trying to rescue a damn kitten.

I needed to get this over with. "Now or never. Just do it, Kate!" And with that rallying cry I grabbed him and pulled him to my chest. His claws held on to me and I felt his body vibrate with his purrs. I looked down the embankment. Now I had to make my way back down. This time with no hands to hold on to the fence, as both were clasping this mess of a cat. Tense, I carefully picked my way with each step down the slippery ice plant on the steep embankment, arriving at the bottom without incident.

In what felt like a one-take action sequence, I threw the car door open, tossed the kitten in, grabbed my keys, started the car, rolled up the window—before the rescued cat escaped! I turned to look at him. He was perched expectantly on my center console, waiting and watching my hurried antics. He was bones. Skin and bones…and purrs.

Next morning at the vet's office, they insisted on a name. I stood in front of the receptionist, shaking my head.

"I'm not going to name him. I don't want to name him."

The receptionist raised her eyebrows and cocked her head, her fingers hovering over the keys of her computer.

"Please don't make me name him. I can't keep him. I have a very small house."

She waited. This same scene must have happened a lot here.

I wondered if it always turned out the same way. "Okay, we'll just type in k-i-t-t-y."

"No, don't write 'Kitty' on the chart. I don't want to call him Kitty." Something told me his name was Simon.

Simon spent the next two weeks sequestered in my bathroom, my only bathroom. I gingerly opened the door whenever I needed access, pushing my foot in ahead of me to keep Simon from rushing the door, nudging him out of the way if he made an attempt to escape. I needed to keep him away from my other pets, the vet said, until the lab results came in and they gave him a clean bill of health.

So until that approval came through, I had a four-pound, voraciously hungry, frustratingly messy roommate. A *loud* roommate who lived exclusively in my bathroom. His tortured cries reverberated off the tile when he heard me stir in any part of the house. In an effort to calm him, I'd visit for long periods of time, just sitting on the edge of the tub. Talking seemed to quiet him down, so I talked. The look in his eyes made me feel that he could answer back.

"My mom died, Simon," I whispered.

"When?" he would purr, rubbing his cheek against mine.

"Two years ago, but it still hurts."

"I know," he would squeak, "but then somebody comes along and helps." He reached out a paw to tap my nose.

Simon talks to everything and everyone. He has a sweet *meep,* high pitched and soft, when looking up at me; a *brrrrr* chirp when he asks my older, "can hardly be bothered" cat relentlessly for playtime; and he gives a *merrwrrrow* to the dog whenever their eyes lock. All very different sounds, very specific and very Simon.

Simon believes he has an imaginary friend. When he plays with crumpled-up paper, he growls and chirps and looks around and plays…with somebody. Not me. Not my other cat. Not my dog. He is alone. It is the craziest thing to watch. The tiny noises he makes scare the bejesus out of my big, scary dog.

Since I found him on the way home from a writing class, perhaps he is a writer, too. He has a special fondness for laptop keyboards. The first time it was the letter *x*. I found him batting something small and black—the key off the keyboard— around the floor, like a hockey player practicing with a puck. The next time it was the *t*. He leaps up and pounces on the unattended keyboard. No letter is safe as he picks whichever one he pleases to pry off and play with. The third time it was *b* and *e,* double the fun. They recognize me now at the computer repair shop.

The little ice-plant kitty was the most loving creature I had ever met. I thought I'd left my capacity for love squashed flat on the cobblestones in Italy, but Simon taught me my heart was still there, strong and healthy, after all.

Sometimes I look at Simon and think back to that night on the side of the freeway. I think I saved Simon, but maybe he saved me.

★ ★ ★ ★ ★

Where the Need Is Greatest

Tish Davidson

I have been a volunteer puppy raiser with Guide Dogs for the
Blind for ten years. Donna Hahn has been raising guide dogs for
at least twice that long. She has shared tips on socializing puppies,
has helped me with difficult dogs and has encouraged me when my
dogs failed to make the grade as guides. We have traded puppy-
sitting chores and dog stories. Donna has loved every guide dog
puppy she has ever raised. But one dog was special.
This is Donna's story.

Donna could hardly control her tears as she mounted the
platform at the outdoor graduation ceremony. A light
breeze ruffled the flag. The audience waited, polite and at-
tentive. The graduates sat, alert and poised. The flag had been
saluted; the speeches made; the staff and students congratulated. Now it was time to take the final step and send the
graduates out into the world to fulfill their mission.

Donna stopped beside one of the graduates and rested a
hand on his shoulder. "Raising a puppy is an act of love and
faith," she began. "When a puppy comes into your home, he

comes into your heart. He is a part of your family. You give him all the time, care and love you can. Then, almost before you know it, that curious, wriggling, uncoordinated puppy has changed into an obedient, mature dog, ready to return to Guide Dogs for the Blind and take the next step in becoming a working guide.

"I'm thrilled and happy that Llama—" she indicated the golden retriever next to her "—has become a working guide. But I'm sad, too, because it is always hard to say goodbye to someone you love." She picked up Llama's leash and handed it to Gil, Llama's new partner. "Goodbye, Llama. You are a special dog."

The crowd murmured in appreciation, and some in the audience sniffled audibly and reached for their tissues. Then the graduation was over. Soon Llama and Gil were on their way to Vancouver, Canada, and Donna was on her way home to Newark, California, knowing there was a good chance she would never see Llama again.

Llama was the third puppy the Hahn family—Donna, John, and their daughters, Wendy and Laurel—had raised for Guide Dogs for the Blind, but he was the first to complete the program and become a working guide. He had come into their life fifteen months earlier, a red-tinged golden retriever with white hairs on his face and muzzle that gave him a washed-out, unfinished look. "An ugly dog," Donna had said at the time. But soon his looks didn't matter.

At first, Llama was as helpless as any new baby. "Neee, neee, neee," he cried when he was left alone. He woke Donna in the night and left yellow abstract designs on the carpet when she didn't get him out the door fast enough. Donna patiently cleaned up the accidents. Soon Llama learned "Do your business," one of the early commands that every guide dog puppy learns, and the accidents rapidly decreased.

Like all guide pups, Llama was trained with love and kind words, rather than with food treats. Soon he would follow Donna through the house on his short puppy legs, collapsing at her feet when she said, "Sit," happy to be rewarded with a pat and a "Good dog."

Llama seemed to double in size overnight. By the time he was five months old, he was accompanying Donna everywhere. It wasn't always easy. Llama had to learn to overcome his natural inclination to sniff the ground and greet every dog he met on the street. At the supermarket he learned not to chase the wheels on the grocery cart. At Macy's he learned to wait while Donna tried on clothes. With a group of other puppies in training, Llama and Donna rode the ferry across San Francisco Bay and toured the noisy city.

In May Donna was summoned for jury duty in superior court in Oakland. Of course, she took Llama. Privately, she hoped that his presence would be enough to get her automatically excused, but the plan backfired. For a week, Llama lay patiently at Donna's feet in the jury box while Donna attended the trial.

All too soon, a year was up, and the puppy that had wagged its way into Donna's heart was a full-grown dog, ready to return to the Guide Dogs campus in San Rafael and start professional training. There was only a fifty-fifty chance he would complete the program. Working guides must be physically and temperamentally perfect before they are entrusted with the life of a blind person. Donna had given Llama all the love and training she could; now his future was out of her hands.

Llama passed his physical and sailed through the training program. When it came time to be matched with a human partner, the young golden retriever was paired with Gil, a curator at an aquarium in Canada. Matching dog and human is a serious and complicated ballet in which the dog's strengths, weaknesses and personality are balanced against the human's personality and lifestyle. When done well, an unbreakable bond of love and trust develops between human and dog.

Gil and Llama were a perfect match, and their bond grew strong and true. Gil had never had a guide dog before. Once home, he found that Llama gave him a new sense of confidence, independence and mobility. Every day they walked together along the seawall to Gil's work at the aquarium. In time, everyone grew to know Llama, and Llama grew to know all the sights and sounds of Gil's workplace. For ten years, Llama was at Gil's side every day—at home, at work, on vacation, and on trains, planes and buses.

Meanwhile, at the Hahns', Wendy and Laurel grew up and moved away from home. John and Donna continued to raise pups. Their fourth dog became a family pet. The fifth became a working guide in Massachusetts, and the sixth a service dog for a physically handicapped teen.

While they were raising their seventh pup, Donna's husband, John, a fit and active air force veteran, began having stomach problems. An endoscopy revealed the bad news. John had advanced gastric cancer. Thus began a long series of treatments and operations to try to catch the cancer, which always seemed one step ahead of the surgeon's knife. It was a grim, sad, stress-filled time. Soon John could no longer take any nourishment by mouth. With John's strength waning daily, the family came to accept that he had only a few months to live.

In October, with John desperately ill, a call came from the Guide Dogs placement advisor. "Donna, we just got a call that Llama is being retired. He's been working for ten years, and all that stair-climbing and leading tours at the aquarium have caught up with him. He has pretty bad arthritis. Gil is coming down to train with a new dog. I know John is terribly sick, and the last thing you might want to do right now is take care of an old dog, but Gil specifically requested that we ask you if you could give Llama a retirement home. He can't keep Llama himself, but he wants him to be with someone who will love him."

"Of course we'll take him," said Donna, never hesitating.

Several days later Donna drove up to the Guide Dogs campus to pick up Llama. She paced back and forth across the receiving area as she waited for a kennel helper to bring Llama to her.

"Do you think he'll recognize me after ten years?" she anxiously asked an assistant in a white lab coat.

When Llama arrived, moving stiffly in the damp morning air, it was not the joyous reunion she had imagined. Llama seemed pleased to see her, but in a reserved, distant way. An hour and a half later, Llama was back at the house where he had spent the first year of his life.

Donna pushed open the front door. "John, we're home." Llama didn't hesitate for a second. He walked in, turned and headed straight into John's bedroom, as if he had been going there every day of his life. From that moment on, he rarely left John's bedside. Although he was too old to guide, Llama had found a place where he was needed.

Llama was a careful and gentle companion for John. When John got out of bed, pushing the pole that held his intravenous feeding bottles, Llama was beside him, ready to protect him, but careful never to get in his way or get tangled in the medical apparatus.

"I don't know how that dog always seems to know exactly what you need, but he surely does," said Donna more than once.

"He was sent to take care of me," John replied.

By the end of the month, John's condition had worsened. The hospice nurse administered morphine. Donna was afraid the drug would make John disoriented and that he would try to get out of bed and would fall over Llama, so she ordered the dog to leave the room.

"Llama, out."

Llama, who had never disobeyed a command, didn't budge.

"Llama, out."

Llama didn't move a muscle and remained planted by John's bed.

The next morning, however, Llama began to pace frantically back and forth through the house.

"What's wrong with him, Mom?" asked Wendy, who had come home to help her mother.

"I don't know. Maybe he's sick."

The pacing continued all day and into the evening. At 9:30 that night, John passed away. Llama stopped pacing and lay quietly by the door.

"He must have known the end was near," said Wendy.

Llama lay at the door, refusing to move, forcing people to step over him. For three days he grieved, along with the rest of the family. On the fourth day he got up, went to Donna and placed his grizzled head in her lap. He had found someone else who needed him.

Today Llama and Donna are rarely separated. They visit neighborhood friends, both dog and human, daily. They go to Guide Dogs meetings, take walks around the lake and occasionally go to the beach. A neighbor has made Llama a ramp so that he can avoid stairs and get in and out of cars. The dog Donna had given a home and her heart to, and then had sent out into the world to help another, had brought that love back to Donna when her need was greatest.

I cried the first time I heard the story of Llama. The second time I heard it, I knew it was a story that needed to be shared. Give yourself to a dog, and you will get love and loyalty in return. Dogs know when you need them most.

Too Many Cats in the Kitchen

Maryellen Burns

Knock! Knock! Knock!!

Six-thirty in the morning! My husband, Leo, and I wake up. Someone's incessantly knocking on the door downstairs. I panic. Who is it? A loved one had an accident? A neighbor found one of our cats dead in the street? I try to shake off my anxiety and the five cats that had rooted themselves to my lap and legs all night.

We stumble to the door. My friend Angela is there. "I'm sorry to come over so early," she says, "but I'm supposed to shoot a commercial for Safeway grocers at seven-thirty and my scheduled location is kaput. You have such a wonderful kitchen. Could I possibly bring a film crew here in an hour?" Her British accent adds an extra note to this early morning request.

My first thoughts are, *Leo has to teach and the kitchen is a mess.* We haven't cleaned up from dinner last night. Piles of dishes are in the sink and on the stove. We'd need to hide cat bowls and kitty litter, and vacuum up *mucho* cat hair.

Second thought? *Yes!* We spent two years restoring our kitchen and are proud of its 1910 Craftsman features: a six-burner, double-oven Magic Chef range, lush redwood-veneer cabinets, a black-and-white soda-fountain floor and old-fashioned comfiness.

We look at each other. A lot needs to get done. Leo rushes to the kitchen to feed cats, clean and make coffee before dressing and going to work, while I attempt to de-cat the living room.

An hour or so later a crew of eight gathers on the front porch—producer Angela; three men with camera gear; Rosa Nosa, our fluffy tortoiseshell, who has rushed out to greet them; and three outdoor cats, who scramble to hide.

Opening the front door is a struggle because Nishan, our little disabled, back-legs-all-tangled-in-on-themselves cat, is parked in front of it.

I finally get the door open, and a sullen-voiced man, the director, asks, "How many damn cats do you have?"

"Nine," I tell him. "Or possibly more. You never know who they brought home last night."

"There aren't going to be any cats in the kitchen, right?" he asks.

I assure him that the kitchen can be shut off from the rest of the house and it won't be a problem.

Brushing cats away from his legs, he hurries through the living room and into the kitchen, as if he knows the way.

"We need to set up. No time for niceties," he says.

I follow him, and there is Rosa, sitting on the butcher-block island, looking every bit the superb hostess she is.

He picks her up and plops her roughly to the floor. "I said no cats in the kitchen!"

I pick her up, reassure her and take her outside.

"What have you done? Angela said your kitchen had a slightly messy, warm, lived-in look. You've cleaned it. Now we'll have to dirty it again!"

Angela and I look at each other. I can tell that this guy is a major pain in the neck, and I hope I can get through a whole day with him in my house. He gives the room a cursory look.

"I like the stove. I want a pot of water, steam rising from it. Mess up the counters. I want fresh vegetables, canned tomatoes, a flour sack spilling out. Move the butcher block to the center of the room. It should be the focal point. What's that cat doing here? I thought I told you to remove *all* the cats!"

Angela picks up the cat. It's Rosa Nosa again. She starts to purr, presses her red nose against Angela's face. Meanwhile, Hephzibah and Honky, the two oldest cats in the household, wander in, looking for food and water. They jump up on the kitchen table, demanding attention.

For the first time, the director spots Nishan hiding under the kitchen table. She scurries out, dragging her useless hind legs. The director looks disgusted. "What is it with these cats? Get. Them. Out. Of. The. Kitchen. Now!"

"Oh, Terry," pleads Angela. "The talent won't be here for an hour. Let the cats be. We'll clear them out before we start filming."

He looks as if he might relent, but something in the tone of his voice spooks the cats. *This is not a cat person.* They scatter. Except for Rosa, who insists on taking up residence beneath the butcher block with Nishan, her shadow.

To understand Rosa and Nishan's relationship, you need to know a little about how we came to keep them. Rosa was born about three months after my mother died, one of six kittens from Little Guy, Mom's faithful companion throughout her illness. Of all the kittens she was the prettiest, the liveliest, a furry lump of playfulness with an air of responsibility, a dignified poise and a beautiful red patch across her cute little nose. Everything about her reminded us of my mother, Rose. We wanted to keep her but couldn't justify it, because she had so many offers of a home and we had so many kittens to place. We gave her to Monica, a little girl who lived down the street.

Within twenty-four hours, Monica was on our doorstep, a squirming kitten in hand, face and cheeks swollen and red. She was allergic. Would we keep her until she could give her to a new home on Monday? My mother had always said she'd return one day as a madam of a cathouse or as one of Leo's cats. There was a reason this cat had come back to us. We were meant to keep her.

A year later Rosa and Giselle, a loveable stray we had taken in, bore kittens within a few days of each other. A couple of weeks later Giselle moved her kittens atop a bed in Mom's old room, except for the runt, a tortoiseshell that looked a little like Rosa. Leo picked her up. For the first time we realized she had twisted, deformed hind legs. "I don't know if this one is going to survive," he said, carrying her to Giselle and placing her at a teat. But Giselle rejected her and moved the other kittens again. This happened two or three more times.

Leo is softhearted. He hates to see any little critter suffer. Obviously, Giselle didn't want her. Something had to be done. The next day we took her to our vet.

"If her mother refuses to nurse her, she could die in a couple of days on her own, but she looks like a survivor to me. It's a big responsibility, but why don't you try again? You could feed her by hand, and in a week or two we could put a cast on her legs and try to straighten them."

Home she went. Giselle wouldn't nurse her. That night

she moved the others yet again. Next morning we're lying in bed. Rosa is nursing her kittens under our desk. We see a little face peeking in at the foot of the doorway and then watch the disabled kitten scurry across the floor to Rosa and push all the other kittens out of the way, looking for sustenance. Rosa begins licking Nishan all over and looks up at us as if to say, "What's one more?"

When almost all the kittens had new homes, my niece Penny showed up with six more, barely three weeks old. Someone had abandoned them. Would Rosa nurse them? Rosa didn't hesitate. All kittens were welcome, but Nishan was her favorite. She never grew beyond the size of an eight-week-old kitten. Rosa continued to nurse Nishan for almost two years. Wherever Rosa went, Nishan followed.

They are together now, watching the crew ready the kitchen for filming. The actors arrive. Rosa runs to the door to greet them and lead them into the kitchen.

Everything is ready for the first take. Spaghetti pot boiling on the stove, lettuce washed and dried by hand, husband and wife intimately touching shoulders as they laugh and make dinner together.

"Cut! Where did that damn cat come from?"

There is Rosa, perched majestically on the lower deck of the butcher block, taking a keen interest in the proceedings. I pick her up and put her on the back porch.

The director sets up the shot again. "Camera's rolling," he says.

The salad is being tossed; noodles are placed in boiling water. I see Nishan, who had remained hidden, peer out from behind a butcher-block leg. Within minutes Rosa is back in place, following every move of the camera. The director doesn't seem to notice at first. When he does, he silently picks her up by the scruff of her neck and tosses her out.

Minutes later she is back, arching her back against the director's legs, as if trying to seduce him. Again, he picks her up and tosses her out the French doors.

Before you know it, she's back again, under the stairs. Neither the director nor the crew has noticed there is a cat door. As I wonder if I should block it so Rosa can't get back in, she suddenly leaps from the floor to the kitchen table and then takes another flight to the butcher block.

"There are too many cats in the kitchen!" the director barks and stomps out of the room.

Angela follows him. I hear muffled voices, his strident and nasty, Angela's soft and lilting as she tries to calm him. One actor has picked Rosa up and is tickling her under her chin. She responds with a rumbling purr and a gracious movement of her head.

The director comes back, temper under control, but barely. Angela follows, a catlike smile on her face. "A few more takes and we're done," he says. "I give up."

Rosa remained in place for the rest of the morning, looking like Gloria Swanson in *Sunset Boulevard* demanding her close-up.

"That's a wrap," the director called.

He never broke a smile or thanked us for giving up our house and our time. He just watched silently as the rest of the crew packed up the camera gear, the lights, the food, petted Rosa one more time and left.

A week or so later Angela called to say that the commercial was going to air at 6:00 p.m. on Tuesday and would be rebroadcast for a month or two.

We set up the television recorder, gathered all the cats on

the bed and waited to see Rosa's debut. The commercial ended. The editor had left all Rosa's scenes on the cutting room floor! The ad was okay but we thought it lacked the emotional punch Rosa might have given it.

Rosa, in one of her rare acts of petulance, jumped off the bed. In solidarity the other cats followed her. Only Nishan remained to ease our disappointment. A strong union household, we boycotted Safeway for a while but realized it wasn't their call; it was the call of a director who didn't realize that the biggest joy of all is too many cats in the kitchen.

Transforming U

Suzanne Tomlinson

As a longtime journalist, I never imagined a writing assignment from a popular horse magazine would lead me to personal transformation. But that was exactly what happened when I met a horse with a giant letter *U* branded on his well-muscled neck.

I'd been asked to write a piece about how to have a successful match when adopting a horse from a rescue center. A lifelong horse-crazy gal with horses of my own, I was excited about the assignment.

I interviewed the Grace Foundation director, Beth DeCaprio. She provided some solid information and great tips on how to find a perfect equine partner at a rescue organization. Then she told me about an upcoming project—the HELP Rescue Me Trainers' Showcase. It had grown out of a crisis involving wild horses.

In the Midwest about two hundred of the Bureau of Land Management's mustangs had gone through three auctions with no bidders. When that happens, the BLM brands the horses nobody wants with a big letter *U* to identify them as unwanted. They are no longer the responsibility of the BLM. Most of the horses with this sad scarlet letter go to slaughter operators. These particular two hundred *U* horses were sent to a ranch in Nebraska, where a rancher placed them on his property and then left them to fend for themselves.

The Humane Society of the United States rushed in to help but not before many of these horses died from starvation. Horse rescue groups, including the Grace Foundation, traveled to a rehab center where the surviving mustangs were being held in the hopes that they could be helped. Beth and her volunteers agreed to take thirty-one of the *U* horses back to her center in California, near Sacramento. Other rescue organizations took on the remaining unwanted horses.

Beth came home with the daunting task of finding these horses forever homes. Suddenly an inspiration hit her. Why not pair professional trainers with each of her thirty-one mustangs to give these wild horses seventy days of training and make them more adoptable?

Local trainers took to the idea. They came to the Grace Foundation and each picked out a mustang. At the end of the training period Beth brought the whole gang—mustangs and their trainers—to the big annual horse expo in Sacramento to show off. She called it the Trainers' Showcase. Each trainer demonstrated to the crowd what had been accomplished in those seventy days of training. I watched in the audience as thirty-one horses and thirty-one trainers entered the arena to show what an untrained wild horse could learn in a very short time. The crowd in the stands was moved to standing ovations again and again. Many of the horses were under saddle and seemed at ease with the chaos of the arena, the lights and the noisy crowd. Some of the *U*-branded horses had learned impressive dressage movements; others jumped obstacles with confidence; all had the beginnings of trust with humans, despite the fact that all the humans they'd met in the past had brought them nothing but hardship and pain. At the end of the event the mustangs were offered for adoption. Would they still be unwanted?

I wrote my story about adopting a horse from a rescue organization, plus a sidebar about the unwanted horses at the horse expo. Editors at the magazine suggested I check on the *U*-branded horses in a few months and find out what had happened to them.

In the meantime my life suddenly, unexpectedly, turned upside down. My seemingly solid twenty-four-year marriage crumbled, damaged beyond repair. For a time I thought the shock and the pain would kill me. I fled to the guesthouse on our property to be alone. In those first few days of facing the ugly truth about a marriage I had thought was based on faithfulness, I asked God for help. I remember praying, *Dear God, if what I feel now is going to kill me, please take me now. But if I am supposed to survive it, please let me rest and feel your peace. Show me your light and I will know I can get through this.*

For the first time in several days I slept for many hours. What awakened me was not the jolting remembrance of the nightmare I was living. It was the brightest light of morning I had ever seen, streaming through window blinds that were closed...the light so bright, so lovingly piercing, it woke me up. Something had shifted in that dark night of the soul. In the recesses of my mind there was a knowing—*I am deeply loved by God and the divine that dwells within me.* The pain, the anger, the unbearable grief just dissolved away. God's peace was all around me and in me. *Thank you, God,* I said to myself. *I have my answer. I can go on.*

In the days that followed I began to count my blessings.

Our children were grown and on their own. I had financial resources. And I had strength beyond anything I could have imagined. Upon filing for divorce, I moved out. I found a nice house on five acres with a perfect setup for horses and moved in, along with two dogs, one cat and my two horses.

Complete healing would take some time, but I was no longer afraid to face the truth. I also knew I had to plumb the depths of my own emotions to try and understand why I had been burned by the scorched earth of betrayal time and time again throughout my life.

I thought of the *U*-branded horses and realized, though I didn't carry that letter outwardly, I carried it inwardly. To most people, and even to myself on a conscious level, I was a happy, optimistic, career-driven woman with lots of love in my life. I had children I adored and many relationships I treasured. But I had been drawn to men who seemed to love me on one level and hate me on another. I would start out with the warm glow of feeling cherished. But invariably over time the relationships brought a cold, sad message—I was unwanted.

My mother delivered that scarlet letter *U* for "unwanted" when I was just a girl. She was a troubled person, depressed and addicted to alcohol, which further twisted her mind. Underneath it all, there was always a spark of meanness. I tried to steer clear of her sting and just let it drift past, but the day came when her darkness changed my life.

I don't remember what I asked of her. It could have been a ride to a friend's house. I know it wasn't much. She sneered at me, a suspicious, small smile curling her lips. Already I was on alert. *Nothing good is going to come out of her mouth,* I thought.

She said, "Suzanne, dear, you are such a lucky girl, aren't

you? You've had the security and safety of feeling loved all your young life, haven't you?"

Why is she saying these things to me? There is something sinister brewing.

"Yes, poor dear, the truth will confuse you, but here it is. I have never loved you, never wanted you, never cherished you. You are unloved."

People underestimate the power of words. These words, her words, devastated me. It was the deepest betrayal from mother to daughter—an intentional fire set to burn down the trust of an innocent, unsuspecting child.

Looking back over my life, I think my mother loved me. I also think she very much wanted to hurt me. It's hard to reconcile those feelings and actions—loving and hurting seem so discordant. But I have come to understand that her desire to hurt must have derived from some deep wound of her own. Over the years and after her death from the effects of alcoholism, I thought I had forgiven her. What I didn't know was that I carried that wound of her words deep in my subconscious mind, and it colored my opinion of myself. Unwanted. Unloved.

Again I had walked into the fire of someone else's loving and hurting. Had I stayed married to a man for twenty-four years because in my subconscious he replayed my mother's themes?

I had to try and heal this deep hurt, or I was destined to invite betrayal into my life for unlimited visits. But how to heal? How to forgive? That seemed like a tall order. There was another way to keep betrayal from my door and it seemed easier. *Just never love again,* I thought. For a short while that seemed like the best answer. Then I met the plain brown horse with the big *U* on his neck.

I had checked back on the unwanted mustangs from the Grace Foundation's Trainers' Showcase. There on the website I found a listing of the *U*-branded horses. As I scrolled down, I could see in bold letters next to their names the word "adopted"! It was exciting to see that so many of these most unwanted of the unwanted had found forever homes—except one horse, at the bottom of the list. They called him Vigilant. He was a plain brown ten-year-old mustang with a sturdy-looking body and a kind eye. The vet had noted that he had been gelded and was healthy, with no apparent problems other than the trust issues that went along with being severely neglected. There was no happy, bold "adopted" next to this horse's name.

I wanted this unwanted horse. It just felt right to start my new life wanting the unwanted. It would help remind that little girl who resided in my subconscious, she was wanted and loved very deeply. I made a promise to bring that kind of sacred love to my life in any way I could. I had rescued two abandoned dogs, so why not this horse? And this is how Vigilant found his forever home with me. I spoke with the trainer who had worked with him, and she told me that he had a willing attitude but definitely did not offer automatic trust to all who approached. She suggested I start all over again in his training…being careful to first establish that trust.

And so the two *U*-branded souls began their work together. The first week I fed him only over the fence and let him settle into his new space next to my other two horses. He didn't seem nervous but I could tell he was wary. The second week I went into his pasture and tried to approach. He ran from me each time. I didn't try to catch him. I just stood as near as he would let me and talked to him softly.

And then like a tightly closed bud protecting itself from

winter's frost, the horse, like the flower, began to open to me. He let me approach and stroke his neck, moving my hand over that awful *U,* wishing I could erase it. The following week, when I opened his pasture gate, he trotted over to me, inviting me to pat him. When it seemed time to put a halter on, he lowered his head into it willingly.

Still, I moved very slowly with him—one little success at a time. In a month I thought he was ready for some round pen work on a lunge line. I discovered that wonderful foundation the first trainer had established. This horse followed my commands perfectly when I asked him to walk, trot, stop and then move out again. When I asked for the canter, it was clear he had no idea what I wanted, but he tried, anyway, trotting ever faster as I urged him to move out. I changed my communication style. Instead of using my voice to ask for this faster gait, I moved my own legs to the cadence of the canter.

Now he was really confused. I could sense what he was thinking. *You want me to run? But mostly I run when I'm fleeing something threatening. Are you scary?* How could I tell him I didn't want him to run in fear? I wanted him to run in a new way, slower, more controlled, a dance I might one day join him in. I talked to him softly, moving my feet to show him what I wanted, and when he began to gallop too fast, I said encouragingly, "Good boy! Now just slow it down a bit."

One day I just thought, *It's time to get on this horse.* Moving things along very slowly, I put my foot in the stirrup and stepped up to the saddle, then down again. He was so quiet. In a few days I felt sure enough of him to put my foot in the stirrup and swing all the way up and into the saddle. I asked him with my legs and my voice to move out at a walk. He responded perfectly. And what a perfect moment for me. *Never trust, never love again?* This horse had been abused, neglected and betrayed, yet he was showing me *he* was willing to trust again. Who was *I* to shut out the world? If I could build mutual trust with this horse, building it with a human being might be possible. This horse was showing me the way. I would be open to love again someday and then I would know how. *Just take it slow. Build it step by step. Be wary, but be willing.*

I thought back to that moment of deep self-love in my dark night of the soul. That love was a bridge to freedom—freedom from anger, sadness, regret, self-recrimination…freedom to be wholly and holy loved. Now riding this *U*-branded horse, I reached down and stroked his neck. "You are not unwanted and will never again be unwanted. I want you. You are loved." The horse and I had stepped up to our challenges. I was healing that *U* brand in my soul. I would not be a slave to betrayal.

My plain brown horse deserved a name that would transform that sad *U* into something fitting his grandness. Why not *U*nderestimated and *U*ltimately free? Now I open his pasture gate and call his new name. "Good morning, Freedom!" He calls back with a whinny and trots to my side.

★ ★ ★ ★ ★

A Nose for Love

Dena Kouremetis

When my husband, George, and I look back, we shake our heads in disbelief. We didn't find one another on a dating site or throw flirtations to one another across a crowded bar. The brother of my maid of honor, George was a groomsman in my 1982 wedding to someone else.

See, it's a Greek thing. During the ensuing twenty years, I'd spot George at Greek weddings, festivals, funerals, picnics and dances I would attend with my husband. And each time I'd see him, I would ask his sister about him, taking curious note of the fact that he'd stayed single. My knowledge of George extended to his being a gregarious, good-looking family friend that danced well. After my marriage broke up two decades later, however, I was to discover that George was still there, unattached. And when he found out I was about to become single myself, he wasted no time saying he had no intention of missing his chance to finally get to know me. Well, it's just about the most flattering thing a middle-aged woman can have happen to her, isn't it?

So is *this* what they meant by "happily ever after?" Well, almost.

You see, my new love made it clear early on that he had pet allergies and that, although he liked dogs, he would probably never own one. *Pet dander* was a new term to me.

"What happens when you're around a dog?" I asked.

A pained look came over George's face. "My sinuses get stuffed up and I get headaches. Then I get sinus infections and it's awful."

Hmm, really? I'd had small dogs throughout my life. They'd warmed my lap, watched TV with me, melted me with their doleful eyes and filled up spaces in my heart humans simply couldn't. It was tough to face the idea of never owning one again. "Can't you get shots?" I asked.

George looked at me as if I had reduced his affliction to inoculating livestock, and it was there the subject ended.

As things got more serious between us, I rationalized the idea of having the freedom to travel and socialize without worrying about a pet. I could accidentally drop food on the floor or leave a door open without having to worry about a little being scurrying to snatch up the morsel or run out of the house. The freedom began to grow on me. A little.

The day finally came when my daughter walked me down the aisle to George and life began anew. At dinner with some friends not long after we moved into our new home, we learned they were getting a Shima puppy flown down from the Northwest—a shih tzu–Maltese crossbreed, a dog that had become popular over the past few years for its personality, its no-shed fur and, of course, its cuteness factor. Rena and her daughters would excitedly show us photos of their mail-order dog. There was jubilation the day Maxie's doggy crate, containing a floppy-eared, mop-tailed pup, was handed to its new owners at the Sacramento airport. In the end, Maxie would be everything this little family had wanted in a dog and more.

He was adorable, easy to train, smart and absolutely charming. Even people who hated most dogs loved this little guy.

Rena could tell I was smitten with her new four-legged charge. I'd make any excuse to "stop by" for a visit and I loved it when she or her girls would knock on our door with Maxie in tow. And even though I'd watch George begin to sniffle afterward, it was apparent that he became putty in Maxie's paws. Soon a conspiracy began to hatch. Rena began forwarding me by email photos of new Shima puppies she received from the Spokane, Washington, breeder of her own pup.

The short-limbed, big-eyed blobs of fur in the photos were, of course, totally disarming. The pure white ones looked like tiny snowy owls, and the brown ones like diminutive shaggy dogs you could cuddle to death, like the character in Steinbeck's *Of Mice and Men,* if you weren't careful. With each set of photos I forwarded to George, he'd make a remark that I was trying to wear him down. I was. By the time I forwarded the third batch of litter photos to George, it was all over.

"Did you see the black-and-white one?" he calls to me as we occupy our respective home offices in our new house.

"Oh, yeah. He's my favorite," I admit.

A few minutes go by. I hear nothing but the click of George's mouse. Then a feeble voice echoes down the hall to me. "I think we have to go see this little guy."

If I could do a happy dance atop my Aeron chair without killing myself, I would have risked looking like an idiot.

Before he could change his mind, I was busy emailing the breeder, asking questions about the black-furred, roly-poly handful with the white paws and white belly. She told us about his parents, how he was the first puppy that wanted to be held, how large he might grow (no more than eight to ten pounds) and when he would turn eight weeks old—just old enough for him to leave his mama. The next day, knowing our heightened interest level, the breeder snapped more photos of him and sent them hurling through cyberspace. There was one of him standing on her deck, one with him shakily perched atop a rock and another one that was a close-up of his little black-and-white face. We were head over heels in love with our small furry Internet date.

Our minds began racing. Recently we had won the grand prize from a raffle George had entered—a free cruise for two to Alaska. The ship was to leave from and return to Seattle, only one hundred miles from where the breeder lived. So instead of flying, we schemed to take a few extra days and drive up so we could swing by and collect our tiny live cargo.

There was much to do to prepare for a new arrival in our house. As we wandered the aisles of the local big-box pet store before the trip, it was as if we were a couple shopping for baby things. We collected books, talked to on-site trainers and bought tiny puppy toys, not knowing what our new puppy might like. At home, we scoured the Internet for information on bringing a puppy home and found that things had indeed changed since I had owned my last dog. Using crates had become the preferred method of house training, since they emulated the security of the place puppies were born. I had even seen *Dog Whisperer* on TV, a series showing people how to train their puppies without resorting to scaring them by using rolled-up newspapers. It was all about understanding how dogs think and not attributing human characteristics to them. I looked forward to using all the newer techniques with this little guy.

The drive to Seattle was fun and the cruise was glorious. But when we got off the cruise ship and reclaimed our car, it was all about the puppy, which we had already named

Cosmo, for his cosmopolitan-looking tuxedo markings. After several hours of scenic driving, we stood at the front door of the breeder's house like two parents-to-be at an orphanage, waiting to see the child we had received only pictures of. The breeder and her husband were gracious, friendly people with several litters for sale—two Shima litters and a passel of Yorkshire terriers, all of whom looked like tiny *Monopoly* tokens, fully proportioned from head to toe. And then we spotted him. Cosmo looked up at us, wagging his entire body, just before his older brother jumped him from behind. There was no doubt that of the entire gang romping before us, this was the little man of our Internet dreams.

We were ushered into the backyard to watch the toddlers romp in order to see more of his personality. His mom was out there, too, still correcting her pups by occasionally "scruffing" a neck or two. And what personality...Cosmo jumped with his siblings, squatted to take a tiny leak and then, ignoring his playmates, began crawling on top of George as he sat on the grass at puppy level. If this had been a real estate deal, George would have signed all the paperwork and handed over the check before knowing anything more about the property. It was love at first cuddle.

Cosmo is now a two-year-old, incredibly cute member of our household. He greets us every morning as if we had been gone for months and makes our entire day complete before it has even started. It's Cosmic bliss as our little friend licks our feet, nuzzles our necks and heaves big sighs of contentment.

So what happened to the allergies George claimed he had? Yes, he has them. But he makes this doggy relationship work, just as he makes ours work—with love, patience, compromise, understanding and the occasional antihistamine. I like to think of our lives with Cosmo as a three-way love affair of sorts—

the happy ending to a warm, fuzzy fairy tale, just as special as the one about how George magically changed his role in my life from groomsman to bridegroom in thirty short years.

Mother Knows Best

Kathryn Canan

I peered out the bathhouse window from behind the faded yellow-polka-dotted curtains. It wasn't safe yet; they were still out there. Perhaps if I peeked out the door and made a bit of noise, I'd be able to scare them off. I opened the door a few inches; it scraped on the uneven concrete floor, and the hinges squealed. Slowly I closed it again and then opened it, drawing out the unearthly sounds. I tried banging the door and shouting, to no avail.

Mama Moose was totally wrapped up in showing her baby where the best-tasting flowers and shrubs were growing. I wasn't going to take a chance that she would trust me walking past them to get back up the hill to our cabin. Few animals are more dangerous than a moose defending her calf—I had as much respect for her as I would for a grizzly. I'd seen enough reports in Montana newspapers about people who hadn't learned that lesson.

Since I had no real choice, I decided to relax and enjoy the sight, although it was clear Mama wasn't going to win any beauty contests. Bull moose (or male moose) are majestic, but cows (or female moose) can easily be mistaken for awkward, malnourished horses with strange ears and knobby knees. The calf had not yet outgrown its reddish-brown coat; he or she had just been born that spring and would stay with its mother for at least a year.

Our house is what decorating magazines call "rustic." Normally it's not a problem having no bathroom in the cabin. It started life as a small log cabin on an old dude ranch in the 1920s. Previous owners had added a kitchen and a porch and had brought in running water from a nearby creek. My parents, who bought the cabin in 1961, when I was still in diapers, had added electricity but had balked at digging a septic tank. The common bathhouse for the old dude ranch was fifty yards down the hill. A bathroom so far away has its advantages, though. The stars are incredible on a clear night at three in the morning.

Moose, thank goodness, are not nocturnal, so we're usually safe on those midnight treks. We tend to see them in the morning and evening, stopping at what used to be a salt lick behind our cabin, on the way to or from the creek. Recently the Forest Service informed us that "baiting" animals with salt blocks is illegal, even though there had been one on a stump outside the back window for at least eighty years. No matter...the stump is saturated with salt by now and the moose come, anyway. Trouble is, they seem to have gone nuts this year and invaded Camp Senia.

I can hardly blame them. It probably feels like the only safe haven for miles around. Mother Nature went on a rampage a couple of years ago, with gusts of wind up over one hundred miles per hour, which felled lodgepole pines all over the forest. Perhaps it was nature's way of clearing out the pine bark beetles killing her trees. As if the windstorm didn't do enough damage, along came a drought and a bolt of lightning the next summer to finish the cleanup. Fire.

I had an excellent view of the first cloud of smoke from that fire, since I was four miles up the side of the canyon, enjoying the pristine blue sky reflected in Timberline Lake. I don't know where the moose went when that fire hit, but I got myself down the mountain faster than I ever thought possible, grabbed my car keys and drove the twelve miles out of the canyon with the firestorm just behind me and moving fast. I passed firefighters heading up and hoped sincerely that no one would be hurt defending our cabin.

Our cabin neighbors had forced my mother into their car at the first sign of fire. After we reunited in town, we spent a sleepless night and the next day huddled in anxious mourning. Finally, my mother got the call from our friendly forest ranger. Owing to the luck of the wind (and relentless nagging by said forest ranger to create defensible space), twenty of the twenty-five cabins in Camp Senia were spared, and we lost only our woodpile.

To fight this huge forest fire, firefighters worked for the next three months, until the October snows put out the last of the fire. By the time the fire was stopped, it had covered a huge distance, eight miles east down the canyon and three miles to the west from its origin; both sides of the canyon were devastated up to the timberline.

Camp Senia, then, was left as a little island of green surrounded by a seemingly lifeless, charred skeleton. When we returned the following summer, we could see gleaming granite boulders previously hidden by dense undergrowth sitting starkly on the mountainside. Piles of chips, where the rocks had peeled from the intense heat, lay underneath them.

Not everything was black; the first summer after the fire already tiny ribbons of green were beginning to grow along the small streams running down the canyon sides to the main creek near the cabin. It seemed that these little trails were all pointing toward our miraculously saved haven.

So the moose came.

They came to the meadows dotted with blue penstemon flowers, which were already obliterating the sites of the burned cabins. They nibbled tender fir trees and the young shoots of shrubs whose roots had survived the fire. A venerable bull moose reclaimed his kingdom on the islands formed where the creek slows down and widens out, while members of his harem basked in the sun behind our cabin, on a patch of kinnikinnick, a plant that is an evergreen ground cover.

The moose and other animals give back to nature as much as they consume; along with the ash from the fire, they fertilize the new growth. Each summer since the fire, the forest has been blanketed with wildflowers—a varied palette of paintbrush, mountain bluebells, bright yellow balsamroot, orange and yellow monkey flowers, and the blooming promise of berries that ripen sooner in sunnier meadows. The flowers give shelter to new seedlings of lodgepole pine, a species whose cones open only in response to the intense heat of a fire.

At last I watched Mama Moose lead her calf down past the lodge, where guests of the dude ranch used to enjoy Western barbecues. The moose were heading for their own banquet of tender plants growing in the creek, washed down by fresh snowmelt. It was now safe for me to leave the bathroom and head back up the hill to the cabin. Closing the door quietly behind me, I waved toward the moose and sent them a wordless thank-you. A thank-you for reminding me of the natural wonders that have resulted from what had seemed to me, as a cabin owner, like utter devastation.

★ ★ ★ ★ ★

Spotty's Miracle

Charles Kuhn

He came to us as a gift, not asked for or expected. A little bundle of dappled tan-and-black fur accented with black spots. Hence, we named him Spotty. His huge ears made him look like a very small bunny rather than a young puppy whose owner wasn't able to care for a disabled pet.

My wife, Melissa, a schoolteacher, was an easy mark. She has a soft spot for animals and seldom turns an injured or sick animal away. I was an even easier mark. My struggle with progressive multiple sclerosis keeps me home and makes me particularly empathetic to animals with disabilities. So I became Spotty's full-time caregiver.

He weighed in at two pounds. His sweet disposition made you love him from the moment you met him. His eyes trapped your heart, two shining brown orbs that stared up at you in complete innocence. Who could resist that look? We sure couldn't.

His back legs didn't work. I could relate to Spotty's discomfort, having slowly lost most of the use of my own legs. Spotty would never race with the other dogs. I may never toss a football or play golf again.

We hoped his condition might be due to poor nutrition and corrected his diet. He gained a few ounces and, with careful muscle massages and flexion, soon scrambled across the floor. But his limited motor skills never allowed him to walk properly or play with our other dogs. We carried him everywhere—often from the couch to my desk chair, where he slept on my lap in cozy luxury throughout the day, snuggled in the comfort of his favorite blanket. At night he was cradled between us, swaddled up to prevent any bladder accidents. He never heard a disparaging word. Through no fault of his own, his handicapped life offered him enough challenge. We never burdened him with more.

We scheduled a veterinarian appointment for a general health checkup and to see if any light could be cast on his condition. Some sort of neurological disorder was suspected, but the diagnosis went no further. Our daily routine with Spotty continued, until one evening everything changed.

Melissa was in the backyard on a rainy evening, filling feed trays in the aviary. Spotty lay on my lap as we enjoyed our time together on the couch, but as he was prone to do, he stretched his back legs aggressively and propelled himself from my lap onto the cushion next to me. I quickly righted him, but something was terribly wrong. He gulped for air. The color of his gums turned from pink to blue to white. I put my pinkie finger down his throat, thinking he may have swallowed a thread from my sweater or a piece of lint. I turned him upside down and patted his back in a silly effort to perform a doggy Heimlich maneuver. Nothing worked. I grabbed my cell phone and dialed Melissa, screaming at her to get in the house. Within moments she burst in the front room.

I yelled, "It's Spotty! He's dying!" She ran to me, grabbed him and headed out the door. She was gone with Spotty. I didn't even have a chance to say goodbye.

I listened to the rain pelt the roof and said a silent prayer for my wife to drive safely and for Spotty's life. Melissa told me later that she drove like a maniac to the veterinarian's office, steering the car down the rain-soaked pavement as she performed mouth-to-nose resuscitation to keep Spotty alive.

She ran into the veterinarian's office, screaming at the top of her lungs. The doctor jumped into action to save Spotty. After nearly ten minutes of not having a heartbeat or a breath, Spotty came back. The cause of this emergency was unknown. At the time we didn't care. This little angel that had fallen into our lives lived again. Ecstatic, we'd worry about the cause later. For now we had our little miracle back with us.

"Later" came in about sixty days. We had been referred to a very reputable veterinary school in a nearby community. Using high-optic X-ray technology, the doctor soon diagnosed luxating cervical vertebrae in his neck. Any awkward movement that dropped Spotty's chin to his chest could result in his spinal cord being pinched by misaligned vertebrae, which would cut off necessary nerve impulses to keep his heart and lungs working. A surgical correction was dangerous and economically unrealistic. We were told that a do-not-resuscitate order should be followed at his next seizure.

It became our goal to treat every second of the remainder of his life as a gift and to relish the joy of his presence. Each moment of his resurrection was cherished. A month after his diagnosis, tragedy struck. Spotty had been cradled with extreme care every day since we were made aware of his prognosis, carried in a small flat bed with cushioned and slightly elevated edges to prop his head up. We snuck him into the movie theater. We carried him into stores, where one kind shopper saw his ears and commented, "What a cute bunny."

Then, one night, his exuberance took him. He propelled himself aggressively into the corner of his bed, where his neck bent down and the misaligned vertebrae squeezed his spinal cord. In that second the damage was done. My wife tried valiantly to revive him. We lost our precious Spotty that night. Melissa sobbed uncontrollably.

We were devastated. I blamed myself for taking my eyes off him. Melissa was inconsolable. We slept little that night. The next day Melissa dutifully showed up to teach her fifth-grade class. She stifled sobs throughout the day.

On her lunch break Melissa called the teacher's assistant who'd brought Spotty into our lives and told her what had happened. Later that afternoon the woman came to the door of Melissa's classroom with a small puppy. Spotty's twin sister, Sophie. She hadn't told Melissa she had kept Spotty's sister. She didn't think Spotty would live out his life, and she'd planned to give Sophie to Melissa when that sad day came.

When Melissa came home that evening and walked into my office, holding a little spotted puppy with bunny ears, I was dumbstruck. Another miracle had occurred. Spotty had been brought back to us a second time! But that wasn't the fact. Melissa introduced me to Sophie.

Spotty can never be replaced, but Sophie has helped mend the tear in our hearts from losing him. We will never forget Spotty. His incurable zest for life was an inspiration to anyone, but especially to me. When you are helpless to stop a disease that ravages your body, it's easy to feel sorry for yourself. I'm six-two, but I found encouragement from a two-pound puppy. Between us, Spotty and I didn't have a decent pair of legs. I could relate. Another way I feel even closer to Spotty is by remembering that he and I both came into this world with healthy twin sisters, who deliver miracles by their sheer presence on a daily basis. He had Sophie. I have my twin sister, Judy. A miracle to be cherished each and every day.

Sophie will never take Spotty's place. But she has created her own place in our hearts. There are times when I cuddle Sophie and look into her innocent, loving eyes and thank her for bringing such joy into our hearts and for helping me recall her precious brother, Spotty. He will never be forgotten and his memory will always be cherished. She reminds me of that wonderful gift each moment I hold her close to my heart, and I quietly offer my thanks for twins.

★ ★ ★ ★ ★

The Nursery

Robyn Boyer

T he birds started showing up around the same time I was
ready to throw in the towel.

My house, my job, my life were coming apart at the seams.
My home, purchased post-divorce, so carefully styled into a
beautiful, welcoming and feng shui–perfect haven, had become a burden. The maintenance costs and challenges were
eating at my savings, my strength and my nerves.

The breaking point came when, out of the blue and for
no apparent reason, the sliding-glass door between the living
room and the smaller of my two enclosed brick patios spontaneously shattered into a thousand pieces. No errant BB shot,
no thrown rock from a passing kid or truck, no explanation
except maybe poltergeists. This came on the heels of having
to shell out thousands of dollars to replace cracked and up-
lifted sections of my driveway, caused by a tree planted by
the developer years ago in the too-narrow strip between my
drive and the neighbor's.

The homeowners' association had also begun to hassle me
about the house's unsightly rust-stained rain gutters and trim.

My house, built by the developer as a showpiece and to sell lots for big custom homes around a man-made lake, also still had the original roof. That was twenty-two years ago, and there was only so much you could do once the shakes started cracking and curling in the relentless Sacramento summers and shedding after every winter storm. A house of woes.

So there I was, with no more savings, trudging back and forth each day to an underpaid, soul-bleaching job, my health and well-being a crapshoot. When the glass door cracked, I did, too. Sobbing, overwhelmed and bone-weary from the seemingly endless struggle to keep going, I sent an email to my father and a few friends. I see now that it was a cry for help, something I'm not too fond of doing, but there it was: fall into the abyss or ask for a hand.

My father responded by sending me a Wikipedia link explaining why windows sometimes spontaneously break. Another friend said, "I don't know what to say." But my friend Gail, my rock, my beacon, said, "Hold on. You're not going anywhere. I've got your back." She's a cop, and I could hear her commanding voice through the email.

The solution was to sell the house, rent and get out from under burdens too great to bear. Bit by bit, with Gail's support and assistance, I made my way, worrying as I have all my life that this, too, would fall away, pulled out from under me at the most inconvenient time. On the edge, never safe, always on the edge. My close companions Depression and its good friend Anxiety love the edge. They work there to cloud your sense of direction, twine themselves around your heart like a gnarly root, take hold and squeeze the life out of you if you don't chop at them with whatever tools you've got. Worst of all, they rob you of your sense of what is possible.

I put the house on the godforsaken market, which was

still teetering from the international financial meltdown, replaced the sliding-glass door and more sections of the concrete driveway, and had the gutters and trim repaired and painted. Now all I had to do was come to terms with a buyer and the unsettling proposition of moving my life's accumulation of stuff—pushed in one direction by pragmatism and pulled in another by attachment.

And that was when I began to notice the birds around my back patio. At first it was just a pair or two. Little common finches, the males dandied up with orange crests and breasts, the females drab brown with white and tan speckles. Sometimes there would be just three of them, two males jockeying for a female. But then they started coming in droves. One pair turned into dozens, with the occasional odd man out. The twitters and calls of a few soon became a din as the scout birds sent word that bird heaven awaited all who arrived.

What had been designed and built to be an outdoor room for entertaining people became transformed over the spring and summer months into a playground and nesting area for the birds. It was like a theme park for finches, with diaper stations and a drinking and splashing fountain. The copper railings I'd installed atop one of the patio walls to espalier the camellia bushes became a singles bar, a place for males and females to land, check each other out, flirt and hook up. A paned mirror with a shelf became a favorite spot to peck away at their own images for hours, leaving a daily mess of droppings on the ledge and sloppy kisses on the glass. The outdoor fan became a tilt-a-whirl as one after another would fly full throttle, land on a blade and ride the spin round and round until it stopped.

They built their nests above the patio, under the roof's eaves, on top of a broad, load-bearing beam. They tucked them back into the *V* where the beam and the overhang intersected. I watched as they swept in throughout the spring days, carrying straw and lint and long pieces of dried plants in their tiny beaks, sometimes squabbling over materials. At one point a pair decided to build a nest atop one of my outdoor speakers attached to the beam. Not sure this was a good thing, I pulled the makings down before they could get to the stage of patching it all together with spit and droppings. I did this three separate times, but the couple persisted, returning each day with a fresh stash of nest material until I relented. *Okay, you win,* I thought. *It's your imperative and the least I can do for all the delight you bring.*

They took over the backs of the patio chairs, a short hop from the fountain and the copper railings and just a quick flight to the nests above. Some days I'd look out and see the tops of four of the six chairs lined with birds, as many as six or seven to a chair. My cat would often lie in one of the chairs, catching a nap in the afternoon sun. The birds ignored her and she ignored them. Everybody felt safe, I guess.

I'd have to clean up the patio on Sundays for open houses, and even though the birds disappeared while I hosed everything down and, presumably, the females laid low in the nests while lookie-loos poked about my place, once all the strangers cleared out and the activity subsided, the birds returned, reclaiming their rightful place in my backyard.

Once the nests were built and the little blue eggs laid, the females brooded and the males kept company and food steadily arrived. One by one, each nest sprang to life with four or five tiny babies. Although the babies were hidden from view and thus well protected from passing predators, like blue jays, if I moved slowly and didn't startle the mothers, I could see the babies from inside my living room as they poked their tiny gray heads up, beaks opened wide, clamoring in a high-pitched keen for food. Mornings and early evenings, when I was home from work, I'd listen to the sounds of life seeking life and smile with gratefulness.

Soon enough the babies grew too big and had to leave the nests. I watched the parents as they weaned their brood, going from feedings several times a day to just perching on the nest with a "Well, what do you want me to do about it?" look when the fledglings peeped for food. *How do they know what to do and when to do it?* I wondered of the parents. Could I learn some primal lesson, apply it to my own role as a parent, see how much was too much to give or just the right amount? The hard-nosed indifference the parents showed at this point in their offspring's development both impressed and disturbed me.

That was when the worrying started. I feared for the babies' safety from jays. I worried that with all the jostling going on in the now too-small nests, one of them would fall out and onto the bricks. I found a dead baby on the ground, in the planter that bordered the brick, and wrapped it in a gossamer cloth bag. With a heavy and trepidant heart, I buried it deep in the mounded dirt around the camellia bushes. I worried that the babies might starve because their parents somehow weren't wired right, that maybe they'd been passed over when Nature distributed the familial handbook. I worried that the house wouldn't sell, that I'd never find a better job, that I was blowing it as a parent. Like the fledglings, I was on the precipice of my own future, unsure and scared, but unlike them, I was too wound up to trust my instincts.

One by one the fledglings made their way. I'd see them hopping about, testing their wings with a short flight from the patio's brick pavers to the backs of the chairs. From there they might flutter over to the fountain or into the persimmon tree. The persimmon tree, which was finally starting to bear fruit after three years of leaves and not much more, became a way station for them, a safe place to flutter to and hide before attempting the longer flights to the top of the forty-foot-tall cottonwood tree in the neighbor's yard. I knew the babies were going to be okay when they could fly from the copper railings to the top of that cottonwood. It was the highest perch in the neighborhood. And as with the backs of my chairs, I'd see dozens of them hanging out together there, perched on the arched branches at the very top, swaying with the winds.

When I was lamenting one day the growing absence of the birds, my daughter assured me in her knowing and wise way that my fears for the birds, for her and for myself were misplaced and that everything would work out, take its proper course. "Nature's a bitch, Mom. This patio was a nursery. Be glad you gave them that."

Watching the fledglings become fliers calmed me down and restored my hopes. By summer's end the nests had emptied and my bird park had closed for the season. I had the occasional visitors, probably the babies who, now grown, were starting their own round late in the breeding cycle. The persimmon tree produced so much fruit that it toppled over and had to be culled and restaked. Neighbors living on my street bought my house as an investment and I now rent from them; I didn't even have to move. My job prospects are looking up. I've slimmed down and generally perked up.

When Gail jumped in to help, she asked only one thing of me. Her lifesaving assignment for me was to write down what the next twenty years of my life would look like, in other words, what I wanted from those years. As the challenges that once seemed insurmountable fall away, and I search for answers and a life of purpose, I realize that she has made me feel safe…like the birds must have felt when making my patio their nursery. I'm betting they'll return next year. I'll be here, brimming with a sense of the possible, waiting to see what life will bring.

★ ★ ★ ★ ★

Frank Observations

E. G. Fabricant

Every dog deserves a boy, or two.

Smooth-haired and black and tan, Frank came to us—to my wife, my two boys, aged ten and approaching eight years, and me—in mid-1985, on the outskirts of Alexandria, Virginia.

His procurement process was equal parts evolutionary and deliberate. My wife, Geri, grew up with miniature dachshunds. I was a dog-deprived child, growing up in a family with eight children; we span twenty-one years from oldest to youngest. My parents' patience with nonathletic, character-building activities—dancing lessons, music lessons and pet ownership—ran out with my next oldest brother. Their tolerance for dogs ran out even sooner. After four different dogs met with sad fates, my mother put her foot down when I was ten. Literally.

"God*damn* it, Frank! *I'm* not feeding, walking and cleaning up after any more *goddamned* dogs! That's it!"

I remedied this childhood dog deprivation as a young adult, my wife and I rescuing first three shepherd-mix dogs and learning that I could deal with most low- to moderate-shedding dogs. When it came time to choose a family dog, I wasn't sure which breed would work best. We were a family of four with a three-bedroom, detached Federal, and no one was home during school hours. We were two working parents and two pre-hormonal boys. The ideal candidate would be:

Short-haired;

Low maintenance;

Agreeable, but not overly needy;

Long-lived enough to stick around, God willing, at least until the boys finished high school and, preferably, college;

Small enough to (a) manage, um, input and output efficiently enough to foist that and other chores off on the boys, and (b) be unable to do much physical damage above baseboard level when left alone;

And large enough to fend off childhood diseases and to be willing to stand his/her own ground with the boys, as required.

Those considerations, along with Geri's imprinted girlhood bias, led us to a litter of mini doxie pups who, it was mutually assumed, were somewhere on the other side of the AKC tracks—hence, the asking price and lack of complications. Frank was the only one not fighting, frisking and falling all over his outsize feet in that six-week-old way. He sat apart, motionless, and never took his eyes off us. He embarrassed and intrigued us into taking him home.

Okay…about the name. I was against a precious, cutesy name for a small dog. My solution was a *double entendre,* played off the more familiar "wiener" or "weenie" dog, to wit, "Frank." Geri agreed, but my self-satisfaction was short-lived. Not only did I have to explain its meaning, anyway, but friends familiar with my story would invariably ask, with Oedipal gravity, "Why did you name your dog after your father?"

Frank's childhood was a little rocky, attributably mostly to human error—mine. To train him, I combined two crude concepts, "papers" and "outside," and spread newspapers both on the kitchen floor and outside the entrances. Unable to catch him with an urge, I created "sessions." Reaching what I thought to be a respectable interval, I'd take him outside, place him on the papers and wait expectantly. He'd park himself in the middle of the pulp and give me his most tolerant look, as if to say, "Okay, Chief. What's next?" I would stand there in the cold and wet, knowing my family was watching with amusement through the window.

Eventually it all worked out, but this was a dog that wanted someone nearby at all times. Dachshunds are renowned for feeling separation anxiety and taking revenge, and if he felt abandoned, he would resort to his untrained puppy ways. We arranged for a pet sitter to look in on him while we went north to Delaware for Christmas break. On our return she sang his praises, took the check and left. It soon became plain that she'd left the door to the basement open, and he'd exploited that loophole; fortunately, the floor was vinyl tile. In the end, he swallowed his pride, to keep the peace, and trained us.

Frank did us the courtesy of respecting Geri and me as the general governing authority, in that order—mostly because she hoisted him onto our bed one night at his first plaintive puppy plea, which he seized upon as a *carte blanche* entitlement. The eventual compromise was between our California king and a folded quilt on the floor nearby, which we called "Flap." He'd ask routinely for the first, but if ordered otherwise, he'd plod glumly away, ears down, as though wading through molasses—followed by a grand and deliberate show of bedding down on the Flap. (Dachshunds are instinctive burrowers, having been bred to hunt badgers, and they like to sleep covered. Before retiring, they find it necessary to fashion a trench in which to recline safely, so they scratch, dig and hump up their spines while imaginary dirt flies out from under their haunches. Robert Benchley observed that "a dog teaches a boy fidelity, perseverance, and to turn around three times before lying down." For pure amusement, then, this was a value-added service.) To this day, when one of us has difficulty getting settled, the other will bark out that command of yore, "Lie down and go to sleep, Frank!"

Befitting his species-neutral given name, Frank established himself quickly with the boys as "the other brother." He was always available to them without condition or stint for real, adolescent play. To be sure, he enjoyed "fetch the ball" in that maddening, "I've got it now. Come get it, sucker!" dachshund way, but right from the start he was always "we," not "they." While he acquiesced to being a love object for us adults and extended family, including my "Auntie Mame" mother-in-law, Ginny, he was all about Trevor and Bevan to the end of his life. In combat, they both did him the favor of shrieking and flopping around on the floor while he vanquished them at the wrist with his mouth.

Frank adapted himself to their disparate personalities. Trevor was his favorite family-room snuggle buddy because, unlike Bevan, he didn't become so absorbed in MTV's *The Real World* that he neglected his petting and treat obligations. Because he was generally more aggressive, Bevan had to be reminded on occasion of his size-ratio boundaries with a growl or nip. When they were out, Frank waited vigilantly at the front window for them to return. The boys took to calling him Ma Bell because from the shoulders up, with ears elevated, he looked like an antiquated telephone set.

Almost Zen-like in disposition, Frank was made anxious by only three things: going to the vet; fireworks; and water, whatever evil form it took. He handled doctor visits with Gandhi-like civil disobedience, having to be carried and manipulated by hand. We learned to avoid fireworks altogether after taking him with us to watch the legendary National Mall Independence Day celebration from across the Potomac, at the Pentagon, when he was just a year old. He was content in Geri's lap until the first flash bang; then he disappeared—under her blouse. I remember her saying, "I think he's trying to mate with my spine!" From then on, he stayed home. And water? Total freak-out. When the boys were sledding or tubing, he'd run alongside in full cry, biting at the carriage. If the boys were swimming, he'd circle the pool, shrieking and biting the water. The first and only time he encountered the Pacific Ocean, he alternated between running away from the incoming surf and snapping at it on its way back. It was clear to him, and not lost on us, that we were being protected.

Frank never met a guest or a lap he couldn't conquer, without so much as a bark or a whine—in large part because he could stare down the Sphinx without blinking. He'd confront his intended victim and, if not invited aboard immediately, settle in and engage for as long as it took. At their first encounter, my baby sister, Carol, was wary of Frank meeting her husband, Don. She revealed, "He doesn't like whiny, yappy little dogs." It was less than fifteen minutes, door to sofa, before Frank was inside his very happy new friend's shirt.

In short, Frank was not just ours, he was *us,* in whatever incarnation required. He was embarrassed by the whole dog butt-sniffing ritual and considered other canines' loud, energetic curiosity about him undignified. In fact, his only acknowledgment of another's very existence was a cursory woof, uttered after that other creature was safely out of range. For fifteen years, until his brothers had graduated from college and it was the late summer of 2000, he was the perfect relative and ever-accommodating host. Bevan was competing in the Olympic trials, trying to win a spot in the sport he'd excelled in at college—decathlon. Dozens of family and friends passed through our house to offer encouragement. Frank was already in decline, and the sheer numbers of kneecaps and laps simply overwhelmed him.

On the day Geri and I carried him to the vet for his final injection, it was we who were anxious—upset and tearful. We held and caressed him; as he sensed and yielded to the phenobarbital, he regarded us one last time with that calm, transcendent gaze. "Don't grieve for me," he seemed to say. "It was a good run, but it's time for my karma to be reborn."

Good boy, Frank.

★ ★ ★ ★ ★

Little Orange

Trina Drotar

I first saw the cat one late spring evening, and he seemed to say, "I'm here, and if you can spare a bite to eat, I'd be most appreciative." Of course, he didn't speak those words. In fact, he didn't meow or purr or make any other sound.

When I returned with a bowl of food, he stepped left into the hydrangeas and camellias. I waited for him to approach. He waited for me to leave. I went back inside and peeked at him through the peephole. He sat and ate without greed.

He returned several times, usually in the evening, over the next few weeks, and we formed a sort of dance. He always led. I'd step out, squat and speak to him before extending my hand. He'd take one step back, always remaining just out of arm's reach.

I'd check each evening for Little Orange, calling his name, even though I wasn't sure that he knew he had a name, much less what it was. I'd walk to the sidewalk, searching for him; I'd sneak peeks through the front door peephole; and I'd even check the backyard. Days passed. I was called out of town for two weeks. The caretaker didn't spot Little Orange.

Days and weeks passed, and then one sunny morning, when I pulled the blinds in the living room, I saw him sunning himself in the backyard. "Little Orange," I yelled. I placed some food and water on the back patio. We danced. We kept that appropriate distance. He spent the better part of the day in the backyard, first in the grass, then under the azaleas near the fence. It was much cooler there, in the dirt, under the shade of the evergreens, the red maple and the Japanese maple. He left sometime before dinner.

I looked daily for him. Scanned both yards, looked up and down the street, called his name. I peered from behind curtains and through the peephole, but there was no sign of Little Orange. That was nearly two months ago.

About two weeks ago, on a Monday morning, when I was headed to the store, I saw an orange/yellow presence on the back patio. I ran to the door. The cat was limping, favoring the left side of his body. He was thin, much thinner than the cat I had danced with. I opened the door and went to him, forgetting that we'd never actually had physical contact. He turned his dirty head and hissed, but he didn't run. I backed up, told him he was safe, and assured him that I'd return with food and water.

He hissed as I placed the bowls on the cement. He hissed again as I backed up. He wobbled to the bowls. He didn't sit to eat, as he'd done before. He stood. I also stood as I watched him eat all the kibble in the dish. I stood as he drank from the water bowl. I wept. Where had he been these past months?

"I need a towel and the cat carrier," I said.

I waited until Little Orange had finished drinking before I approached with the towel. I figured that I'd wrap the towel around him in case he tried to bite or scratch. Just then, another stray entered the yard and a chase ensued. I screamed.

I cried. I chased both cats. The other cat had been friendly toward me and had a companion, but I was worried about Little Orange.

Thinking they had both jumped the privacy fence, I ran to the front. One cat. Not Little Orange. I went back through the house to the backyard and spotted him. He ran with all that he had, hobbling and favoring that left side. He leapt at the back fence. I knew we'd lose him if he crossed it. He clung to the top, unable, or as I'd prefer to think, unwilling, to pull his body up and over. I placed the towel around him and brought his toweled body to the house. With my roommate's help, I placed him in the carrier and closed it.

Whatever Little Orange had experienced, I'd never know, but his ordeal increased with the visit to the vet's office where I'd taken my pets for more than two decades.

I'd advised the desk personnel that the cat was feral, that it was injured, and that it was undernourished and probably dehydrated. I gave his name as Little Orange and completed the necessary paperwork before being shown into an exam room. The tech opened the carrier; Little Orange popped his head out, eyes crusted black, burrs on his head; and the tech tipped the carrier. She didn't want to handle this little cat. Still frightened from the earlier chase, Little Orange fell from the exam table before my roommate or I could catch him. The tech simply stood. Little Orange scrambled for the door, hissing.

My roommate picked him up. The tech insisted on taking Little Orange to the back for the exam. We said we'd carry him.

"You're not allowed back there," the tech said.

In hindsight, we should have left then, but we were both

exhausted. We allowed the tech to take Little Orange, and then we paced the exam room until the doctor appeared.

"That cat is out of control. He is an unneutered male, and he scratched me and tried to bite me," she said and continued to call him everything except pure evil.

My roommate and I looked at one another. He'd never been that way, not even when I pulled him from the fence. The hissing, I knew, was his only defense. The doctor suggested this test or that test, but only after we badgered her. Her first suggestion was euthanization. Immediately.

"Can we be there?" I asked.

"Absolutely not," she said, adding that she'd give him a sedative first.

"Absolutely not," we said in unison.

We spent the next thirty minutes phoning a friend who works with feral cats, another who loves cats and yet another who is known for having a solid head. One said that we needed to have the basic tests for HIV and feline leukemia done. Those would inform our next step. The tests came back negative. Good news. One friend then suggested we take the cat to the SPCA for medical care.

The next step was a complete blood panel to rule out kidney and liver disease, which we would have the SPCA do. Another thirty minutes passed before we told the vet that we would take the cat to the SPCA. It took ten minutes for them to retrieve Little Orange.

"He's much calmer," the tech said.

We drove away, intent on going to the SPCA. Turned out that it was closed on Mondays. We took Little Orange home and quarantined him in the spare bathroom. We put blankets and towels down, a litter box, food and water. He didn't jump out of the carrier, as my other cats always did. He remained there until later that night, when I tipped the carrier. I helped him onto the bed we'd made for him out of towels and blankets. Little Orange was covered with burrs.

We made additional calls that evening, with the intention of bringing him to the SPCA the next morning. One friend suggested we try her vet. I phoned Dr. K's office the next morning. We took Little Orange to the office. He hissed once at Dr. K. After the exam, we asked about blood tests. He ordered the tests. He told us that the cat was very ill. He suggested fluids for Little Orange.

We took Little Orange home, his neck fuller because of the subcutaneous fluids he'd received. He licked my finger clean of the canned food I offered and let me know when he was full. We purchased additional bedding for him.

Partial test results that evening indicated no kidney or liver problems. That, combined with the doctor's proclamation that Little Orange had a strong heart and strong lungs, gave us hope. With fluids, food, rest and safety, he'd grow stronger, like another cat I'd rescued several years earlier.

For the next few days, we changed his bedding at least twice daily, fed him by hand and checked on him. When he refused the cat food, we searched for something different. We brought home baby food instead. Beef and beef gravy had the highest iron count. Dr. K's main concern was Little Orange's anemia. His red blood cells were not being replenished. Dr. K indicated that the anemia went beyond the cat's flea infestation. We purchased flea medicine and applied it to his already ravaged body. Flea dirt, we soon discovered, covered nearly every part of his tiny body. He'd likely been lying in the brush for a long time. There fleas had set up house and multiplied and used the already weak cat for their own nourishment and procreation.

On Wednesday I thought he'd died on the trip from Dr. K's office. Little Orange lived. I moved him onto the bedding when we got home. That was the day I began stroking his body. I'd touched his head a couple of times. He'd flinched. He seemed to enjoy the stroking of his fur. I began, also, to cut away the burrs that had wedged their way into his fur.

Thursday seemed to mark a turning point. He raised his head and turned toward the bathroom door. Three times. The baby food, which he continued to lick from my finger, but only after sniffing it each and every time, and the subcutaneous fluids seemed to be working. We had been prepared to take him to the vet that morning. He wasn't ready.

I spent nearly every day, nearly every waking hour with Little Orange during that week. I brushed his fur with an old soft-bristle pet brush. He purred. I doubted that Little Orange had ever been touched by a human, ever been brushed, ever been held. When I changed his bedding, I held him. I pulled his frail, limp body close to mine so that he might feel my warmth and my heart.

Friday brought another injection of fluids. Dr. K reminded us that the office was open Saturdays in case we needed anything. Although there'd been indications throughout the week that Little Orange was getting stronger, Dr. K told us there might be some brain or spinal cord injury, things only specialists could diagnose. Dr. K never once treated Little Orange as a feral—only as our pet. He suggested a cortisone shot, saying that the shot was usually recommended by specialists.

We returned home, and I spent most of Friday with him, brushing him and trying to feed him, changing his wet bedding, removing burrs from all parts of his body. He needed to retain some of the dignity he had exhibited when he came to us. As much dignity as a cat unable to stand on its own could.

Little Orange, or Orange, as we affectionately called the peaceful orange/yellow tabby, refused to eat late Friday night. That refusal continued through Saturday morning. He refused to drink. He was unable to lift his head, his torso or his limbs. I held him, cried, told him that we loved him. He demanded nothing. He never fought.

We agreed that only Dr. K could tend to Orange. The office was officially closed when we arrived, but Dr. K ushered us in. I cried tears for Little Orange, for the life he had never had the chance to experience, for the love we'd shown him, for the other cats who had entered and left my life, and for me. I wanted to save him, wanted him to grow stronger. After all, he had strong lungs and a strong heart, and his kidneys and liver and pancreas were healthy. Years ago, a doctor told me that I'd know when the end was near.

I held Little Orange in my arms as I carried him to the exam room. Dr. K examined him again, said this was best. My roommate and I stroked Little Orange. He never convulsed.

We wrapped his body, blessed him and placed him in a hole we'd dug in front of the azaleas, under the Japanese maple, shaded by the red maple, near the spot he'd rested two months earlier. We marked the spot with a white fence, autumn leaves and a ceramic garden hummingbird.

★ ★ ★ ★ ★

The Old Barrel Racer

Elaine Ambrose

By the summer of my twelfth year, my parents had already decided that I was a problem child. There had been too many calls to the school principal's office to discuss my noisy and disruptive behavior in class. (Obviously, they failed to appreciate my spirited, creative nature.) And my teachers had complained that I daydreamed too much. (Couldn't anyone recognize a potential writer here?) And my parents were weary of my fights with my brothers, noting that the boys never questioned the rigid rules of our home. (My brothers later suffered from painful ulcers and other health ailments; however, I did not.)

I grew up on an isolated potato farm near Wendell, Idaho, a nearsighted, left-handed, goofy girl with wrinkly hair and absolutely no ability to conform. Outside of farm chores, the only activity for youth in the farming community of one thousand was a program called 4-H. Desperately hoping it would help me focus, my mother enrolled me in a 4-H cooking class, with the admonition that I behave and not embarrass her. I failed both assignments. When it came my turn to do the demonstration in front of the group, I dropped a dead mouse into the cake batter because I thought it was a brilliant way to spice up the boring meetings. But the leader, one of the town's most prominent women, thought otherwise, and she called my mother and told her I was never welcome in her home again. My mother is still mad at me more than forty years later for the public humiliation.

My great escape from the chores and challenges of life on the farm was to ride my horse, Star. As we galloped through the forty-acre pastures, I hollered with delight when she jumped the ditches and raced to the far end of the field. Sometimes I would lean over, lace my fingers through her long white mane and push my boots against her flanks until she ran full speed, ears back, nostrils flared, with a force of freedom that no bridle could control. When she finally stopped at the top of a hill, her sides were heaving and covered with sweat. Her entire body shivered as she calmed down, and I would jump off and loosen the cinch on the saddle. For me, the exhilaration was worth the fear of falling.

Star was a big white horse, over fourteen hands high (almost fifty-eight inches from the ground), and had been trained as a prizewinning barrel racer. My father had acquired the horse from a man who owed him money, and the horse was all he had to give. At ten years old, she was past her prime for the rodeo, but I didn't care. She was my passport to liberty, andI loved her.

During the summer of 1964, I worked in the fields during the morning and rode my horse every afternoon. I knew how to catch her in the pasture, bring her to the barn and put on her bridle and saddle. I would be gone all day, and no one ever checked on me. Probably, they were just as eager to have me out of the house as I was to leave. After every ride I brushed Star's hide and fed her oats. Sometimes I brought her an apple or some sugar cubes. My brothers referred to her as an old gray mare, but to me, she was a gorgeous white horse who could run like the wind. And she was my best friend.

One day I learned about a 4-H club for horses. It took expert negotiation skills and outright begging to convince my parents to let me join. "No more dead mice!" I assured them. With the help of the club, I learned how to ride my horse as she raced around three barrels set in a dirt arena. She knew what to do, and all I did was hang on for dear life. She loved the full gallop after rounding the third barrel, and within weeks, we were the fastest team in the club.

"You should ride her at the barrel race at the Gooding County Fair and Rodeo," my 4-H leaders said, encouraging me. "And she should do well, even though she's not so young anymore." Again, I resorted to theatrical pleading to receive my parents' permission. I also needed silver cowboy boots, a purple saddle blanket and a purple vest to ride with the 4-H club. That required extra days of working in the field for one dollar an hour, hoeing beets and weeding potatoes. Soon I had enough money, and I was ready for the fair and rodeo at the end of August.

Two weeks before the fair and rodeo, I used bleach and water in a bucket to comb through Star's long mane and tail to make them gleaming white. Then I saddled her for a solo practice in the pasture. Just as we were riding toward the first barrel, a flock of pheasants suddenly flew up in front of us. Star jumped to the side and I lost my grip. I flew through the air and landed on my right foot. I screamed as it broke.

Star trotted back to me and lowered her head. I couldn't tell her to go get help. My only choice was to get to the three-rail fence and try to climb back on the horse. I grabbed the loose reins and told her to back up. She understood my command and slowly backed to the fence, pulling me through the dirt. We finally reached the fence and I managed to pull myself up on my good foot. Then I climbed up and straddled the top rail.

"Come here, Star," I said. "Easy now." She pressed against the fence so I could fall across the saddle. Then I sat up, secured my left boot in the stirrup and reached for the reins. That was when I noticed her mouth was bleeding, because the bit had rubbed it raw while she was pulling me. That was the only time I cried.

We rode back to the barn and found one of the hired hands, a gnarly old guy named Titus. He helped me off the horse and into his pickup truck. "I'll get you home and then take care of the horse," he said. "And I have some ointment for her mouth." I was grateful.

Going to the doctor was an inconvenience for many farm families. It just wasn't done without considerable effort and a good reason. "Are you sure it hurts?" my father asked. "Maybe it's just sprained?" After much debate, reinforced by my contorted expressions, my mother decided to take me to town to see the doctor. I closed my eyes as they cut off my jeans and sliced through my new silver boot. I heard mumbling as my swollen foot was examined and x-rayed. Then I felt the cold, messy cast being applied to my foot and leg.

"Stay off of it for six weeks," the doctor said, and the words echoed like a prison sentence.

"But I'm competing in the barrel race at the rodeo in two weeks," I said.

My mother and the doctor laughed.

I did not see any humor in the situation. "I'm riding," I said with all the conviction I could muster.

The doctor handed me some crutches and patted my head. "Go home now, dearie, and get some rest," he said. That was when I knew I would ride.

The following day I called Todd Webb, my 4-H leader, and explained the situation. He seemed reluctant to talk with my parents about the barrel-racing competition. "I just need help getting on Star," I said. "She knows what to do. Please let me try."

Todd Webb approached my father that night and, after a few shots of Crown Royal, convinced him that all I had to do was sit on the horse. And basically that was true. Somehow my father agreed, and I was thrilled.

The day before the race, Todd Webb and several 4-H club members came around with horse trailers to get the horses. By then, I was using only one crutch and could maneuver quite well with my clunky cast. We drove to the stables at the fair grounds and unloaded the horses, our gear and extra bales of hay. Star seemed nervous, so I brushed her hide and sang my favorite song from our lazy riding days—"We'll Sing in the Sunshine," by Gale Garnett. The song had the perfect cadence for an afternoon ride.

The next day we all arrived early to prepare for the race. The right leg of my jeans was split to cover the cast. The club members assisted in hoisting the saddle onto Star, joking that I would need to split any prize money with them. Star's mouth had healed, but I decided to pull a hackamore without a bit over her head. I struggled onto the horse and took the reins. I felt comfortable, except the cast caused my leg to stick straight out, and I knew it would hit the first barrel as Star galloped around it.

"Tie me down," I said to Todd Webb. He hesitated but

then agreed. He used a small rope to secure my right leg to the stirrup.

"Don't fall," he said. "Or we're both in trouble."

We trotted to the arena and joined the other riders. I supported my weight on my thighs and left boot as we rode in a slow lope around the arena. I could feel Star getting tense. She had owned this competition many years ago, and I knew she was eager to return. "Easy, Star," I murmured. "We can do it."

There were seven riders ahead of us in the race, and we were last. They all posted times between twenty and fifteen seconds. Star's ears were rigid as we eased into the chute. I matched her breathing as we waited for the countdown. Suddenly the gate flew open and Star shot out in a fury of speed. She leaned around the first barrel and my cast rubbed the side. Then she ran toward the second barrel and circled it so sharply that I could touch the ground. Then she sped toward the third barrel. We rounded it and headed toward home. Dirt flew, the crowd cheered and my cast banged against the rope as I rode the relentless force of pure energy. I knew my magnificent horse was running to win. We crossed the finish line in fourteen seconds and the crowd went wild. The clumsy problem child and the old horse were the improbable winners.

I don't remember all the details after that. I know I looked into the stands and saw my parents and brothers and couldn't believe they were cheering for me. The five-hundred-dollar prize money, a fortune back then, was added to my college savings account. Star and I never raced again. After that day she became slower and less eager to run free. We still took regular rides, and she would pick up the pace as I sang. But we had nothing else to prove.

My foot healed, I entered high school and I didn't have

much time to ride. Star spent her last days roaming the fields, and every now and then she would raise her head, point her ears and break into a full gallop. The last time I saw her, she was jumping a ditch on the far side of the pasture. She died while I was away at college, and my mother called and asked if I wanted to see her before they took her away. "No," I answered. "She'll always be alive for me. Every time I need to get around an obstacle, I'll feel her power." And that's how it remains for me, the wild child who finally grew up with the help of an aging horse and a pounding passion for freedom.

The Dog Who Wouldn't Bark

Meera Klein

The black-and-white photo was old and yellowing, but I could clearly make out the proud stance of the dog and his mistress. I could barely make out the words penciled on the back of the fading photograph: "Leela and Chuppa, 1951."
My mother and her beloved dog.

The cool mist swirled around Leela and smothered her in its wet embrace. She shivered and wrapped the woolen shawl more tightly around her slender body. The late November days in Kotagiri were chilly and dismal, nothing like the warm tropical nights she was used to. Leela's sigh sounded loud in the gray silence as she paused to take a deep whiff of the fading jasmine blooms on the vine by the front gate. It was then she heard the sound, the tiniest whimper, which she would have missed if the world hadn't been so silent. She reached up and unlatched the metal gate and stepped onto the patch of grass. In the dim twilight she could make out a small bundle lying on the wilted jacaranda blooms. When she looked closely, she saw it was a tiny shivering puppy. She couldn't bear to leave it there on the side of the road. She relatched the gate and walked into the kitchen using the side entrance.

The kitchen was warm and cozy. Her mother, Ammalu, was seated on a small wooden stool in front of the hearth, stirring a pot of lentil stew. The sharp scent of cumin mingled with the wet puppy smell. Ammalu wrinkled her nose.

"What do you have there?" she asked, getting up to take a closer look at the black-and-tan bundle in Leela's arms.

"Oh, Amma," Leela wailed. "Look what someone dropped off at our front gate."

The puppy seemed to know it was being inspected and opened its tiny jaws and yawned, stretching out a minuscule pink tongue.

"Not everyone has your kind heart, my daughter," Ammalu sighed. "Remember what our neighbor Sister Mary told us?"

Leela nodded and held the puppy closer to her chest. Their nearest neighbor, an Anglo-Indian everyone called Sister Mary, lived a few miles down the road and was a feisty animal lover.

"Be warned. Villagers get rid of their unwanted pets by dropping them off at the bungalows in the middle of the night. Most of us are only too happy to take in these dogs and cats. It's a shame, though, because not everyone wants a stray and that is the end of the poor animal," she'd lamented.

That will not happen to this little one, Leela silently vowed. Mother and daughter dried the puppy and fed the hungry creature some rice gruel. Soon the little dog was curled up on a pile of rags in front of the warm hearth.

The next morning Ammalu mixed a little rice and vegetable broth in a beautiful ceramic pan decorated with deep purple flowers and urged the little puppy to eat out of the fancy bowl.

"Amma, why are you using such a nice dish for the dog?" Leela protested.

"Leela, you know I don't like to use these tainted containers."

The tainted containers Ammalu was referring to were part of a collection of dinnerware left behind by the previous owner. After the declaration of independence in 1947, many British decided to leave India rather than live in a country no longer ruled by Great Britain. Rather than pack up an entire household, some of them left many things behind. One such Englishman was the owner of the charming bungalow that was now Leela's home on the outskirts of the remote hill station town of Kotagiri, nestled among the famous Blue Mountains, or Nilgiris.

When they moved into the charming red-tiled house in late 1948, they found the musty rooms filled with large pieces of wooden furniture. The cabinet doors were inlaid with ceramic tile in beautiful geometric patterns. An intricate carved folding screen in one of the three bedrooms provided privacy and beauty. The dining room boasted a large china buffet, complete with silver soup tureens, round and oval serving platters, big serving bowls and a tea set. The delicate moss-green tea set, made of the finest bone china, would never be used, though. Like most upper-caste Indians, Ammalu's family was vegetarian. They had no intention of eating or drinking from vessels used by strangers and nonvegetarians. At the first opportunity Ammalu invited friends, neighbors and acquaintances from the surrounding areas to come choose from the lovely Spode plates and Wedgwood dinnerware. So the puppy happily ate off the Spode chinaware and drank from his Wedgwood saucer.

The German shepherd turned out to be the most patient of animals. He waited for Leela or Ammalu to get up each morning and let him out. He would wander around the front yard, sniffing at rosebushes and lifting his leg against the spindly poinsettia tree. He would then lie on the kitchen floor, his bright blue eyes following Leela's every movement.

"He really is the most silent dog," a friend remarked to Leela. That was when she came up with the perfect name for her new pet, Chuppa, or "the silent one."

She tried out the new name, calling, "Chuppa!" Immediately the puppy sat up, straight and proud. He cocked his head and looked at Leela as if waiting for a command. From then on Leela spent countless hours with the young dog, teaching him simple commands. Chuppa was an intelligent pup and wanted to please Leela. He became the young girl's constant companion. He would greet her joyously, albeit silently, every afternoon when she returned from school. He draped his long tan-and-black body across Leela's doorway. The pair was a common sight as they went on long walks among the tea bushes and apple and pear orchards.

One evening, when Ammalu made a teasing gesture toward Leela, pretending to hit her, Chuppa immediately sat up and stared at Ammalu and emitted a soft warning growl.

"Chuppa thinks I was going to hit you!" Ammalu exclaimed. "What a good dog. Don't worry, Chuppa, I would never hit my girl." Ammalu bent down and petted the agitated pup, who settled down, his head resting on his folded paws, as if he understood Ammalu's words.

Leela decided to teach the dog commands to make sure he would know when a threat was real and when a family member was just playing. The dog took to the lessons as if he was a sponge soaking up spilled water.

Two years later Chuppa was a full-grown German shepherd with thick black-and-tan fur and bright blue eyes. He was a familiar sight in the little village and allowed young children to pet and fuss over him. But his soft eyes were always on Leela.

A few months later, their postman, the deliverer of news and mail, had some disturbing gossip. "Did you hear about the thefts?" he asked Ammalu and Leela one afternoon. "There has been a rash of thefts in the area and residents are asked to keep their gates locked."

The following spring Ammalu and Unny, Leela's older brother, had to make one final trip to their ancestral village to take care of some business, and Ammalu was not happy to leave Leela.

"Don't worry, Amma. Chuppa will keep me company at night, and during the day Mala and her husband will be here," Leela assured her mother.

Mala and Lingam were local villagers who came to help Leela's family with household chores. Ammalu and Unny were expected to be gone for about five days, and after giving Mala and Lingam many instructions about the household and Leela's personal safety, they finally left.

That evening Leela made sure all the doors were locked before retiring to the living room. A fire in the hearth made the room snug and comfortable. Chuppa settled down in front of the fire and Leela curled up on the sofa with a Sherlock Holmes mystery.

"Why didn't the dog bark?" she murmured to herself.

Chuppa glanced up with a questioning look in his blue eyes.

"Don't mind me, Chuppa. I'm just talking about the clue

in this story," she assured her pet, who sighed and went back to staring at the golden flames.

The crackling fire was the only sound in the room and Leela found herself drifting off. Chuppa's low growl woke her up.

"Shh…Chuppa. It's just the fire."

But the dog didn't settle down; instead he stood up and looked toward the front hallway. The coarse hairs on his neck were standing up and his body was tense and alert. Leela was alarmed at the dog's stance and got up to stand in the living room doorway. She was as tense as Chuppa and tried to hear what had disturbed the dog.

Then she heard it, the slightest grating of metal as the front gate was opened. Chuppa growled beside her. She put a hand on his head, wondering what to do.

"Is anyone home?" a woman's voice called out from the front stoop. Leela knew whoever was out there had probably seen the warm glow of the light through the living room window, even though the cloth curtains were drawn shut.

Leela took a deep breath and walked into the dark hallway. She turned on the porch light and lifted up the curtain to peer through the front window. She could make out the figure of a woman and a man standing on the front porch steps. The woman raised a slim hand and knocked on the wooden door. Leela looked back at Chuppa and gestured for him to stand behind her. The dog obediently went into the hallway, where he was hidden in the shadows behind his mistress.

Even though she dreaded opening the door, Leela decided it was better than waiting for the couple to perhaps break the glass and force their way in. She pulled the door open and peered out.

"Who are you, and why are you knocking on my door at this time of the night?"

The woman laughed, a sound that was nervous and at the same time somehow threatening. "Sister, we are just poor pilgrims on our way to the temple on the hill. Can you spare us a hot drink or a few paise?"

"I'm sorry, but my hearth is out for the night and I have no change. Perhaps you can find hospitality farther down the road," Leela said.

"Listen here, sister," the man snarled, pushing the woman aside. "We are not asking for a few paise like beggars. We are demanding you hand over your necklace, earrings and anything else of value you have in the house. I don't make idle threats." As he spoke, he pulled out a knife, the blade glinting in the overhead porch light.

"I don't like threats. I suggest you leave," Leela said, trying not to sound as frightened as she felt.

The man answered by pushing the door aside and taking a step to come inside. A deep rumble from the hallway stopped him in mid-stride.

"Chuppa, come here," Leela called out to her faithful companion, who came to stand beside her. He bared his teeth and he gave out a menacing growl. The couple stared at the German shepherd.

"Now, I suggest you leave before my dog gets impatient," Leela said to the couple.

The man hissed in anger. "A dumb animal isn't going to stop me," he said in a low tone as he stepped toward Leela, his knife raised.

"Chuppa, get the knife," Leela ordered in a firm voice.

Without a moment's hesitation, the dog leaped and grabbed the man's hand. The knife clattered to the ground. The man yelped in surprise. Leela quickly kicked the knife out of his reach. The dog let go of the man's hand and waited for his next command.

"Good dog. Now get him," Leela said.

Again the dog leaped and, using his full weight, brought the man down. Chuppa placed a heavy paw on the man's chest and bared his teeth. The woman cried out, and the dog looked at her with his soft eyes and pulled back his lips to show his sharp white teeth.

"Call off your dog," the woman cried. "We meant no harm."

The silence was broken by a murmur of voices.

"Miss Leela, are you all right?" a voice asked from the driveway. It was Lingam. He was carrying a smoky homemade torch in his hand. Behind him there were several villagers.

"Lingam! I am so glad to see you," Leela called and sighed in relief. "Chuppa has caught a man who was threatening me."

Lingam walked up to the porch steps and looked down at the figure on the ground.

"These look like the couple who have been robbing houses," he announced. "We heard they were out tonight, and came by to check on you. But it looks like you can take care of yourself." His white teeth flashed as he grinned at Leela.

"It was Chuppa who saved the day," Leela said. "Chuppa, let him go."

The German shepherd looked down at the man and growled again before moving slowly off him. The animal went to stand beside Leela, looking up at her with adoration shining from his bright blue eyes.

Leela bent down and hugged the dog. She buried her face in his doggy fur. "Thank you, Chuppa," she whispered.

"Woof." Chuppa's bark was short and soft. Leela laughed out loud. That was the one and only time Chuppa ever barked.

For years the dog was my mother's faithful companion in Kotagiri. When he died of old age, my mother was heartbroken. Chuppa was the last pet she ever owned.

★ ★ ★ ★ ★

In Touch with One's Felines

Ed Goldman

T he crying starts as soon as the car starts. "It'll be all right," I say as softly as I can, while still fighting to be heard. "Daddy loves you," I add, figuring there may be some doubt on her part.

I'm already soaked with perspiration by the time I reach the end of the block, the crying now reaching such a feverish, intense pitch that I debate pulling over and reprimanding her. But how can I? She won't understand and won't care that this is proving more traumatic for me than it ever will be for her. So I take a deep breath, crank up Mozart's Turkish March on the classical station and keep telling myself, *The hospital is only a mile and a half away....*

Every three days I take my wife's seventeen-year-old cat, Sabrina, to the Sacramento Animal Hospital for intravenous fluid treatments. They slow down her metabolism, and that keeps her from burning too many calories too fast. Early in her treatments, she weighed four pounds and eleven ounces. Now she's up to six pounds and two to four ounces, depending on how much of her dinner and then our dinner she eats the night before.

I inherited Sabrina when my wife, Candy, and I began our life together four years ago. The little cat is beautiful and calls to mind a black-and-white Puss in Boots. She also has lungs that would prompt even an opera conductor to say, "Easy." When I drive her to the treatments, she howls from the moment I strap her carrier into the backseat until the moment when I get her home, unstrap the carrier and let her strut back up the stairs to the house, as though she went to the vet only because she felt like it.

Sometimes between the hours of 4:00 and 6:00 a.m., she yowls, which is worse than howling, from the first floor of our three-story home. It's a home with a contemporary, open floor plan. This means the only sound barriers are the earplugs I keep on a shelf behind my pillow.

I'd never had a cat before, only a couple of dogs. My first dog was a rescue dog, in the truest sense of the word. One evening my first wife (bear with me, as there are a total of three) and I were riding back from dinner with another couple in Long Beach, California. As we came to a stoplight, I noticed there was a very panicked mutt on the island separating the opposing lanes of traffic. She was panting heavily, and that was her only activity since she was, literally, paralyzed with fear. Since my wife and I were passengers, I asked my friend not to go when the light changed (we made many friends that evening). I jumped out of the car, hunched down on the island, about twenty feet from the little dog, and put my arms out. "Come on," I said as softly as I could above the din of traffic, the shouted assertions about my parentage (our *many* friends), the cursing and the honking from the cars behind us.

Miraculously, the dog dashed into my embrace. I all but tossed her into the backseat with my wife and jumped in the car with an athletic grace that surprised everyone in the car, including the dog and me. My friend gunned the car through the intersection just before the light turned red.

Back in our one-bedroom apartment, a block from the ocean, we let the little dog smell her way around before she settled in for the night on the bathroom floor. This turned out to be a measure of her intelligence, because sometime later she experienced an attack of diarrhea, which she thoughtfully dealt with by quickly climbing into the bathtub.

As the days went by, we advertised in the local newspaper that we'd found her (she had no ID tag and this was many years before the invention of the puppy microchip). We hesitantly named the dog Portia—my wife loved Shakespeare—in the hope that we would keep her.

No one answered the ad after a tense ten days. By then, we had taken Portia to the vet (she was fine), had caught her up on her shots (as best as the vet could determine) and had plied our landlady with champagne, chocolates and a hefty damage deposit for allowing us to violate the apartment building's no-pets-or-surfers edict (the latter was implicit; the former clearly spelled out in our lease).

As the years went by, we fell in love with Portia, moved to Sacramento and promptly fell out of love with each other. I adored the dog but knew it would shatter my soon-to-be ex-wife even more than the divorce would if she also had to surrender our dog to me. So when she asked if she could keep Portia, I said, "Of course." Part of me wanted to push for visitation, but I realized that as much as I would miss my dog, in the long term she'd be far better off with my ex-wife.

My second dog was a rescue dog, too, from the SPCA. I was married to Jane, my second wife, whom I would live with for twenty-nine years, until her death. We got the dog when our daughter, Jessica, was three and a half years old. Jane had always been afraid to have a dog because she suffered from allergies that could easily escalate into asthma. But since our daughter loved animals so much and clearly had a gift for communicating with them—she surreptitiously petted the kangaroos at the San Francisco Zoo, which was strictly *verboten*—Jane asked her allergist what sort of dog she could have that would cause her the least discomfort. "Get whatever you like and we'll adjust your shots," he said.

This came as a shock to her. All her life she'd been told—by uninformed family doctors and a mother who would say, "Who needs the trouble?"—that a dog, *any* dog, unless it was completely shaved and drenched in aloe, would cause her grief. "I'd have had dogs all my life," she said.

Camellia, a German shepherd–Queensland herder admixture, was just eight weeks old when we adopted her. She and our daughter quickly became quibbling siblings, to the extent that when we were enrolling Jessica in a private school and she was asked if she had sisters or brothers, she responded, "I have one sister an' she's a doggy."

Camellia lived with us until she was fourteen (and my daughter was seventeen) and contracted cancer. By this time, my wife was also five years into her nine-year battle with breast cancer. Camellia's losing battle became far too emblematic of the direction our lives would take in the next couple of years: my wife's condition would turn terminal, our daughter would leave home for college, and I would have to learn, or to pretend, that everything in life had a purpose.

I could never stand cats. Part of my animus derived from the fact that I'd always been allergic to them. Another part sprang from the fact that cats just didn't seem needy, dependent, grateful and sloppy enough to make them loving pets. Cats just never seem to need anyone's help. Fact is, I like to be depended on, I like to protect and I like to help. I have the same problem with children once they're old enough to ask you to leave their rooms.

And while I lived with Sabrina and tolerated her, I never really saw myself as a cat owner—not in the way I'd been a dog owner to Portia and Camellia. Until one day, not long ago, a feral neighborhood cat strolled into our backyard and began to hassle Sabrina. She quickly burst into an aria that had me running downstairs from my office into the backyard and removing the intruder, which I threw for a thirty-yard incomplete pass (unless you consider a camellia bush a receiver).

Wow. Where did that come from? I wondered, standing on the grass, waiting for my heartbeat to calm down. My rage and violent reaction surprised me. Since when was I patrolling the garden to protect a cat? I knew enough about cats by then not to await a thank-you note from Sabrina or even a casual brush against my leg as she stalked stiffly back into the house. *Weird,* I thought, shaking my head and brushing the stray cat hairs off my hands. *Just weird.*

A few nights later Jessica came to dinner and asked for my help with a project with a looming due date. The request was barely out of her mouth before I nodded in agreement. "Sure, of course. Let's get started. I'm ready right now."

And that was when I realized why I'd come to Sabrina's rescue. One of my kids had been in trouble. I'd done what any loving father—or cat owner—would do.

★ ★ ★ ★ ★

Kissing the Whale

Pam Giarrizzo

Laguna San Ignacio is not a destination people generally think about when planning a vacation to Mexico; indeed, most people have probably never even heard of it. It lies on the Pacific Ocean side of Baja California Sur, but visitors don't go there to swim or scuba dive or lie on the beach. Flying into the desert near the lagoon in an airplane so tiny they can't even stand up straight in it, they may start to question why they decided to go there at all. But they are there because they have heard about the *laguna de ballenas amistosas* (lagoon of friendly whales) and they want to see if the stories are really true.

Two years ago I was one of those people, although I wasn't actually the person who was supposed to be there. My husband, Phil, was, since he had been part of a successful campaign a few years earlier to prevent Mitsubishi Corporation from building a salt plant at the lagoon, which serves as the nursing grounds of the California gray whale. He had been asked by others who had been a part of the campaign to go with them and see the whales for himself. After all the arrangements had been made, pressing business matters arose that kept Phil from taking the trip, and he asked if I would like to go in his stead.

I had gone whale watching before, crowded with strangers along the rail of a large tour boat off the coast of Monterey, fighting seasickness and straining for a glimpse of a whale a quarter of a mile in the distance. I had no desire to take a trip like that again. But I knew that this was not going to be that kind of whale watching. My husband had been told stories about camping out on the beach in Mexico, close enough to hear the whales breathe in the stillness of the night. That sounded like a once-in-a-lifetime whale-watching excursion, and I was grateful for the opportunity.

I packed my gear and flew to San Diego, the jumping-off point for the trip. The chartered bus ride with my fellow whale watchers from San Diego to a small private airport across the border in Tijuana was uneventful. When I saw the small planes we were about to board, I suddenly understood why I had to list my weight on the trip application and was instructed to bring no more than thirty pounds of luggage. It looked like only a dozen or so passengers would fit inside each plane. I found myself worrying about whether or not I had been entirely truthful when I listed my weight, and whether I might have packed a few more things than I really needed.

With a certain amount of trepidation, I climbed the steps to the plane's entrance, hunched forward and squeezed through the narrow passage that served as an aisle, dropping into the first open seat I saw. The lavatory was separated from the cabin by only a flimsy curtain. After takeoff, the person sitting in the last seat in the plane began serving the in-flight meal by reaching into the cooler supplied by the tour operator and passing snacks and soft drinks forward until everyone, including the pilot and copilot, had something to eat. I was beginning to wonder what I had gotten myself into.

Fortunately, the plane touched down without incident on a dusty airstrip in the desert, where we were met by vans and driven several miles to the water's edge. We grabbed our luggage and boarded pangas, small fishing boats about twenty-two feet in length, which delivered us about forty-five minutes later to the Rocky Point campground at Laguna San Ignacio. We unloaded the boats bucket-brigade style, found our assigned cabin tents and received a brief orientation about the camp.

After a quick lunch we headed down to the water and climbed back into the pangas for our first ride out to see the whales. In addition to the pangateers who piloted the boats, there was a naturalist aboard each boat to point out the birds—black-and-white surf scoters, with their striking orange bills; parasitic jaegers, conducting midair attacks to steal fish from the mouths of hapless gulls; and other denizens of the lagoon, such as sea turtles, moving effortlessly through the water. Whales could be seen in the distance, breaching most of their bodies' length out of the water's calm surface or spy hopping just enough to see who was in the vicinity. Bottlenose dolphins appeared from nowhere, bow riding in the surf stirred up by the pangas, much to the delight of all the passengers aboard.

Suddenly, the pangateer cut the throttle, slowing the boat to a quiet glide along the shimmering water. He and the naturalist were especially alert then. The whales that had seemed so distant a moment ago were now a mere fifty feet away. We all held our breath; this was what we'd been waiting for. Slowly, an enormous barnacle-covered gray whale mother made her way toward the panga, which was about half her length. She was followed by her shiny black calf, which, even though it was only a few months old, was already as long as the boat. The whales were only a few feet away, and we were at their mercy, hoping that the stories we'd been told about the friendly whales of Laguna San Ignacio were true, and that they wouldn't upend our panga and spill us into the frigid waters of the lagoon.

"Lean over the side and splash a little water toward them with your fingertips if you want them to come closer," the naturalist advised. There was no question that we wanted the whales to come closer. This was the moment we had dreamed of. The mother whale appeared to show her infant what to do next. She eased closer and closer to the boat, until her head rose up out of the water mere inches from the side of the panga. As she met our gaze, we reached out eagerly and began to stroke her scarred gray head, whispering soothing words to let her know that we, too, were friendly. The encounter continued for a minute or so, before she dived down and resurfaced several feet away on the other side of the boat.

Her calf, who was learning this behavior from his mother, inched closer to the boat, much to our delight, as we couldn't wait to stroke his smooth black head. His body had not yet been invaded by the barnacles and sea lice that had attached themselves to his mother's skin, nor had he suffered the injuries from run-ins with ships or other creatures that had left his mother with deep scars. We continued to pat every part of him that we could reach until his mother finally swam away and he followed after her. We had all heard about people who had managed to actually kiss a whale or rub the baleen plates in its mouth, which are used to filter its food, but for us on our first day in the lagoon, it was enough just to be able to touch the whales. It is not an overstatement to say

that this demonstration of trust from creatures who have suffered so much over the centuries at the hands of whalers and
other humans was a life-changing experience for me and all
the other passengers aboard the tiny fishing boat.

The gray whales of Laguna San Ignacio were not always
friendly. They could not afford to be. After the captains of
European whaling ships discovered what a fertile hunting
area these nursing grounds were, the waters of the lagoon ran
red with the blood of slaughtered whales. Then the mother
gray whales would attack the whaling ships ferociously in a
futile attempt to save themselves and their calves. The whalers called them "hardheaded devil fish" and learned to fear
them, even as they harpooned them by the hundreds, hunting them almost to extinction. Not until 1949 did the International Whaling Commission end this bloody practice, once
again allowing mother gray whales to give birth to their calves
in the peaceful sanctuary of the lagoon and to prepare them
for the long migration north to the Bering Sea and beyond.

For decades after the hunting ended, gray whales and local
fishermen maintained an uneasy truce, staying as far away
from each other as possible. The story of how that all changed
is legendary in Laguna San Ignacio. One day in 1972 two local
fishermen were out in their panga when they saw a female
gray whale heading for them. They tried to get away, but the
whale kept coming closer, going so far as to swim under the
boat at one point and actually lift it out of the water. After she
lowered the boat, she continued to swim near it, making eye
contact with the fishermen until one of them finally reached
out his hand and touched her. This was the beginning of a
new era in the relationship between humans and whales in
Laguna San Ignacio. News of the friendly whales began to
spread, and people began to arrive from locations near and far

to enjoy this mystical experience for themselves. Now tourism has joined fishing as an important source of income for the people who live near the lagoon, and they have become very protective of their whales.

Over dinner in the evenings we learned about the gray whales and the lagoon from the naturalists who had been hired for the season. I had the impression that everyone who made the journey to Laguna San Ignacio must be deeply touched by the experience. It seemed to me that no one who had stroked the head of a baby gray whale would ever see a Save the Whales bumper sticker in the same light again. It would no longer be just a slogan; it would become a sacred trust.

But after a few trips out onto the lagoon, I began to worry that I might be part of the problem. "Should we be encouraging them like this?" I asked Kate, the naturalist who accompanied the panga I was in one afternoon. "Should we make the whales believe that people are their friends, when on so many levels we are not? Will my loving caresses somehow take away the baby whale's ability to recognize danger if she comes across a whaling ship during her northward migration?" Kate agreed that normally this would be cause for concern, but she assured me that the gray whales exhibited this behavior only in Laguna San Ignacio, where, thankfully, they are protected by laws and local sentiment.

I allowed her words to soothe my newly troubled conscience, but I continued to wrestle with the question of whether we are wrong to allow the whales to become so comfortable with us. After all, one of the cardinal rules of wildlife rehabilitation is to refrain from trying to turn a wild animal into a pet, which means that contact with humans is kept at a minimum. The whales have no need for rehabilitation, as they are already in the wild, but it seems as though the same principle would apply.

Part of my dilemma is that I don't know what's in it for the whales. They approached us, after all. We didn't approach them. The fishermen in 1972 were trying to get away from the whale, but she persisted in forcing their acquaintance. When my fellow whale watchers and I went out into the lagoon, the pangateer didn't chase after the whales. He waited for them to come to us. The whales aren't looking for food, since food is not the primary reason they stay so long in Laguna San Ignacio, and no food is given to them by anyone in the pangas. There are those who believe that the whales seek interaction with humans in order to form a close bond and thereby ensure that we won't threaten to harm them or their calves again. But I know of no research that would support this anthropomorphic theory.

Maybe I'm overthinking this. Maybe I should just trust the whales. If they perceive that there is value in making overtures to humans, who am I to say there is not? Still, I worry.

In our two trips a day out into the lagoon, I don't think we ever went without a visit from a whale, although the tour operators always caution that there is no guarantee of whale encounters. We all became quite adept at coaxing the whales to the side of the panga so we could pat them, but I had an unfulfilled desire to kiss a whale before my trip ended. That seemed a little more difficult, though. Reaching my arm far enough over the side of the small boat to touch a whale with my hand was one thing, but leaning my whole upper body far enough out to kiss the whale was another matter entirely.

On the last day of my trip, I watched for my chance. I would have loved to kiss a mother whale, if for no other reason than to thank her for trusting us with her calf, but it seemed to me that the mothers always hung back just a bit, making us work a little harder to reach out and touch them. The calves, with their exuberance of youth, were more likely to come closer. With a heightened sense of awareness, I watched as a gray whale calf swam toward the panga. I began to ease up off of my seat and reach out into the water. I splashed a little water in the whale's direction, leaning a little farther out of the boat the closer he came.

Suddenly he was rubbing up against the side of the panga, and everyone was stroking his satiny skin. It was now or never, I thought, and I leaned as far out as I safely could and kissed the side of his head. And then, with salt water still clinging to my lips, I gave him another kiss for good measure. Afterward, I alternated between a feeling of almost giddy excitement and an overwhelming desire to burst into tears. It was an intensely emotional experience, one that I would never have thought possible just weeks earlier.

I had to be in Monterey on business several months ago and I had a little time to kill before my meeting started. I took a walk along Fisherman's Wharf and saw people waiting to go out on a whale-watching cruise. It seemed to me to be awfully late in the season for that, so I stopped and took a look at the trip board set up by one of the cruise operators to find out what they expected to see. It announced recent sightings: Killer whales! Blue whales! Gray whales! And I found myself wondering if any of *my* gray whales were off the coast of Monterey now. Would anyone on that whale-watching cruise, fighting nausea and being jostled by other passengers, see my whales? Would they see the mother whale to whom I felt such gratitude for trusting me with her calf? Would they see the baby whale that I kissed? Probably not, and even if they did see those gray whales, they couldn't possibly feel the same bond to them that I now feel.

Perhaps reasonable minds can differ as to whether it's a good thing or not for people to have such close encounters with whales as I did in Laguna San Ignacio, but one thing is certain: having kissed a baby gray whale, I will always feel that the responsibility for his fate and the fate of his species is in my hands.

★ ★ ★ ★ ★

In the Nick of Time

Sue Pearson

Family and friends each wrote goodbye notes and put them inside a grave marker, a memorial box that read Beloved Friend. One handwritten note read, "We will love you and miss you forever." My granddaughter's note read, "We will never forget what you did for so many, especially me. Thank you." I tucked in a faded piece of newsprint, a story from almost a dozen years before. The first line read: "When life is moving very fast but everything seems to be in slow motion, you can be sure nothing good is happening. The events speed up the action. The fear slows it down."

Holding the delicate newsprint in my hand, I could still see it all so clearly—Nick was still a puppy then, really—a Lab not yet two years old. Adam was the twelve-year-old friend of my son, Evan. What began as an adventure on a mountain river on a bright, warm, sunny June day was to take a sudden dark turn. It was the day before the first day of summer and the river beckoned. I told the boys they could only go wading and only in one shallow section of the river, upstream, and only if I went with them. It was that compelling an idea to them, even if Mom had to come along, so off we all went, including Nick the dog, to sample the first of summer's refreshments. We arrived at the spot I had dubbed "safe" and the boys proceeded to roll up the legs of their jeans. Nick splashed along the shore, enjoying the cold water rushing by but in no hurry to join the strong currents bent on finding a more tranquil home in the valley. I had taken Nick's leash off to let him play and I stood on the shore, watching the boys and the dog.

Life couldn't be better. Everyone was having one of those moments of simple pleasure that we look back on years later and realize was in fact a treasured memory…one of the reasons life is so sweet. The next moment Adam was joking with Evan…giving him a twelve-year-old's challenge. "Go all the way under, Evan. I dare you!" Evan was laughing and hesitating. Suddenly it was Adam who was all the way under. He'd slipped on the rocks. He was immediately swept into the unforgiving current. In those split seconds, which have now become vivid snapshots of terror engraved in those parts of my brain reserved for life-and-death reactions, I remember thinking I was watching a tragedy unfold. I ran to the edge of the water and yelled for Adam to catch the dog leash I was about to throw. I missed. He missed. He went under water again, surfaced and looked up at me. His eyes, wild with fear, seemed to plead, "Help me!"

I saw paramedics arrive after Evan ran back to the cabin to get help from his dad. I saw them pull Adam's lifeless body from the chilly water and work on him for an hour. I saw Evan sobbing on the shore, forever changed. I called Adam's parents. There would be no birthday party next Saturday. Instead a funeral. I could never forgive myself for letting the boys go in the water. Adam's loss would weigh us all down for the rest of our lives. None of us would love the little cabin in the mountains again. This landscape would be a tangle of pain and grief and sorrow.

But none of this happened. In those split seconds of heightened awareness I saw a blur of yellow fur flash by. It was Nick. He jumped in the water and swam to Adam as the current thrust the boy away. I saw Adam grab a handful of fur and skin like his life depended on it. It did. Nick never hesitated. He swam to shore, pulling Adam with him. Adam climbed out of the water, shaken and shouting at the same time, "Nick, I love you!" Nick shook himself off and casually walked over to me and sat down.

Thank you, God. And thank you, Nick—for saving us in the nick of time from a lifetime of grief, deep sorrow and regret.

My hero dog, Nick, lived to be thirteen, and not only was his a good life in the country, with ten acres to explore and rule, but it was a life full of more heroic deeds. He had that courage in his DNA. In the years after he saved Adam's life, he was always on duty to perform more acts of courage on behalf of everyone nearby, casually nudging a toddler out of harm's way near a bucking horse, defending a neighbor against an attack by another dog, helping my granddaughter overcome a fear of dogs. He was most dramatically protective of me. When a visiting dog rushed me at full speed, catching me behind the knees to flip me into the air, Nick was there. I landed on a hard slate patio…heard something snap…my femur. The dog was on top of me instantly, mauling me. A snarling Nick with his hackles up bit the dog, pushed the dog away and then kept it at bay until help arrived.

As we closed the memorial box with our notes, which we'd tucked into a plastic bag to keep time and weather from destroying our tributes, we held hands and prayed at Nick's final resting place in a sunny spot on my ranch. "We thank you for this guardian angel who saved lives, chased danger into retreat and washed away fear."

Standing there in the sunlight now, I try to imagine what heaven is like for dogs. I know one exists, because God wouldn't let these loyal creatures go with no reward. It must be a place with not just ten acres, but a million acres, with an eternity of holes to dig and smells to sniff. If it turns out there really are pearly gates to heaven, I see Nick waiting there for me, leash in his mouth, looking forward to another long walk.

Wednesday in the Wall

Chris Fowler (Roller Derby name: Cherry Madness)

*The softness of the kitten was a relief in my hands. Her small
black form had been wedged in the confines of the brick wall.
Now she was safe with me.*

It was a Wednesday, a chilly October afternoon, as I worked
quickly to unload supplies in a pre-WWII warehouse in
downtown Sacramento. This cold warehouse with redbrick
and lead-lined walls is the proud home of my team, the Sacred
City Derby Girls, a women's flat-track Roller Derby league.
It is said to have originally been a WWII ammunition storage facility, then a candy factory sometime in the sixties. Its
history is then lost for a few decades. After several years of
neglect it was home to a "bounce house turned rave night-
club" venue. We acquired it at an auto auction a few years ago
and now had a training ground for a team exuding feminine
strength and endurance, a team of derby girls. On this blus-
tery fall day, three members of Sacred City were brought to a
stiff standstill with the softest "meew" from inside the walls.

"Stop!" I suddenly yelled to my husband, Clayton. He was

affectionately known within our derby world as Mr. Madness. My friend Michelle stopped, too. She skated under the handle "Her Meechness." She had these amazing, long, strong legs that made her an asset to our team. They both froze, looking at me to figure out what I wanted. "Did you hear that?" I whispered.

"Meew."

There it was! Oh, it was so small. That was the precious, squeaky sound of a newborn cat. We moved softly to the east wall of our building and waited for one more.

"Meew."

There it was again, the sound of a tiny new kitten, coming through the half-a-century-old brick and mortar. We stopped unloading the truck and instantly became a Roller Derby kitty rescue team. This kitty needed our help. As the team medic, that is what I do—I respond to those who need me, whether on the track or, now, in the alley.

But where exactly was this cat? In the wall? Yes, and we were on the other side of the wall, separated by a long enclosed alley. To get there we'd have to move a gigantic sliding steel door that had come off its rusty old track. It took all three of us to muscle that heavy steel door open enough for one of us to slide through. It made a horrible scraping noise on the concrete floor. We stopped. There was silence.

"Meew."

It was still there! Slightly louder now, letting us know of its whereabouts. I slid through and was in the alley, surrounded by almost pitch blackness at first. My eyes adjusted. I felt along the cobweb-covered wall. There were no lights. The dim afternoon haze through the cracks in the roofline was no help.

There were two white, midsize industrial trucks parked in the alley. They came into view quickly and I recognized them as belonging to our neighboring business. It was a tight fit, a shimmy to squeeze by, and I got dusty webs on my clothes as I brushed against the wall. I could hear Michelle as she was sliding along the same wall, following me on this rescue mission.

We had not heard a sound for a few minutes. I made my way down the alley, softly calling out, "Kitty, kitty, kitty." I hoped we weren't too late....Finally, there it was. One final sound was all we needed to locate our target.

"Meew."

Just behind an oddly shaped alcove in the alley was a very slight, very hungry jet-black kitten. As I later discovered, a girl. She seemed hesitant to emerge from the wall, but she was curious. She did not object as I reached into the wall for her. She was so small. She looked at me with her green eyes. I might have been the first human she'd ever seen.

I snuggled her against my shirt. We shimmied our way back down the alley to the steel door and slid through. Once back in the well-lit warehouse, we did a full survey. She was darling. There were no apparent injuries, but yes, a flea or two. And now that she'd been rescued, she would not stop talking.

"Meew, meew, meew, meew!"

It was a constant flow of sound, like an infant's attempt at communicating. It was as if the kitten was saying, "This baby needs to be fed and bathed! Prompt attention please!"

Scrambling around the warehouse and rummaging through our cars, we found a few things. Kitty was placed in a cardboard box with a soft blanket and some water. The water spilled within moments as she wanted to leap and jump and play. She was so small, we were afraid she would get wedged in another nook in the warehouse. So we closed the box and watched it hippity-hop around the floor as she objected to her confinement.

We'd all planned to work on the building that afternoon, but now those plans were canceled. I loaded up our impatient orphan and took her home. Once she was bathed and cleaned up, she settled right in with a litter box and some food. It was time to search for a loving family. I love cats, but I already had two. A third addition was not a wise option. Someone else would have to be persuaded to take this kitty in.

I thought of a solution. Another Roller Derby girl, Tiffany, with raven-black hair and the skate name Pink Devil, had a penchant for wayward animals. A dog with one ear and a kitten with one eye were just two of now five animals that shared her home. Maybe she needed a tiny black kitten....I convinced her to come over for a visit. I was certain if I could just get her to meet this little wallflower, she would be smitten. Unfairly, I cajoled her with text message pictures and tales of the kitten's rescue.

She responded quickly, and soon enough we were all three sitting on the floor of the garage. I watched Tiffany and the new kitten interact. She'd recently lost a beloved pet, and it was clear she was quite taken with the midnight-colored feline. Our gentle little rescue walked over to her adoptive mom and climbed into her lap, snuggling into the folds of her skirt. I described her rescue from the wall the day before, and Tiffany nodded in approval as I detailed how we had all moved the steel door together. She stroked the kitten as I talked.

"So," I asked gently, hoping to seal the deal, "what do you want to name her?"

"Well, it is October," she said. "She is black as night. Her day of rescue is very fitting. We shall call her Wednesday."

★ ★ ★ ★ ★

Hammer

As Told to Morton Rumberg

This is the story of Hammer. He was unconscious when I met him for the first time. Our animal control officer had seized five pit bulls, charging their owner with being an unfit caretaker and with cruelty to animals. The house they lived in had been condemned because of accumulated filth, debris and fecal matter. The animal control officer took the dogs to a veterinarian for examination. Four were young dogs: one young male, a breeding female and two young females. They were moderately to severely underweight, filthy, and infested with fleas, hookworms and whipworms. The male had numerous bite scars, especially on his legs and head, but all the dogs were friendly and surprisingly trusting. And then there was Hammer.

Hammer was attached to a short, thick chain that could easily be used to tow a truck. The chain weighed twenty-seven pounds. The spike anchoring the chain to the ground weighed another ten pounds. Hammer was the guard dog, the fierce protector of the only home he knew. The owner said that he had to keep Hammer chained because he was so aggressive. Hammer had to be tranquilized to enable the veterinarian to examine him safely.

Hammer was a pit bull; a large, full-grown, heavy-boned dog, but he weighed only fifty pounds. Every part of his body was witness to the hell his life had been. The details were grim. He was emaciated—every rib, every bone in his spine was clearly visible. Bite scars were visible all over his body. His ears, severely cut in the "fighting crop," were swollen, inflamed and badly infected. A fist-sized growth, probably an untreated tumor, protruded from his side, and several smaller tumors were located elsewhere on his body, including in his groin area. He had an open abscess on his front leg.

His entire abdominal area was blackened from a long-term, untreated bacterial infection. His neck and throat were raw, inflamed and infected from pulling against the chain. He had an unforgettable rank odor of filth and infection. His canine teeth were broken, and all his other teeth were worn down almost to the gums, probably from chewing on the chain. It was impossible to estimate his age, given the condition of his teeth and his overall physical condition. He could be anywhere from five to fifteen years of age. That was Hammer.

Their veterinary exams completed, the dogs arrived at the shelter. I carried Hammer, still unconscious, to a run that I'd padded with blankets to keep him from hurting himself when he awoke from the tranquilizer. Through that long evening the youngsters were photographed, vaccinated, dewormed, bathed and dipped. They accepted it all trustingly. And then there was Hammer.

The shelter staff checked on him often as he began to wake up. He followed our every move, as if he was trying to understand what was happening. Finally, we finished our initial care for the youngsters, but we hadn't vaccinated Hammer.

Even the friendliest dogs can be unpredictable as they're waking from anesthesia. Common sense said to forget it, and just leave him alone, but that was not our way. One staff member held Hammer's head in a bear hug while another vaccinated him. He barely struggled and we began to wonder how vicious he really was.

Our animal control officers, the veterinarians and the Commonwealth attorney did an outstanding job putting the case together against the dogs' owner. The court upheld our petition to have the owner declared unfit to provide proper care for the dogs, and awarded their custody to the animal shelter. A few weeks later, in criminal court, the owner entered a plea of guilty to the charge of animal cruelty. But the wheels of justice moved slowly and the dogs would be with us until the case was finally closed.

Meanwhile, at the shelter the dogs had been put on a special feeding regimen for malnutrition. Hammer's food was laced with antibiotics for his many infections. All five dogs gained weight steadily and their condition visibly improved from day to day. The youngsters were friendly with everyone on staff. And then there was Hammer.

Hammer would jump on his cage door as people approached, barking with his distinctive deep, yet hoarse voice. He used his food and water bowls as Frisbees, shaking and tossing them around. We gave him heavy, tip-proof water and food bowls and a thick rope toy to shake. He demolished the frame of his metal dog door one day by constantly barreling into it. He didn't want to stay outside during inside cleanup or be inside when we cleaned the outside. His weight and his strength improved daily, but his ears needed topical medication on a regular basis and his skin needed medicated baths. He still smelled horribly.

As lead officer for Hammer, I visited him after hours, when the shelter was quiet, plied him with dog biscuits and talked to him, trying to earn his trust one step at a time. It took a while, but I finally was able to pet him through the bars, then enter the kennel with him and finally medicate his ears. He began to trust me and it was a wonderful feeling.

One night I put a slip lead around his neck and led him through the empty shelter to the grooming room. I invited him to jump in the tub. He had no idea what to expect. The next step could be dangerous. I reached under him to pick him up. Would he let me? We were both surprised it went so smoothly when I placed him in the tub. He looked very warily at me when I turned on the hose, but he let the warm water cascade over him. Owners sometimes encouraged aggression by turning a hose on their dogs, so I was alert to any sudden move he might make, but he put up with it. Perhaps he understood I was trying to help him. He grunted and groaned with delight as he was lathered and massaged, turning different parts of his body toward me for more massaging. The next thing I knew, his huge front paws were on my shoulders and this fierce guard dog was giving me sloppy doggy kisses. I had a new friend named Hammer.

One by one he learned to know and trust several other staff members. We gave each of the pit bull youngsters big rawhide bones. They devoured them in record time. Hammer's teeth were so worn down that he couldn't really chew his, but he loved to carry it around. We began taking him to our fenced exercise area after hours. At first he'd run a few feet and stop, expecting to be jerked back by his chain. Little by little he began to explore and leap and run. When we called him, he would run to us for belly rubs, rolling in the grass on his back, giving us big openmouthed groans of pleasure.

He didn't know how to fetch or play with toys, but he loved the attention and the freedom. He continued to gain weight, soon weighing in at sixty-two pounds, with no protruding bones and a shining coat. He was enjoying his new life.

Too soon the final date for the owner to appeal the court ruling arrived. The following day we held Hammer's head tenderly while we euthanized him—his story could end no other way. He was what he was: a large, powerful dog who had been taught to fight other dogs and distrust people. This disqualified him from ever being adopted. At the shelter we had a friend named Hammer. We're proud that we were able to let him know love and trust and simply enjoy being a dog, if only for a short time. We're proud, too, of our other animals, the ones adopted by loving families.

This is what we do. Everyone who works at an animal shelter has stories like Hammer's. Our work may not be understood or appreciated. We do it for the animals because we are all they have. We take them in, give them food, a clean place to live and medical care when they need it. We try to place them with people who have a lifetime of love and care to give. We enjoy them for the time we have with them, and when we say goodbye, whatever the circumstances, we say it with love. We may never change the system or society or the world, but if we continue to care and to take pride in what we do, we *can* make a difference—one day, one animal, one life at a time.

★ ★ ★ ★ ★

Quiet Vigil

Sue Pearson

She stands in the corner, looking out on the road. This is the only spot in the field that isn't shaded by large, sheltering, beckoning trees. The sun is beating down on her tired body. Her haunches are hollow, with skin stretched tight over hip bones that protrude. Her back is swayed. Her shoulders are bony. Her head is bowed. She stands and she waits.

"Have you noticed that skinny horse in the pasture along the road to your house?" My neighbor and I sometimes run into each other at the feed store, and today she was concerned about this sad-looking horse standing in the blazing sun with its head hung down, looking forlorn and neglected.

I know this horse. Our lives are intertwined. The story is very different than it appears. To be sure, there is suffering, but along the way there is an invitation to trust in a higher power—a chance to experience the nearness of God. Shiloh and I both have been touched by grace, our paths connected by some divine guidance.

Spiritual growth is often difficult, and this chapter in my growth began when a health crisis sidelined me from a successful career as a journalist and pushed me into early retirement. Friends said, "Just stay at home and play with your horses." And while that sounded appealing, it also sounded a bit self-centered. An organization called Wonder, Inc., offered a chance to make a difference, not in the world or even in my community, but in just one life...the life of a child in foster care.

And so I became a mentor to MJ, an eight-year-old with hair the color of wheat, eyes that sparkled, a personality that said, "I can and I will" again and again. It's the quality the people in child protective services call resilience, and MJ has it. Her enthusiasm won my heart. "When can we start having adventures?" "Can you teach me anything?" "I love to learn!" I explained to MJ that, according to the rules, I had to have three home visits before we could start going out and doing things together. Each time I came over, I brought what I thought were interesting craft projects for us to do in her foster home, things like egg decorating, scrapbooking and beadwork. She dove into each project but didn't have much to say. Where had the earlier excitement gone?

"Is there anything on your mind, MJ?" I asked.

"Yes, there is," she said. "When can we get outta here and start having fun?"

"Okay. Next time, I promise, we can get out of here and start having fun." I laughed. I told her a little bit about myself. "I have five children—one girl, four boys—and mostly they are grown and gone from home. In six months my youngest boy will graduate from high school and leave for college."

MJ threw back her head and turned to me, her long ponytail flicking from side to side. "Well, aren't you lucky to have me now!"

I laughed at her spunkiness. Looking back, this was the moment I fell in love with her, certain a lifetime bond was in the making.

We went to plays, concerts, the zoo, skipped rocks at the river, hiked in the mountains, played with my dog; and when a neighbor offered to loan me her child-safe pony, I gave MJ riding lessons. I knew from my long years of riding and caring for horses that these animals offered an extraordinary learning experience. In honing good equestrian skills, a lot of pretty amazing life skills get formed and sharpened. Things like leadership, patience, responsibility, self-confidence and more. MJ was a little scared when she first got on Diamond, but with slow and steady guidance from me, she was ready for her first horse show within eight months. We borrowed show clothes, and together we groomed Diamond until the pony gleamed.

In the show arena, I had to let go of MJ. No more helping. She was on her own now. I leaned against the arena fence, drumming my fingers nervously on the top rail. I must have held my breath the entire time, because when the judge announced the results, with MJ awarded first place, the air came rushing out of my lungs in one huge whooping shout of joy. The smile on MJ's face could have lit up the universe. I was helping her with what is all too often missing in the life of a foster child—the opportunity to thrive. The surprise was how much she gave back to me. I felt energized and needed.

Suddenly MJ was at a crossroads. From her social workers she learned she would either return to her biological mother, be put up for adoption or stay in foster care until she aged out of the system at eighteen. Every option seemed scary.

While the unknown was looming, the thing MJ was most concerned about was me. I had indeed filled the role Wonder, Inc. had intended—to be a constant presence, the one who followed through on promises and offered a fount of unconditional love.

"I'm worried we won't be able to be together." The usually upbeat MJ was somber.

I did my best to reassure her. "Honey, as far as I'm concerned, I'm with you for life. Even if you get tired of me someday, you'll have a hard time getting rid of me." I hoped she would smile but she didn't. It's hard to trust when trust has been broken. I knew I would hang in there no matter what, but MJ wasn't so sure.

In a matter of weeks MJ's mother lost her parental rights, and thus going home was no longer an option for MJ. Social workers sought to find a family who would adopt her, and three times she was moved. I saw MJ try her hardest to bond with the new parents, accept different rules, adjust to new schools, find new friends and just fit in. But every time she did these things, she was expected to do it all over again somewhere else.

The people who study the effects of the foster-care system on children say these kids experience more post-traumatic stress than war vets. Having now seen it up close, I understand.

Through each move I stayed connected, though the foster families lived many hours away. MJ told me she had high hopes for the second foster home. "The room they had fixed up for me was so pretty. I thought I could be happy there." When I visited after the third move and took her out to lunch, she was desperately unhappy.

At the noisy café, she leaned in close and said, "I told myself to just hang on, because I knew when you got here, you would make everything all right. Get me back to the other family quick, okay?"

I choked back tears. "Oh, MJ, I don't have these magical powers. I can't make everything all right. The only thing I can do is be your friend and love you through all the good times and bad times. I will hug you when you are sad. I will listen when you need to talk. I will be your cheerleader for life. Someday you are going to have a life of your own design and it's going to be wonderful." Now we were two broken hearts. Hers because I wasn't the hero she wanted me to be. Mine because I had to take away that illusion. I cried most of the way home.

Later I made plans with a stable near MJ to bring our borrowed pony for day trips so she could continue her riding lessons. I began to map out a routine and dream up new adventures. I knew there were some problems in the new family and that MJ was not doing well in school. I thought the foster-care people would give this patched-together family time to work everything out. I was wrong. The director of Wonder called. "Sorry to have to tell you this, but MJ has been moved yet again, and I don't have the new contact information. We'll just have to be patient."

What! Be patient? Are you kidding? I couldn't believe what I had just heard. Four moves in six months! I was angry. How could a system meant to protect these children bring so much additional trauma into their lives by shuffling them around? MJ was in a state of perpetual emotional whiplash. No one should have to endure this chaos, much less our vulnerable, powerless children. This time I wanted to shake things up… take some people down…bring the system to a reckoning. I vowed to call on my journalism skills to right this obvious wrong.

But the assault on the system would have to wait until Monday. Some weeks before, I had signed up to spend that weekend at a spiritual retreat, a monastery in the mountains, looking out over the sea. Within the first few hours I felt a tremendous calling. I kept sensing a message....*Be quiet. Lose the anger. Wait without judgment.* But what was happening to MJ and so many other foster children was just wrong. Something should be done. Then that message again. *Be still. Be open.* I listened. As hard as it was, I shed the anger and the judgment. I would hold a quiet vigil, because I had made a decision to trust this piercing message.

Monday afternoon the director of Wonder, Inc. called me. "MJ has a new foster home and guess where it is." Well, it could have been anywhere in the state. I wasn't in the mood for games. So to be flippant, I spat out the name of the unlikeliest place—the tiny country hamlet where I lived.

"Yes!" the director said. "That's where MJ's new home is."

"Don't be kidding around with me," I said.

"No, no kidding. In fact she lives just down the street from you," he replied.

God winked. I am sure of it. I was deeply humbled.

Three years have passed since I heeded God's message to lose the anger and wait. MJ is flourishing in a stable family with a foster mom and dad who have good values and great parenting skills. They, and I, are committed to helping MJ succeed in life. She is doing well in school and has joined the ranks of preteens everywhere, with girlfriends, sleepovers and a lot of giggling.

A few months ago she and I went to visit a friend of mine who operates a horse rescue center nearby—a place called the Grace Foundation. My friend, Beth, knew of my mentoring journey with MJ. She said, "If you are ready to adopt a horse,

I have one I have been saving for just the perfect home. MJ, would you like to meet Shiloh?"

And that is how Shiloh came to live in the front pasture at MJ's house. The horse had been badly neglected, starved and left in a barren field to die. MJ is taking excellent care of her horse, giving her plenty of good hay and clean water. The horse is groomed and stroked tenderly every day. MJ rides her on a nearby trail or bareback in the front field. Shiloh and MJ have a bond. They both know about betrayal and hardship.

The mare trots across the field in the morning as MJ walks from her house to the bus stop. It's not far. In the corner where the fencing meets, the horse can see her best friend being taken away in a big, noisy yellow box. She has no idea where. But she is willing to suffer the searing heat of the sun to wait there for MJ. Shiloh trusts her quiet vigil will end when her friend is returned in the afternoon. A passage from the Bible frames this scene: "In silence and in hope will be your strength."

As MJ steps from the bus and walks along the fence line to the house, the horse trots from the corner to the other end of the pasture to follow her home. They both have learned that love is worth waiting for. So have I.

★ ★ ★ ★ ★

A Life Measured in Dog Years

Hal Bernton

I married into the basset-hound breed.

One day in Twin Falls, Idaho, after running the Snake River Canyon from rim to rim, I met a slender, young woman at a post-race picnic. Her basset hound grabbed the sandwich in my hand, and the owner, Ann, soon claimed my heart.

That was more than twenty-five years ago. Since then, Ann and I have shared many memorable moments with the gentle, long-eared, keen-nosed and often stubborn hounds.

There were bassets at our wedding and one on our honeymoon.

When my newspaper career took us north to Alaska for eleven years, our bassets joined us as we hiked through grizzly country, fished for salmon and picked fall berries in alpine meadows. In one memorable experiment, we briefly hitched our bootee-clad basset, Homer, to an Iditarod racer's sled for a pull through the snow. But bassets as sled dogs never quite caught on.

When we moved to the Pacific Northwest, Ann decided she wanted to check out field trials, which give your hound a chance to match his scent and tracking skills against other bassets. We joined a small, eclectic band of basset-hound brethren who have kept field trialing alive in our region. Most come from Washington and Oregon, and a handful from as far away as Idaho and California.

These dogs were initially bred in France as low-slung hounds that could help hunters pursue small game. The field trials are a way to honor this hunting heritage. The trials are held along a stretch of land in southwest Washington that is piled with Mount St. Helens's ash dredged from a nearby river. This land has been reclaimed by a motley mix of Scotch broom, Himalayan blackberries and grasses, all of which provide prime cover for rabbits.

These competitions typically begin soon after daybreak. Most participants form a line, known as "the Gallery," and walk forward slowly, beating the bushes with sticks or poles in hopes of flushing out a bunny. Eventually, someone cries "Tallyho!" as a rabbit scurries out of the brush. Then two bassets are walked up to the point where the bunny was last seen. They are left on the bunny's trail for several minutes. That's enough time for two judges to decide which of the dogs does a better job of following the scent. (Hunting is forbidden at field trialing, and bassets are bred to flush out game, rather than track it down and pounce on it. And the dogs are caught and leashed long before they would have the chance to catch and harm the rabbits they pursue.)

At first, field trialing didn't hook me. I thought the people were too intense and the pace was awfully slow, and many of the dogs often were surprisingly uninterested in following the rabbit scents. My dog, Winston, was a complete bust

and finished far back in the pack. But Ann was not ready to give up on Winston. She was convinced he eventually would figure things out. He had been born at a humble kennel in Oregon's Willamette Valley, one that had not produced any renowned field-trial dogs. But on our walks and weekend outings, Winston always had his nose to the ground, so Ann was convinced his mythical "lightbulb," which one of our field-trial friends had talked about, would turn on.

It did. After a few field trials, Ann took Winston up to the point where the rabbit was first spotted. He inhaled deeply and began to howl. A wild, exuberant howl that he repeated again and again as he sniffed his way through the field. Winston took a red ribbon that day. In the months and years that followed, he won enough ribbons to gain the title of a champion. In 2008 he finally had enough placements to reach the highest level of achievement—grand field champion.

All this was not accomplished without controversy. Judges assess the dogs on a number of traits, such as desire, determination, endurance and "proper use of voice." Winston had plenty of critics who thought he was too quick to howl. Some called him a babbler who somehow fooled the judges by howling when he didn't really, truly smell a rabbit. Over time, the criticism eased, even if it did not fade entirely, as Winston aged and grew more refined in his approach. He would move more slowly, bark less often, and he once successfully followed a rabbit's scent across a difficult stretch of sandy roadway.

There was plenty of competitive fervor at the field trials, sometimes too much, as a few nasty disputes flared up. There was also romance. Though most of the field trialers were well into their fifties, sixties or even seventies, one younger couple began their courtship while tramping through tall creek-side

grass in search of rabbits. They ended up getting married. We all attended their wedding ceremony, held after a long day of field trialing. There were also sad moments. Some dogs died. Some field trialers died, and we tried to honor their passing by ensuring their dogs—brought down by surviving spouses—continued to compete.

In the spring of 2010 Winston was diagnosed with a blood cancer. Over the summer he gradually faded away. He would bleed internally, then regain strength and then bleed again. On our twenty-fifth wedding anniversary Ann and I went to stay at a hotel in the Columbia River Gorge. Winston was so weak that he had to be wheeled on the luggage cart to our room. He passed away the next day, and we buried him in our backyard.

Ann said she wouldn't get another basset for at least a year. The illness had been so long and drawn out, and she wasn't ready for another basset. She was upset that we had even tried to leave home on our anniversary. But it was awfully quiet at our house. Our two children had both left for college. At night it was just the two of us, and a lot of basset memories.

Last October I was driving down Interstate 5 near the basset-hound field-trial grounds. I realized there was a competition that weekend and stopped by to say hello. Everyone offered condolences about Winston's passing. Then a friend suggested we consider adopting a two-year-old basset named Maverick. He had spent two months with a family in Oregon. Things hadn't worked out, and he had just been returned to the kennel of his birth. Maverick had beautiful lines and those soulful basset eyes. He came right up to me at the field-trial grounds and put his paws on my lap. I gave him a hug and took a bunch of cell phone pictures of the dog to show Ann.

Today, Maverick is a much-loved member of our family,

although we think he sometimes struggles with our suburban lifestyle. Maverick had lived most of his puppyhood at a wonderful place, Tailgate Ranch Kennels on Whidbey Island, where he spent his days playing in the fields with his siblings. He was a country boy, and he initially seemed a bit insecure. He frequently sought to jump in our laps or snuggle up against us as we sat on the couch. And he could be spooked by small things, such as the sound of rattling paper.

But he was passionate about hunting. That made walking a chore, as he strained on his leash and often refused to move past a promising scent of a squirrel or cat. So in the spring we brought Maverick to the field trials. In his first competition he was a dud, just like Winston had been. But the second time around, he came to the line and gave a howl. Then another and another as he raced off through the Scotch broom.

The Green Collar

Sheryl J. Bize Boutte

Dogs were not among my mother's favorite things. Begged for and then promptly neglected by each of her five daughters, or promising and then failed watchdogs for my father, they were just an extra chore for my mother. On more than one occasion she would yell from some corner of the house, "If you don't feed that dog, you are going to find him stiff in the backyard!" Sometimes that threat would propel one of her girls into action, but more often, the playdate or the telephone call or the party would take precedence and the dog du jour's stay at our house would come to an end.

So it came as a complete and utter shock to all of us when one day in 1980, my mother came home with a fluffy brilliantly white toy poodle she had already named Pierre.

Somehow this Pierre had managed to break through Mom's decades-long avoidance of all things dog and capture her heart. Her devotion to him was proven even more when, at scarcely three months old, he required a serious and expensive operation. We thought for sure he would be counted among the "temporary" dogs we had growing up, but again to our surprise, Mom took him to the vet hospital, paid the bill without a word and walked the floor during his surgery as though he were one of her children. It was clear that Mom and Pierre had a special bond, and looking back, I think even he knew it.

Pierre fit perfectly into Mom's life at that point. At a moment when her children sometimes placed conditions on giving her time and attention, Pierre was constant and unwavering in his loyalty. He asked no questions, never talked back and did not have any other obligations. He was calm, quiet and stealthily present, an escape from the sometimes raucous sibling rivalry, which often shattered mom's peace. He looked her in the eyes when she spoke to him and seemed to listen and understand. It was as though their destinies had been divinely intertwined by forces beyond our control or understanding. And even though he was "Mom's dog," he was always happy to see us and, acting as the perfect host, greeted us warmly when we arrived at the front door to the family home.

Then, in 1981, at the young age of fifty-three and scarcely a year after bringing Pierre home, my mother died suddenly. The shocking loss of the person who was literally the glue that held us together created a fracture in our family that has never been mended. Pierre grieved along with us during those dark days of turning off life support and during the heavy emptiness that followed. Like us he shunned food, looked for her in the house and inhaled the lingering scent of Youth-Dew in her clothes to invoke her presence. During this time, Pierre transitioned from Mom's beloved pet to the living vessel in which memories of her were stored.

When my father could no longer live with the memories that filled the house he had shared with my mother, he took

Pierre with him to his new house and later to a small apartment, after the last of my sisters got married and moved away. The cramped apartment soon became too small for the lively and energetic Pierre. It was then that Pierre came to live with my husband, my young daughter and me.

Struggling against the leash my father held, freshly groomed and decorated with a new bright green collar, Pierre pranced across the threshold of our front door. After greeting the three of us, he ran through his new home, exploring each room. While it was understood that Pierre had an extended family, it was also clear that he would live out the rest of his days with us. During the ensuing years, Pierre kept my mom ever present and brought us joy, calm and unfettered, pure devotion. His regard for us enhanced our regard for each other. He was regal and anointed, with the countenance of a true gentleman.

With his seven pounds of assumed swagger, he ruled his backyard kingdom, protecting it from raccoon, cat or bird interlopers who dared to set foot on his hallowed turf. He could jump three times his height and never licked a face without permission. We laughed when he would bare his teeth and bark to protect us from strangers or perceived harm. When an acquaintance came to visit and unkindly referred to him as a "little rat," he was forever banned from our home.

No matter the season, when the sun would reach a certain point in the sky, Pierre would use his nose to turn over his bowl, signaling he was ready to eat. The sound of the electric can opener would send him bounding into the kitchen in anticipation of food. He loved to ride in the car, running from the back to the front and to the back again, never disturbing the driver. He luxuriated in bubble baths and would turn over without prompting for the soothing heat of the blow-dryer. And while he was undemanding and patient, he was every inch the proud and high-stepping poodle. He was happiest after grooming and would throw his head and shoulders back and strut with the bearing of a lion.

When I used my air popper to make popcorn, Pierre would scoop up the flying kernels from the kitchen floor. (To this day, when I use that air popper and have to get the broom to sweep up the errant kernels, my husband and I will say in unison, "Where is Pierre when we need him?") When we needed a hug, Pierre would place his face on our shoulder, and we could almost hear him tell us everything would be all right. Pierre was our unruffled constant when we needed it most.

In 1995 it became clear that Pierre's health was failing. By then he was seventy-six in dog years and had lost sight in one eye and most of his teeth. He was no longer the luminous white ball of boundless energy, but a lethargic, yellowing shadow of himself. As it had happened many years before with my mother, it became clear that life was leaving him and we had to make a decision.

So while our daughter, who could not bear to say goodbye, packed the rented minivan we were using to drive her to college, my husband and I took Pierre for his last car ride to the vet. The vet took one look at Pierre and told us his time had come. On a hot August day, on what would have been my mother's sixty-ninth birthday, my husband and I tearfully removed Pierre's green collar and said our goodbyes.

We drove home in silence. There were no words. We immersed ourselves in the other life-changing event before us: our daughter leaving home for her freshman year of college. We had planned it this way on purpose so we would not have time to dwell on the loss of Pierre. We were forced to focus on what was ahead.

★ ★ ★

There is no doubt in my mind that Pierre came at the right time for all of us. For my mom, he was the one who doted on her when all others seemed to have fallen away. And during what turned out to be the last year of Mom's short life, Pierre gave her the gift of unconditional love. For the rest of us, Pierre was the only thing that remained calm and steady after she died, a time of family upheaval and change. He filled a void that would have been left open and unresolved. He was a connection to my mother that we all needed to keep from falling off the cliff. He was also an entity unto himself, independently loved and cherished.

Every now and then, I open the desk drawer in the kitchen and look at the green collar. It still contains small tufts of Pierre's fur. After all these years I am still amazed at the power this ten-inch slash of fabric has to evoke such strong emotion and vivid recollection. Holding it in my hand starts the video of Pierre gazing up at Mom. Then, as the camera is pulled back and the image widens, Mom's smiling face comes into the frame. As a physical manifestation of memory, the collar provides the tangible closeness Mom and I always shared and I continue to need.

I could stretch out the green collar and encase it in a frame. I could hang it from my rearview mirror or have it sewn into a quilt. But I prefer to keep it unencumbered but latched, as if to form the halo I am sure still floats above Pierre's head.

★ ★ ★ ★ ★

Growing Together

Louise Crawford

When I first met my dog Lily, she was living with a foster-dog mom. I drove about an hour to get to the foster home, intending to meet a short-haired, small black dog that would fit my house and my backyard. However, when the foster-doggy mom opened the door, my eyes were drawn to another dog, which stood amid this herd of barking dogs, not making a peep.

She just stared up at me with her big brown eyes and trembled. This dog was clearly terrified, and so was I. I felt an instant sympathetic bond, but what if she wasn't a dog looking for a home? What if she belonged to the household? And what if I really wasn't ready for this dog ownership step?

"What can you tell me about this one?" I asked the woman in charge, pointing at the orange-and-white, fluffy-eared sweetie. "Is that your dog or a foster dog?"

She looked down at the trembling dog. "Her? Oh, she's new. Just came in. We haven't even gotten her photo up on the website yet. We're calling her Lily."

My heart leapt, and I blurted, "That's the dog I want!"

Immediately I regretted saying it. The thought of having my own dog and being completely responsible for it was something I was really struggling with. Yes, I know most of the world is at ease with the idea of owning a pet, but not me. It had taken me three years in counseling to get to this point. My childhood was a hard one, and the aftereffects have left me with serious issues of self-worth, particularly when it comes to doing or having something that is just for me. Not for others, just for me. A dog would be just for me, and secretly I still wondered whether I deserved that.

When I bent down to get closer, I noticed one of Lily's ribs poked out and she shook in terror. Had she been mistreated, too? I didn't try to pet her but just stayed still. She was so small. I looked up at the foster mom. "What kind of dog is Lily?"

"The vet thinks she's part papillon and part Chihuahua," she said. With a laugh, she added, "Her ears could be from either breed."

Lily's ears reminded me of a fruit bat's. They stood up like two radar dishes on the top of her head, alert for any threatening sound. This was not a dog that would relax and trust easily.

At the foster mom's suggestion I went to the couch and sat down. Within minutes Lily had jumped up and settled on my lap. It was love. This was the dog I wanted. Because Lily was so new, I couldn't take her with me that day. I had paperwork to complete, and she needed to be spayed and have a tracking chip implanted so she'd never get lost again.

I stayed and stroked Lily's soft fur, hating to leave her there. Then I went home and told my daughter happily, "I found a dog!" I'd initially wanted a short-haired dog that wouldn't shed, but once I met Lily, I didn't care if I had dog hair all over my house, or if my house smelled like "furry animals."

It became more obvious that Lily had been mistreated, as well as abandoned, when my daughter and I drove out to pick her up the next week. Lily still didn't make a sound, while all the other dogs barked in excitement at the door. This time I noticed the poky rib again and how she retreated when I came near her, then nipped at me when I tried to pet her, letting me know I was moving too fast.

I sat on the couch with my daughter and the foster mom, and we chatted while Lily slowly gathered her courage and came into the room. After a few minutes she jumped up onto the couch between my daughter and me. We both let her smell us and finally she let us pet her.

Armed with dog food, a book on dog behavior and the name of a vet for emergencies, we drove home. Little Lily rested on a soft green blanket on my daughter's lap. She poked her head up once in a while to peer out the window, but other than that, she stayed put and made no sound. Once we were home, I put Lily's blanket on a small beanbag chair in the living room. It was meant to be her bed. She lay down on it, her eyes wide with fear, her little body shaking, and didn't move all evening. Before bedtime I took her into the backyard and she peed. Then I brought her back inside and she slept on her bed all night.

I planned to do this right—I wasn't going to just plop a dog in my house and expect it all to work. I'd taken a week's vacation from work so we could get to know each other. Our first day I hung out with her and watched her explore the house. When I sat on the couch to watch TV, she sat next to me. That night she slept on the couch instead of her bed.

I'd never imagined I would let a dog sleep on the couch,

or anywhere except on its bed or in its crate, but here I was, happy to let her sleep on the double recliner. I stood in the doorway, smiling down at the sleeping dog. This adorable little fluff ball, all curled up in the corner of the armrest was my watchdog! *Life would be perfect,* I thought, *now that I have a dog to call my own.*

But the next morning Lily wheezed and coughed like she was trying to cough up a hair ball. She sounded like she might die. What had gone wrong already? What didn't I do right? Terrified, I put her in her crate and drove to the vet. She whimpered and clawed and cried the entire drive, which was horrendous, because it was New Year's Eve and the traffic was awful. It took an hour to get there. She was scratching to get out of the crate, crying and coughing like I was the meanest owner in the world, and her new mom was a basket case.

You know what they say about owners? That if the dog has a problem, treat the owner. Well, I think the vet saw that I was not coping well: my tears and my statement "I think my dog's dying!" clued her in. She ushered Lily and me into a room, came in and calmed us both down, then took Lily in the back to examine her. By the time she placed Lily back in my arms, I was no longer hyperventilating or crying.

"Lily has kennel cough and needs antibiotics," the lady vet said, smiling reassuringly. "I'll give her a prescription, and you can pay for it out front."

As I held this warm, wonderful fluff ball in my arms, I realized that in my panic, I'd left my purse, my wallet and, most important, my Visa card at home. I tried calling home, but my daughter wasn't there, so after being reassured Lily would be fine, I drove home with her, got her settled and drove back to the vet to pay for the medicine. Happy New Year!

The next few days I watched Lily anxiously, waiting for her

cough to go away. The first sign she felt better, and safer, was when she went to the front window and barked at a passing car. This was Lily's first bark! For a little dog, she had a fierce bark, but I didn't want her barking all day, so I encouraged her to go to the window and look out before barking, using my voice and treats.

During the week I was home, I worked with her, teaching her to sit, lift her paw and shake, and "dance." She liked dancing for treats best! I'm currently playing fetch with her and teaching her the commands "jump" and "down." She taught me, as well. After she spent a couple of nights on the couch, when her cough worried me, I put her doggy blanket on a chair next to my bed and let her sleep there. After two more nights, she was sleeping on the end of my bed, then right beside me, curled up in the small of my back or the crook of my legs. At first I worried that I might injure her when I moved in my sleep, but I quickly learned that if I moved, she moved. She was quite adept at taking care of herself.

When I took her to a local vet to make sure she was over the kennel cough and to get heartworm and flea medicine, I discovered that Lily seemed terrified of men. One look at the male vet, who was not at all threatening, and she peed on the steel table, shook, then barked. When he tried to put a muzzle on her, she was not having any of that, and I was so traumatized by then, I thanked him and took Lily home. I could see that the two of us both had healing work to do.

In the meantime, I tried to bulk her up. Taking a tip from the movie *As Good as It Gets*—if you ever saw the movie, you may remember the scene where Jack Nicholson feeds bacon to Greg Kinnear's dog—I started adding in a tablespoon of bacon bits to her food. Uh-oh. Big mistake. She loved the bacon, but she also started putting on weight!

When I took her for a six-month checkup to a female vet who had been recommended by a friend and was close to home, the vet told me, "Your dog needs to lose about two pounds." Since I teach weight management classes (as well as write suspense, romance and fantasy fiction), imagine my chagrin at hearing *my* dog was overweight. I worked on eating a healthy, low-fat diet, yet I was feeding my dog bacon. I left the vet's office determined to stop the bacon treats cold turkey and stick to dog food for Lily.

Of course, my resolve nearly crumbled when Lily gave me the biggest sad-eyed stare the next morning, her sweet little face asking, "Where's the bacon?" Oh, dear. This wasn't going to be easy, was it? The vet had warned me, "Small dogs are notoriously good at getting their owners to feed them bad foods," so I steeled myself with the knowledge Lily would live a longer, healthier life if she was fed properly, then went and bought appropriate doggy treats for small dogs, along with some "banquet-style" food made by the same company that made her dry food. I mixed a fourth of the can of wet food in with her dry food twice a day. At first she held off eating, to see if I'd relent and feed her bacon again, but once she accepted the bacon was gone for good, she ate her food—sometimes with a mournful expression. I wonder if after two and a half years, she dreams about bacon?

Over the next few years, Lily and I slowly fell into a routine. We walked about thirty minutes in the morning; then I fed her and went to work. When we first started our walks, Lily barked in warning at every car, person and dog we passed. Gradually, over time, she went from full-out barks to mild warning growls, to curiously sniffing at other dog owners and their dogs in brief "meet and greets."

When I asked my daughter, who was in and out of the

house for college classes, what she and Lily did while I was at work, my daughter laughed. "She just sleeps on your bed or your pillow all day, then races to the door when you get home." Before I put my key in the dead bolt, Lily was on the other side of the door, waiting joyously for me to come in, her tail wagging so hard, I thought she'd wag it off, her little body jumping up and down with excitement, and her rather long tongue trying to get a few kisses in when I crouched down to pet her and say hello. She really did become my dog, a dog solely focused on me.

Nothing gets healed overnight, and we both still have scars from our early years. Lily still has one rib that sticks out, perhaps the remnants of a swift kick to the side when she was a small puppy. She is still skittish around strangers. I'm still working to heal emotional wounds from my childhood. But together, Lily and I can focus on the present rather than the past.

★ ★ ★ ★ ★

The Improbable Cat Lover

Jennifer O'Neill-Pickering

I had always thought of myself as a dog person. This was because of a country upbringing, where our dogs performed double and even triple duties: herding animals, policing the property and serving as a family member before this was fashionable. I didn't grow up with cats that were pets. Cats took care of varmints in the barn.

This changed in my early thirties, when my friend had to choose between her apartment and a kitten that, her landlord said, "wasn't part of the rental agreement." She called on the phone in tears, asking if I'd consider adopting her half-grown cat, Lady.

"Well, I'm not exactly a cat person," I said. "Let me think about it after I meet Lady." We made a date for me to meet her pet the next day.

I sat in her studio apartment, looking down at Lady, who had already done loopy loops around my pant legs, marking me as part of her territory. *What a sweet cat,* I thought as she jumped in my lap and curled up into a purring ball.

"Well, it looks like someone's already made up her mind," I observed.

The next day I called my friend to say, "Yes, I'd take her." As we drove away, I thought about all the positives of having a cat. People with cats had lower blood pressure, and didn't cat owners live longer than people without felines? I recalled a story my supervisor had shared. Her pet had the habit of using her as a human trampoline and had discovered a lump in her breast, which turned out to be a cancerous tumor. The cat had saved her life. With these thoughts swirling around in my mind, I drove Lady to her new home. My friend had assured me that Lady was not a "hunter" and that no "feathered" or "furry" gifts would be deposited on my front porch or on bed pillows. Thankfully, she was correct in this prediction.

When Lady first came home, she stepped right out of her crate, walking like she had just graduated from kitty-cat charm school. She jumped up on my favorite living room wingback chair, a queen on her throne. She was stubborn and wasn't going to give up the chair. If I sat in it, she'd join me and then climb on its top and pretend she was a warm scarf, wrapping around my neck and shoulders. I decided she might need her own chair and so I bought another—for myself. She also decided quickly that the bed was a more comfortable place to sleep than the cat bed I'd provided. If she slept on the bed, she deserved a soft pillow to spin dreams on.

She was called Lady because she walked like a lady in four dainty white boots. These contrasted with her jet-black coat and the white diamond pinned on her chest. She also could have been named Diamond. Her eyes were almond shaped and the color of amber and seemed to read minds. Chatty might have been another suitable name for Lady, because she always had something to say and talked nonstop from the moment I stepped through the door.

She was quite the social butterfly, which was a surprise, because I'd read cats were solitary in nature and territorial. Not true of Lady. She had two neighborhood chums: a rotund tabby and an enormous Russian blue. The pride liked to hang out on top of the garage and watch the goings-on of the neighborhood. Each night, when I pulled into the driveway, Lady greeted me feetfirst, jumping on the hood of my car from the roof of the garage.

Eventually, I met a wonderful man and we bought a house in a new neighborhood. Lady was not pleased and sulked in one of the bedrooms for several days. She finally forgave us and quickly claimed her new space, marking all the furniture and doorjambs about the house. We did not yet have a cat door, but Lady soon adapted. One evening, as we sat with friends over glasses of wine, there came a knock at the door, followed by another.

"Are you expecting more guests?" one of our friends asked.

"Yes, just one," I replied. "Would one of you mind getting the door?"

Before one of them could reach the door, there was another knock.

"Whoever it is, is impatient," said our friend who'd offered to get the door. She opened the door, and there sat Lady, one paw lifted behind the screen door, ready to "knock" again.

Lady stopped, looked up with blinking amber eyes that asked, "What took you so long?"

Not long afterward, we introduced a new cat into our family, Mr. Peach. Lady soon taught him to knock on the door, too.

★ ★ ★

My husband was a musician and a music teacher. We had a piano in our living room for his students. Each week an assortment of them filed in and out of our house for their piano lessons. Lady was an astute student, too, and took a seat on top of the piano during the lessons. We soon learned she had a good ear, because cats can't read music, can they?

One blistering mid-July evening, we sat in lawn chairs on the back deck, sipping lemonade and fanning ourselves. The Delta breeze from the coast had finally begun to rustle the old walnut tree, announcing autumn's arrival and the promise of relief from the heat. The screen door was open and we heard the tinkle of piano keys. The music stopped and started again, this time with more bravado. We crept into the house, curious to see who the musician was. Lady strolled back and forth across the keys, playing her dissonant repertoire, and then stopped and took a bow, pointing her head toward her two outstretched paws.

Over time I learned Lady had eclectic tastes in the arts. I had studied fine art at SUNY Buffalo in New York and had finished up my degree in California. I especially enjoyed watercolor for its fluidity and immediacy. But the one drawback of painting in watercolor is that once the color meets paper, the marriage is forever. I put a great deal of planning and thought into my paintings before putting the brush to paper. Sometimes my paintings take several months to complete.

I had been working on a large painting with complicated patterns entitled *Seated Woman with Camellias*. The color palette for this painting was purples, reds and blues applied in delicate layers of glazes. The painting was to be hung in a few days time in a local gallery. I often kept my tools of the trade—brushes, palette, paints and water—set up on my drawing board to make it easier to get right to the task.

The painting was complete and I decided to go out for lunch to celebrate with a friend. When I returned, I again looked at my painting to see if there were any finishing touches that needed to be made before it was framed. To my horror someone *had* made some changes. My eyes followed a trail of small muddy paw prints that led from the drawing board onto the painting. The tracks, of pale mud, thankfully were erasable. But what of that purple blotch on the neck of the woman in my painting? My eyes went from the purple blotch and then back to Lady, who sat in her chair, fastidiously grooming her paws. She looked up at me with her beautiful amber eyes, which asked, "What's wrong? Don't you like the improvements I made?"

★ ★ ★ ★ ★

Psychic Cat

Kathryn Canan

A recent article in Parade magazine compared the intelligence of cats and dogs. According to the author, Kalee Thompson, "dogs are ahead by a nose" since they recognize more words and can be trained to do intricate tasks, serving as sheepherders, police dogs and service dogs. Okay, I'll concede that point. Anyone who tried to use a cat as a guide would end up at the top of a tree or burrowed under the covers of the nearest soft bed. I do take issue, however, with defining intelligence as the ability to be trained to do particular tasks. Our orange tabby, Chewbacca, takes the prize for ingenious, complex problem solving and weird psychic talents.

Unkind family members have described him as a "basketball with a Ping-Pong ball for a head." Certainly Chewie defies the purpose of his prescription-diet cat food: he seems to be missing the off switch that tells him to stop eating when he is full. We recently had to purchase a new raccoon- and squirrel-proof automatic cat feeder for use on short vacations because he had learned to open the old feeder; he would use one claw to delicately pull aside the trapdoor and let the food out whenever he wanted. He had also developed Fonzie moves to set off the feeder—a good whop of the paw in just the right place would send a shower of food down the chute. This new feeder was developed by a man with a similarly ingenious cat. My husband and I are taking bets on how soon Chewie will be able to hack into it.

A helpful cat, our Chewie. When he began marking the carpet in several places near the south wall of our house, we thought he was showing his age or reacting to cats and squirrels running along the top of the fence outside. But no. Turns out we had severe dry rot on that side of the house, and if we had listened to Chewie sooner, we would not have had to buy my husband a whole new wall for his birthday last year. I appreciate Chewie's taste in interior decorating, too; the new oak flooring is a huge improvement over the dingy gray carpet.

Chewie's psychic abilities showed up early in his life. It's true that cats don't fetch the way dogs do, but our cat does have an uncanny ability to find lost objects. I play early music on recorders and early flutes, and although Chewie rudely escapes under the bed at the sight of my soprano recorder, he still tries to participate. Before a performance one year at a local Renaissance fair, I rushed around the house, madly looking for a piece of music I wanted to play that day. It was nowhere to be found. Finally my husband noticed that Chewie was sitting on top of a tall file cabinet, on which he had never jumped before. Slowly swinging his tail to get our attention, he was carefully guarding the very piece of music I was seeking: "A Catch on the Midnight Cats."

Even better than detecting dry rot or locating missing music, Chewie is able to read my emotional wrangling and provide succinct answers to my dilemmas. There was one night in particular when during dinner—nothing Chewie does is unrelated to food—he solved a particularly thorny problem for me.

Growing up, I played the modern flute and piccolo, but in my early thirties I discovered the vast and gorgeous early music repertoire for the recorder and early wooden flutes. I soon joined the local chapter of the American Recorder Society to meet others infected by this bug. I learned about repertoire and style from those who had immersed themselves in Renaissance and baroque music for many years. One woman in particular took me on as her project. She came to my house when my youngest child, Robin, was just a few months old, and we formed an ensemble called Robin's Nest, which rehearsed while Robin napped nearby.

Soon others joined us, and the members of this ensemble nurtured my new enthusiasm and became my closest musical friends. In many ways, a musical ensemble resembles a marriage. Several musicians may "date" each other in informal playing sessions, assessing both personal and musical compatibility. Once a group gels into a regular ensemble, members make a commitment to show up, practice and always give their best. The friendships that form can be intense, since the object of all our work is to create beauty. Leaving an ensemble, then, can feel like a divorce.

Eventually the time came when I was no longer musically satisfied playing with the members of Robin's Nest. We seemed unable to solve problems with intonation, rhythm and ensemble skills, and our repertoire was limited to a narrow period of Renaissance music. I wanted to explore other genres of recorder music—medieval, baroque and contemporary—and I was ready to play at a more professional level. I had already begun to play with other musicians who challenged me in new ways.

It was an agonizing decision. Could I really leave these talented people who meant so much to me? I talked to other musicians about it. I talked to my husband, to my son who is also a musician. I talked to the air, talked in my sleep and I talked to the cat. Everyone listened politely but in the end reminded me that it was my decision alone. The image that kept coming up was of a bird ready to spread its wings and leave the nest. Certainly Robin's Nest had nurtured me for several years, and I was profoundly grateful for that. Month after month I put off the decision, coming home from rehearsals tired and frustrated.

At last one night my husband and I sat at the table, dinner over and the dishes before us. Once again I brought up the topic and said sadly, "I am so ready to leave the nest, the Robin's Nest." My husband sighed, dreading another evening of worrying over the same old topic, to go or stay. He was tired of the discussion. And apparently so was Chewie. In a sudden rush of loud movement he came through the cat door, jumped up on the table and deposited a dead bird on my now empty plate. Placing one paw on the dead bird, he sat up and looked proudly at me. "The bird has left the nest," I choked out when I had stopped laughing uncontrollably. My decision was made.

And it wasn't so bad, after all. My ensemble imported a new member who also played harpsichord. They added baroque music to their repertoire and two members took up the viola da gamba. My departure let them grow in new ways, and our friendships have stayed strong. Recently I have found myself remembering that episode, because I am now facing an empty nest of my own. Robin has just left for college, and Chewie's blunt nesting advice is useful once more.

My husband and I saw all the signs of a teenager ready to

leave home during her senior year of high school. Seniori-tis hit hard, and we sympathized with her tirades over "stupid English poetry packets." She observed curfews but came home not a second too early. Family meals gave way to quick bites grabbed at fast-food restaurants or her own creative pasta concoctions. Somehow I found myself asking permission to use my own car, since her schedule was so full with swim team, film projects and an intricate social life. The college decision was really quite easy; Robin gave serious consideration only to colleges more than three hundred miles away. She wouldn't be popping home on weekends.

Chewie took to sleeping on Robin's bed.

My cousin once told me that when your kids are ready to leave home, you're ready to let them go. I repeated that mantra to everyone who asked me how I felt, hoping I would manage to believe it. When the day came at last, we drove nine hours to her new home and, feeling a bit like rats in a maze, navigated the tightly scheduled move-in procedure. We finished hauling her stuff upstairs to her dorm room, helped her make up her new bed and met her roommate. Suddenly the awkward moment arrived.

"So," she asked, "how long do you want to hang around?"

Chewie and the bird flashed into my mind. "I think we're ready to go." And we were.

Chewie is fourteen years old now, limping slightly from arthritis, and I doubt if he can ever again catch a bird or jump up on the table. But I look forward to his sage advice again, should I ever need it.

★ ★ ★ ★ ★

Maggie

Jerry and Donna White

My wife looked up from the newspaper she'd been reading. "You have to go get this dog."

A dog? We hadn't had a dog in years; our beloved Petunia and Whippet had spoiled us from any possible replacements.

She held the paper out toward me. "Read it. The dog is deaf. No one wants her." I knew by the tone in her voice, we were about to get a new dog.

"But what will I do with a deaf dog?" I asked.

"Train it," my wife replied.

"How can I train a deaf dog?" I pleaded.

"Teach it sign language," she said.

After years of marriage, I knew when I'd been overruled, and the very next day I went to the local pound.

Maggie was a cutie, a half-sized Dalmatian mix with a bobbed tail of all black. Maggie was only a couple months old. It was love at first sight. Attached as I had been to our old black labs, there was something about this little one I could not resist.

From the get-go Maggie was always super-alert to her surroundings. Unable to hear what was going on around her, she had to continually turn her head to be aware of events. When I took Maggie to the fields behind our house for our daily walk, I noticed she would keep a close watch on me. Even when she chased rabbits, she would periodically stop to check on my whereabouts.

As my wife predicted, I taught Maggie sign language. She learned three signals: "Come here," "Stop doing that" and "Look or go over there." We had had two dogs before, and they were all much smarter than me. Maggie was the smartest. She quickly learned to obey my hand signals, but she also realized that she did not have to obey the signals if she did not see them. Maggie developed the habit of not looking directly at me when she had a different idea of what she wanted to do next. She would face slightly to the left or right and could see me only from the corner of her eye. As soon as I gave a hand signal that Maggie did not agree with, she would turn a blind eye and proceed to do as she pleased, even if it meant on several occasions that a deaf dog was crossing a road. Maggie was lucky, as well as smart.

Friendly by nature and always sure of an enthusiastic welcome, Maggie liked to go visiting in the neighborhood. Of course, we had a dog-proof fence, but why should that have slowed her down? There were places to go and people to see.

The sight of someone calling out to his or her dog at the end of a day in an effort to bring it home is a common one— calling the dog's name hopefully at first, then impatiently for a few more minutes, and finally shouting the dog's name in anger before stomping back into the house with a muttered, "Your dog is gone again." But what do you do when the dog is deaf? You make it a point to learn all her visiting spots and check each one when it appears that she has once again climbed a tree.

Maggie's favorite place to visit was the neighborhood Waldorf School on the Unitarian Church grounds. She quickly became a favorite of the children, who called her by name amid a lot of petting. Of course, one of the teachers had to bring Maggie home.

"The children really like Maggie and they always look to see if she is waiting for them at recess," the young teacher said. "She is so cute and friendly. The children want to bring her into the classroom but we cannot allow that."

Maggie visited the school and church grounds many times before we discovered her tree-climbing trick. If Maggie went visiting and school was not in session, she would explore the church. More than once the church administrative assistant called me to inform me that Maggie was there. "Hello, Jerry? Well…Maggie is attending church again." She'd climb on a front-row bench and appear to show great interest in the proceedings. Nobody seemed to mind, but nobody was sure which set of religious beliefs she was observing. She liked all the groups but seemed especially fond of the Buddhist services. Everyone in that group knew her by name.

Since she was a puppy, she'd slept beside our bed, on my side. I still wake at night and reach down to make sure she is covered by her blanket, only to remember she is sleeping in our flower garden. We had to put her down at age twelve. Maggie has been in the garden for over three years now. We miss her every day.

★ ★ ★ ★ ★

Roxanne

Gordon M. Labuhn

It looked like a small, fuzzy black rock in the center of a busy four-lane street. Out of curiosity, I scooped it up as Karen and I zigzagged between cars on our way to get a steaming cup of coffee at our favorite greasy-spoon café. The fuzz ball was wet, soft, and it wiggled. The newborn's eyes were still matted shut.

"It's a kitten!"

In our café booth, we sipped our brew and Karen dipped her napkin into a glass of water to administer a therapeutic bath. Other customers gathered around our booth to see what we'd found and to share in the rescue. For a bassinet, the waitress loaned us a large coffee cup lined with a napkin. The kitten was so tiny that her head didn't even clear the rim. We named our newborn Rocky before we realized its gender; then we renamed her Roxanne.

Like every newborn, Roxanne required and received considerable TLC. We set up a nursery in the bathroom and embarked on a journey to save her. No matter what we tried, we couldn't get her to take nourishment. With an eyedropper, we thought we succeeded in getting one or two drops of warm milk into Roxanne's mouth, but we weren't sure.

In desperation, we rushed to the local veterinarian's office. Gently the vet examined our tiny friend and we were given ointment for her infected eyes. "You should know this now," the vet said gently. "She isn't likely to survive." Instantly, Karen and I became undaunted, determined to win her battle for life. Roxanne had no one but us to care for her.

Karen, a registered nurse, took her ten days of accrued vacation time to work a miracle. Our six-year-old neighbor, Julie, volunteered to be an assistant nursemaid. Young girls are a great help to newborn kittens during the day, but nights were a struggle.

Our rescue Roxanne's routine went like this: every forty-five minutes, day and night, the eyedropper wet kitty's lips with warm milk, and four times a day the ointment was applied to her eyes. After two days Roxanne's eyes were getting better. Ours, on the other hand, were getting redder. Sleep deprivation chipped away at our stamina.

Progress in feeding was slow, but with persistence nourishment dribbled into our infant drop by drop. On day four Roxanne tried to walk. Wobbly and unsure, she promptly fell into a saucer of milk. It was drink or drown. She quickly weaned herself off the eyedropper. We cried.

Like every parent of a newborn, we worried about what the future would hold. Young Julie had fallen in love with Roxanne and was desperate to keep her, but pets weren't allowed in her family's complex. Both Karen and I traveled for business frequently; we couldn't take care of her long term. Once Roxanne was over her initial survival crisis, we planned to seek a permanent home for her.

Karen taught Julie how to knit, and together they made a

one-inch-wide, five-inch-long soft strip, which I dubbed a bookmark. When Roxanne was not sleeping on the bookmark, she played with it vigorously. She was becoming a wide-eyed scamp, always on the move. Her prognosis for life turned from gloomy to hopeful.

The twists and turns in a kitten's life are not much different than for any vulnerable newborn. I was scheduled as a guest speaker at a meeting in a Springfield, Illinois, hospital. Roxanne couldn't be left alone, of course, so at the age of three weeks she had her first long-distance car trip in a towel-lined cardboard box. She was accompanied by a saucer, a baby bottle of milk, a dab of soft kitten food and her woven bookmark. Karen came along on the trip and planned to wait for me in the car and read while Roxanne slept.

On my way to the meeting room in the hospital I passed a nursing station. One nurse was crying softly as her coworkers gathered around her.

"Anything I can do to help?" I asked.

A nurse at the edge of the small group shook her head sadly, still looking at her friend, while she whispered to me, "Oh, it's so sad. This morning she accidently ran over her daughter's kitten."

Ah, I could help, after all. I whispered in return, "Don't let her leave. I'll be right back."

Believe me, there is no greater pleasure in this world than to give a gift of love to a wounded soul. Karen and I brought in Roxanne with her box, saucer, bottle of milk and yarn bookmark. Willeen, the crying nurse, adopted Roxanne quicker than a cat could blink. She left work with the goal of taking her daughter out of school for the day to have a healing celebration. We had found a permanent home for Roxanne where the bonds of affection would be strong.

Story's end? Not quite!

A year later it was my good fortune to be scheduled for a return visit to Springfield. On our trip Karen and I reminisced about our experience in saving Roxanne. Was she still alive? Did she have any major health problems? Would we get a chance to see her? When we arrived at the hospital, our questions were answered by Willeen, who was waiting for us at the door.

"Roxanne is fine. Would you like to see her?"

"Yes, we would love to," we said in unison. A quick trip to Willeen's home during the lunch hour was arranged.

It was a thrill for Karen and me to see Roxanne comfortably lounging in an old apple tree. She was so black and silky, so at peace with her life. *Amazement* is a weak word to describe our shock in discovering the tattered and faded yarn bookmark draped over Roxanne's perch. We coaxed her to come down. Roxanne picked up her bookmark, came down the tree bottom first, made a beeline to her cat door and disappeared into the safety of her home.

"I can't believe it," I said. "She still has the bookmark that Julie made, after all this time."

"Yes," Willeen said. "She carries it everyplace she goes. Last year I washed it, and she sat on top of the washing machine and meowed the whole time it was being washed. I felt so sorry for her that I gave it back to her without putting it in the dryer."

Roxanne still holds a place in our hearts. I like to think that Karen and I, like the bookmark we gave her, hold a small place in hers, too.

★ ★ ★ ★ ★

High Energy

Mark Lukas

I t's a crisp, sunny Sunday afternoon in Central Florida as Zak heads down the driveway and turns his truck onto the street, towing his new Jet Ski and trailer behind him. A placid golf course community with dogwood-lined streets, our new neighborhood is perfect for a family of four. *We'll all be happy here,* I think, still standing in the garage with tools in my hand, as Zak turns and waves to me. This is the last time I'll see my sixteen-year-old son alive.

Just minutes before we'd had a father-son chuckle together as Zak searched for bolts to install the new license plate on the trailer. Listening to his fingers riffle through the metal in the nuts-and-bolts storage bin, I asked him what he was looking for. "I need bigger nuts," he answered back casually. Immediately he froze when he registered what he'd said to his dad. He turned and looked over at me with a sly smile. He knew what a mistake that comment was.

Sixteen-year-old boys have very little fear; they all think they're invincible. Zak and his friend from the high school soccer team, Jason Lewis, died that night when the Jet Ski sucked up a line from a crab trap, disabling the engine. They'd set out into the Gulf of Mexico at about 2:00 p.m., and when Zak didn't show up for dinner with our friends that night, we tried not to worry. A cold front blew in from the North, and the Coast Guard would not search over the water because of the fog. A fishing boat found the boys nine miles out the next morning. They hadn't made it through the night, dying of hypothermia.

Zak's death was the beginning of the end of my life as I knew it. My twenty-year marriage dissolved; my relationship with my daughter faltered. I lost my whole family the day Zak died.

Zak was my hero. His life was full. He lived to play. He was very popular and he loved people. I think his goal in life was to make people laugh. His popularity came from being a great athlete; he was always one of the first picked and everyone wanted to be on Zak's team. True, Zak was not a good loser, but he was often a winner. By the time he was twelve, he was dribbling a soccer ball past me and his soccer coach, laughing as he zipped by. He played soccer at a high level on a traveling competitive team, and he played varsity soccer as a high school freshman.

Zak didn't like working out alone with a soccer ball. At a professional soccer game we'd gone to watch as a family, he thought he spotted the answer to this dilemma: during the opening ceremony an amazing border collie dribbled a soccer ball with incredible speed and skill. We met up with the owner after the game.

Zak reached down to pet the border collie and asked, "What's the dog's name?"

"Silk," the proud owner told us.

That was it. We were hooked on the idea of having a soccer dog like Silk in our family.

"Zak, if you had a dog like Silk, would you put down the video games and go outside for soccer every day?" I asked him.

He smiled and nodded.

We purchased an Australian shepherd with the intent of teaching her how to play soccer. Did it really happen? No. With our busy lives, no one put the time into the training. Instead of being a soccer dog, Kobe ended up being really good with a Frisbee.

Soon after Zak's death I found myself living alone. It was time to try and teach a dog how to play soccer. It was, I thought, a way in which I could feel somehow close to Zak. I derived some small comfort in following through on something we'd talked about doing together. When I went to pick out a border collie pup, there were two males roughing each other up and a scrawny little female who just sat there and watched her brothers fight. I pointed at the female. "I'll take that one." I named her Ms. Z after Zak. At first she was an awful lot like Zak—feisty and high maintenance, full of energy and very demanding. How could I channel this into soccer playing?

Turned out that I owned the perfect training ground—a fourplex housing unit. One of the units needed a new floor put in, and to save money, I was doing the work myself, down on my hands and knees every day, putting in new tile. The puppy would go with me every day and roam around the apartment while I tried to get things done. Of course, she wanted to play. To keep her occupied, I had a hard rubber ball that was really too big for Ms. Z to get her mouth around. I tossed the ball and she chased it. A simple game.

She would whine and talk to the ball, venting her frustration and inability to get her mouth around it. Once she maneuvered the ball back to me, I stopped whatever I was doing and I heaped big praise on her and then threw the ball again. After a couple days of this and no small amount of doggy swearing and frustration, she finally learned how to maneuver the ball to me. One day something seemed to click in her mind: she realized that she had to bring me that ball if she wanted me to play with her.

Anyone who has ever spent time with a border collie knows that they need a job. Bred to herd, if they don't have something to do, if they don't have several hours of exercise a day, it won't be pretty. Sooner or later they will eat your house. Soccer became Ms. Z's job. She was getting pretty good at it, too. After a few weeks of playing soccer every day, we went to visit my sister and her twin eight-year-old girls. One of the girls tossed the ball to Ms. Z and she caught it! I still remember their excitement and astonishment.

Catching a soccer ball between her wide open mouth and her paws has become Ms. Z's signature statement. As time went on, Ms. Z really started to think all humans were born to play soccer with her and she would adore anyone who would touch a soccer ball. She would play with anyone. It didn't matter where you were or what you were wearing. If you touched the ball, then you became her instant best friend.

I started to wonder just how far this could go. I went out and purchased two female border collie pups and named them Sweeper and Keeper, and did they ever live up to their names. Then I found Bek—yes, he is named after David Beckham—in a litter of brown-and-white border collie puppies. My intention was to become a soccer dog breeder and trainer. With three females and one male, this would be the start of something big. Soccer Collies was formed.

Soccer Collies is much different today than when we started. The business has evolved from a one-on-one encounter with a soccer dog to a group activity. Here's a description of what we do: groups of kids ages two to ninety-two play the goalkeeper position as an incredibly talented soccer dog scores goals. A lot of goals! It's a competition involving speed and agility, as the dogs quickly show their human competitors who has faster feet. There's always laughter, especially when adults play against the dogs.

In the past years Soccer Collies have worked everywhere—from companies like Google and Purina to sports organizations like Major League Soccer and Women's Professional Soccer. My dogs have entertained the crowd at places like the U.S. Open, Nokia Plaza and the Staples Center.

Training soccer dogs and promoting the soccer dog movement have become my life's purpose. Nothing will ever replace my son, Zak, but working with the dogs gave me a reason to live again.

★ ★ ★ ★ ★

About the Contributors

Elaine Ambrose
Elaine Ambrose is the co-author of *Menopause Sucks* and *Drinking with Dead Women Writers*. Her short stories and feature articles appear in several anthologies and magazines, and she owns Mill Park Publishing. She organizes "Write by the River" writers' retreats in Idaho and creates a sassy blog called "Midlife Cabernet." Find more details at www.ElaineAmbrose.com.

Hal Bernton
Hal Bernton is a journalist who works for *The Seattle Times*. He lives in Portland, Oregon, with his wife, Ann, and their basset hound, Maverick.

Sheryl J. Bize Boutte
Sheryl J. Bize Boutte is a Northern California writer and management consultant. More of her short stories, poetry and commentary can be seen at www.sjbb-talkinginclass.blogspot.com/.

Robyn Boyer

Robyn Boyer's daytime job is to write about public policy, politics and people. This is the first story she has written about animals. She lives in Sacramento, California, and has a daughter and a cat.

Maryellen Burns

Maryellen Burns has been involved in the word trade for more than forty years, working with writers, publishers, libraries and booksellers in editing, research, public relations and events planning. Her work has appeared in newspapers, literary anthologies, *Smithsonian* and *Cooking Light*. When not writing, she's engaged in helping others get their words on the page and into the marketplace. Visit her at booktalksacramento.blogspot.com.

Kathryn Canan

Whenever the family cabin in Montana is buried in snow, Kathryn Canan lives in California with her husband and two psychotic cats. She is a freelance writer, Latin tutor, and early music teacher and performer; she has recorded CDs of medieval and Renaissance music with Briddes Roune and the New Queen's Ha'penny Consort. Her master's thesis on Anglo-Saxon medicine has made her one of the few experts in diseases caused by malevolent elves.

Louise Crawford

Louise (AKA L.F.) Crawford writes under both names depending on the genre. In her next Blaize/Zoloski mystery, *Blaize of Trouble,* Blaize rescues a bulldog after his owner is murdered, wrestles her bra from his slobbery mouth, solves a kidnapping and plans her wedding, all in the same week! For darker suspense/thriller Dexter fans, check out *Born in Blood,* and for more information visit Crawford's websites: www.lf-crawford.com and www.louisecrawfordbooks.com.

Tish Davidson

Tish Davidson writes and lives with dogs in Fremont, California. Her nonfiction has been published by Scholastic, Adams Media, and many magazines and newspapers. Currently she is writing a mystery novel whose main character is a professional pet sitter. Davidson can be contacted at tish_davidson@yahoo.com.

Trina Drotar

Trina Drotar (poet, writer, visual artist) has been widely published and is currently working on *In the Night Garden,* a collection of poetry, prose and art. Cats in need always find her. Reach her at TrinaLDrotar@gmail.com.

E. G. Fabricant

E. G. Fabricant writes and lives in Sacramento, California. His first short story collection, *Matters Familiar,* is available in e-book format from Barnes & Noble, iTunes, Smashwords and Sony. Connect to E. G.'s blog and sample stories online at egfabricant.com and follow him as egfabricant on Facebook and Twitter. His email is egf@egfabricant.com; if you prefer pulp over electrons, write to him at P. O. Box 19170, Sacramento, CA 95819-0170.

Chris Fowler

Chris Fowler is a born and bred California girl who divides her time between her devotion to family, the fire department and roller derby. She is an aspiring non-fiction writer. This is her first publication.

Pam Giarrizzo

Pam Giarrizzo is a retired attorney living in Northern California with her husband Phil, a political consultant. Their son, Zack, is a freshman in college. Pam is a founding member of the Sacramento Women's Action Network (SWAN), a giving circle that provides funding to nonprofit organizations serving the Sacramento area. She also serves on the boards of the California Museum for History, Women and the Arts, and the Camellia Network, which assists young people who are transitioning from foster care to adulthood. She is the author of the *Sacramento Vegan* blog, which identifies restaurants in the Sacramento area offering menu choices for vegans.

Ed Goldman

Ed Goldman is a daily business columnist, the author of 4,000 newspaper and magazine features, three books and the musical *Friday@5.* His new comedy, *Jews Don't Kayak,* will be produced in early 2013. Contact him at goldman4@earthlink.net.

Meera Klein

Meera Ekkanath Klein is a writer who lives in Davis, CA, with her family. She is currently working on a story about her coon hound, Duke, the original dog of leisure.

Dena Kouremetis

Consumer journalist, author and would-be shrink, Dena Kouremetis loves to examine life from a midlife perspective. She is a national columnist for three channels at Examiner. com, has authored, co-authored and contributed content to dozens of books, and loves to speak to groups about how our online presence says volumes about us. She welcomes visits to her website at communic8or.com.

Charles Kuhn

Charles Kuhn is an accomplished writer in the areas of mystery, non-fiction and adventure. He has published short stories in various magazines, self-published and writes for local writers groups, including the poetry group for the local Sacramento Multiple Sclerosis Association. Mr. Kuhn and his wife reside in Citrus Heights, CA.

Gordon M. Labuhn

Gordon M. Labuhn is the author of *Murder Has Two Faces* (2011), a feature article journalist for a Detroit newspaper, the screen writer and movie producer of one nationally promoted movie, a winner of the National PR.PI award, and has won first place in the Bayview writers essay competitions in 2008.

Mark Lukas

Mark Lukas, a Soccer Dog Guru, travels nationally with his famous Soccer Collies. The world's greatest soccer dogs, Ms. Z and BEK, rescued Lukas from old age. Now they bring back child-like behavior to everyone who has forgotten how to be a kid. Not to mention the Soccer Collies help train and adopt soccer dogs as they promote youth soccer and dog rescue. SoccerCollies@gmail.com.

Jennifer O'Neill-Pickering

Jennifer O'Neill-Pickering is a writer and an artist living in Sacramento, California. Her writing is featured in many publications including *Sacramento Anthology: 100 Poems, Earth's*

Daughters, Sacramento News and Review and *Medusa's Kitchen.* Her poem, "I Am the Creek," is included in the Sacramento site-specific sculpture, Open Circle. She's published two books: Poems with the *Element of Water and Mandala Art, Poetry,* and *Instruction.* Contact her at her blog, Jennifer's Art and Words or at jenniferartist@att.net.

Sue Pearson

Sue Pearson has been a journalist for more than 30 years. Writing is her passion and animals fuel her soul. She has staked out a little piece of heaven on 6 acres in the Northern California foothills where her four horses, two dogs and a cat inspire her every day.

Morton Rumberg

Mort Rumberg was a volunteer at the Animal Welfare League of Alexandria, Virginia, for eight years, where the story of Hammer was told to him by the director of animal welfare. He has written several novels, one of which has won a national award, and many short stories that have won awards in national competitions. He now resides in Gold River, California, with his American Eskimo dogs, Yuki and Kori. Visit his website at mmrumberg.com.

Finley Taylor

Finley Taylor lives, works and writes in Northern California. She and her husband are thrilled to be expecting twin girls in summer 2012, but Finley will always consider Bridgette her first "kid."

Suzanne Tomlinson

Suzanne Tomlinson lives on a ranch tending her beloved

horses. She has learned how to be her own best friend and is grateful for the journey that has led her to inner peace.

Katherine Traci

Kate (or Katherine) Traci is a beach girl at heart who now lives in Surprise, Arizona, with two cats, including the heroic Simon, and one dog, who might be her furry soul mate. She patiently waits for her next adventure on a dark starry night in the Arizona desert.

Jerry and Donna White

Jerry White had a career in the military and in real estate. He now teaches in the Earth Science department of a local community college. Donna White is a retired nurse who now spends her time in the garden. She is known as the "compost lady" of the neighborhood.